This book was written by

Eon Harper
Dietmar Küchemann
Michael Mahoney
Sally Marshall
Edward Martin
Heather McLeay
Peter Reed
Sheila Russell

NMP Director
Eon Harper

NMP Research
Edward Martin

MATHEMATICS FOR  SECONDARY SCHOOLS

5

RED TRACK

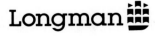

Longman

The front cover shows a detail from *Swinging*, by Wassily Kandinsky (the painting is reproduced in full on the back cover). He was born in 1866 in Moscow and died in 1944. Kandinsky was one of the founders of 'pure' abstract painting.

Wassily Kandinsky *Swinging*
© ADAGP. Paris, DACS, London, 1989 (photo: Tate Gallery)

Longman Group UK Limited
Longman House, Burnt Mill, Harlow, Essex CM20 2JE, England
and Associated Companies throughout the world.

© Longman Group UK Limited 1990

First published 1990
ISBN 0582 22517 5

Set in 10/12 Times
Printed in Great Britain by Scotprint Limited, Musselburgh

PREFACE

This book and the three companion books, Year 4 Blue Track. Year 4 Red Track and Year 5 Blue Track cover all Levels in Key Stage 4 of the National Curriculum and provide a complete two-year Examination course for all grades of the GCSE Examination.

The course builds upon the Years 1–3 Red Track and Blue Track course of *NMP Mathematics for Secondary Schools*. Each book contains Review sections which revise the mathematics introduced in Years 1–3. The course can thus be used by schools which have hitherto not used NMP materials in the foundation years.

The Blue Track books for Years 4 and 5 provide for GCSE Grades C/D to G; the Red Track books provide for Grades A to C/D. Further details can be found in the Teachers' File for each track.

NMP was founded in 1981 to develop teaching and learning materials suited to the emerging new syllabuses and National Criteria. The material was researched and evaluated at the University of Bath and written by practising teachers and professional educators.

Each text provides for pupil–pupil and pupil–teacher discussion, oral and mental work, skill and practice work, written and calculator work, problem solving, investigation and extended assignments for GCSE coursework. Each of these aspects is integrated into the text to provide the variety of learning opportunities required by the various GCSE Boards and the National Curriculum.

The text falls into two Sections, A and B, whose Chapters contain Review, Consolidation, Core and Enrichment material. The relationship of these to GCSE needs is explained in detail in the Teachers' File.

ACKNOWLEDGEMENTS

We are grateful to the following for permission to reproduce photographs: John Birdsall, page 106; Beken of Cowes, page 14; J Allan Cash, page 50; Croydon College (photo Joyce Farrelly), page 218; Egyptian National Library, Cairo, page 160; Holt Studios, page 49; Honda, page 61; Network (photo Laurie Sparham), page 10; Philips, page 60; Planet Earth Pictures (photo J Bracegirdle), page 115.

Other copyright material:
Department of Health and Social Security, page 11, extract from leaflet FB23 '*Young people's guide to Social Security*'.

Illustrations by Oxford Illustrators Ltd and cartoons by Martin Shovel.

CONTENTS

REVIEW

Two shapes are *similar* if corresponding angles are equal *and* corresponding sides are in the same ratio.

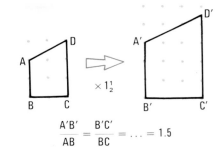

$$\frac{A'B'}{AB} = \frac{B'C'}{BC} = \ldots = 1.5$$

■ Draw a pair of quadrilaterals whose corresponding angles are equal but which are not similar.

■ Draw a pair of quadrilaterals whose corresponding sides are in the same ratio but which are not similar.
Triangles are a special case; they are similar if corresponding angles are equal *or* corresponding sides are in the same ratio.

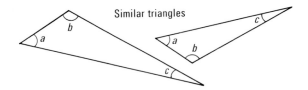

Similar triangles

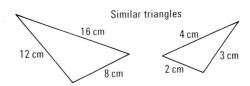

Similar triangles

CONSOLIDATION

1 a) In the triangles ABC and PQR, what is the ratio

   (i) $\dfrac{BC}{PQ}$ (ii) $\dfrac{AB}{RQ}$ (iii) $\dfrac{AC}{PR}$?

   b) Are the triangles similar?
   What is the reason for your answer?

   c) What is the ratio of the areas of the two triangles?

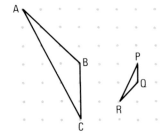

2 Here are some sketches of triangles.

   a) In each case decide whether the marked angle is smaller, the same, or larger than the shaded angle A. Do not measure any angles: the drawings are not meant to be accurate.

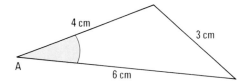

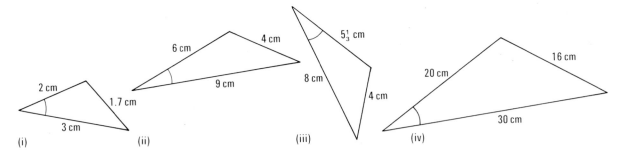

(i)   (ii)   (iii)   (iv)

b) Are these marked angles smaller than, the same as, or larger than angle A in part a)? Explain your answers.

(i)

(ii)

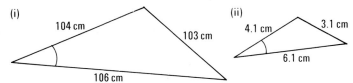

3 Two of the triangles A, B, C, D are similar. Which two?

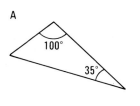

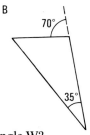

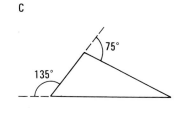

4 a) Which triangle is similar to triangle W?

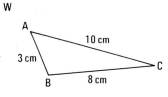

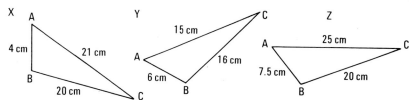

b) Write down the ratios $\dfrac{AB}{BC}$ and $\dfrac{AB}{AC}$ for each triangle. Explain how the ratios can be used to check the answer to a).

5 Triangles ABC and XYZ are similar.

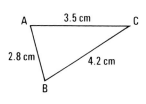

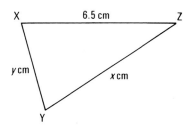

a) Here is a way of finding the length of XY. Copy and complete the working:

$$\frac{XY}{XZ} = \frac{AB}{\square}$$

So $\dfrac{y}{6.5} = \dfrac{2.8}{\square} = \square$

$\times 6.5\!: y = 6.5 \times \square$

So $y = \square$

The length of XY is $\square$ cm.

b) Use the method in a) to find the length of YZ.

CORE

Congruent figures

███ TAKE NOTE ███

The shapes in this tiling pattern are all identical. They are exactly the same shape and size. We say that they are *congruent*.

This tiling pattern is made from two sets of congruent shapes. The large triangles are all congruent, and the small triangles are all congruent. The small triangles are similar to the large triangles but not congruent to them.

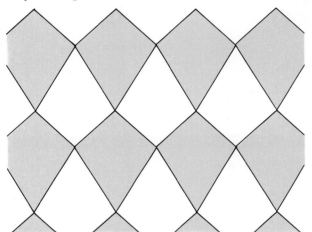

1 a) In the *Take note* above, what is the scale factor for enlargement for the small triangles and large triangles?

b) We can identify other sets of congruent shapes, for example: (You will need to ignore the colours.) Sketch two examples of your own.

2 A square can be made from

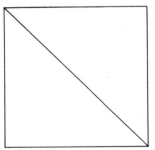

Two congruent triangles

or

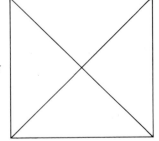

Four congruent triangles

or

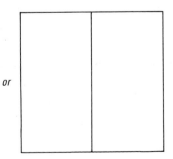

Two congruent rectangles

... and so on

a) Make a sketch to show how a parallelogram can be made from four congruent triangles.

b) Every kite can be made from two pairs of different congruent triangles, and two congruent parallelograms. Make sketches to show how.

A1

3   a) Do these produce *congruent* shapes (or objects) or *similar* shapes (or objects)?

A   A slide projector   B   A jelly mould   C   A date stamp

b) Name two examples of your own of things which produce

(i) congruent shapes (or objects)   (ii) similar shapes (or objects).

Try to give a 2D and a 3D example for each case.

ACTIVITY

4   You need a ruler and a compass.

a) Triangle PQR is drawn full size.

Draw a triangle that is

(i) congruent to it
(ii) similar to it.

b) Draw a triangle that is congruent to triangle ABC.

c) Draw a triangle with one 7 cm side and 50° and 70°
angles which is *not* congruent to triangle ABC.

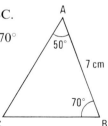

CHALLENGE

5   Triangle ABC has two of its sides 6 cm and 10 cm long. One of its angles is 40°.
Triangle PQR also has two of its sides 6 cm and 10 cm long, and an angle of 40°. But ABC and PQR are not
congruent.
Draw each of them, full size.

EXPLORATION

6 a) A regular pentagon can be divided into three pairs of congruent triangles.

   Find other ways of dividing it into congruent triangles. Make sketches.

   Try other regular polygons. Write a report to explain what you discover.

   b) Investigate other congruent shapes which make up regular figures. For example, a regular hexagon can be made from congruent trapeziums.

   Write a report about what you discover.

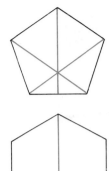

WITH A FRIEND

7 It is possible to draw two quadrilaterals whose sides are identical in length, but which are not congruent.

   For example,

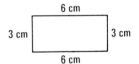   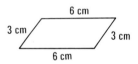

   Decide between you if it is possible to draw two different (that is, non-congruent) figures in cases A to J. If you decide it *is* possible to draw two *different* figures, do so.

A   Two quadrilaterals with the same sized angles.

B   Two quadrilaterals with the same sized angles and the same length sides.

C   Two triangles with two pairs of angles identical to each other.

D   Two triangles with two pairs of sides identical to each other.

E   Two triangles with one pair of angles identical.

F   Two triangles with one pair of sides identical.

G   Two triangles with a pair of identical angles and a pair of identical sides.

H   Two triangles with a pair of identical angles and two pairs of identical sides.

I   Two triangles with three pairs of identical sides.

J   Two triangles with two pairs of identical angles and a pair of identical sides.

A1

━━━━━━━━━━━━━━━ TAKE NOTE ━━━━━━━━━━━━━━━

Triangles whose sides are the
same length must be congruent.

Triangles with two equal
sized angles and one pair of
corresponding equal
length sides must
be congruent.

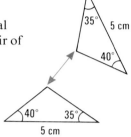

Triangles with two pairs of
equal length sides and the
angle *between them*
equal must be
congruent.

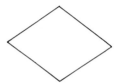

━━━━━━━━━━━━━━━ ASSIGNMENT ━━━━━━━━━━━━━━━

8 Think of quadrilaterals
with four sides all 2 cm long.

a) You are told that two of the shapes also have an equal angle. Does this mean that the two shapes are
congruent?

b) If you say 'No' in a), how many angles must be identical before we can be sure that the shapes are
congruent?

c) Now think about quadrilaterals whose angles are right angles. You are told that two of the shapes have
one pair of corresponding sides the same length. Does this mean that the shapes are congruent?

d) If you say 'No' in c), how many pairs of corresponding sides must be identical before we can be sure that
the shapes are congruent?

e) Investigate convex kites.
What is the minimum we
must know to be the
same about two of them
before we can be sure
that they are congruent?

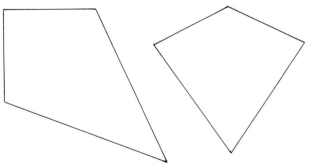 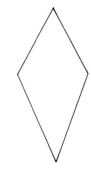

f) Investigate some more quadrilaterals, such as squares, rectangles, parallelograms, trapeziums ....
What is the least we must know about two of each type before we can be sure that they are congruent?

ENRICHMENT

WITH A FRIEND: THE SIMILAR SHAPES GAME

A1

1   You need dotted squared paper.

Player 1 chooses a whole number scale factor (for example, × 2). Player 2 marks two points A and A′ (keeping them fairly close to one another).

Player 1 now draws a line AB and an enlarged (and parallel) line A′B′.

Player 2 now draws a line BC and an enlarged (and parallel) line B′C′.

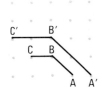

The chosen points A, B, C, etc. have to be on the original dot lattice. Play continues until a player is forced to draw a line that crosses a previous line or veers off the page. The other player gains a point. The first player to score 3 points wins.

2   You are told that **ABCD** and **ABEF** are parallelograms.

Explain how you know that triangles ADF and BCE must be congruent.

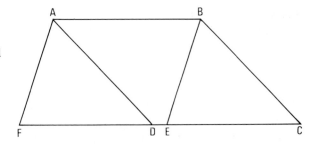

3   Copy and complete this explanation to show that triangles ABE and BCE are congruent.

AB = BC (given)

∠EBC = ☐° (angles on a straight line sum to 180°)

So ∠ABE = ∠EBC

∠BAE = ∠BCE (......)

Hence triangles ABE and CBE are congruent (two angles and a corresponding side are equal).

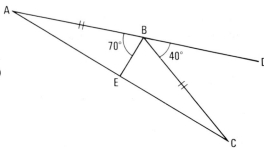

CORE

Wages and salaries

================= WITH A FRIEND: WAGE CHALLENGE =================

1 When you work you can be paid in various ways:

per hour	for example,	£3.75 per hour
per week	for example,	£420 per week
per month	for example,	£1200 per month
per annum (year) or p.a.	for example,	£15000 per year.

Assuming that for each of the rates above, the number of hours work per day is 8, there are 4 weeks in a month, and there are 11 of these working months in a year, which rate of pay is best?

================= TAKE NOTE =================

Working hours are often fixed, for example, 9:00 a.m. to 5:15 p.m. with an unpaid hour for lunch. If you work more than these hours, this is called *overtime*.

Normally you are paid more than the standard rate for overtime.
For example, Ahmid works in a timber yard. His working day is 8:00 a.m. to 5:00 p.m. with a one hour unpaid lunch break (that is, an eight hour day). He often works two hours overtime from 5:00 p.m. to 7:00 p.m.

His *standard* pay rate is £3.60 per hour.
His *overtime* pay rate is £4.90 per hour.

2 Read the *Take note*.

a) How much does Ahmid earn per day when he does two hours overtime?

b) This is the work record card for Ahmid for one week.

How much did Ahmid earn for the week?

| | STANDARD | | | | OVERTIME | |
| | a.m. | | p.m. | | | |
	Start time	Finish	Start time	Finish	Start time	Finish
Monday	8:00	12:00	1:00	5:00	5.00	6:30
Tuesday	8:00	12:00	1:00	5:00	—	—
Wednesday	8:00	12:00	1:00	5:00	—	—
Thursday	8:00	12:00	1:00	5:00	—	—
Friday	—	—	1:00	5:00	5:00	7:00

ASSIGNMENT

3   Wage earners are paid at the end of every week. Salary earners are normally paid every month.
Bus drivers, bricklayers and shop assistants are usually wage earners.
Teachers, nurses and accountants normally earn salaries.
Collect some examples of job advertisements from the newspapers. Compare the amounts people earn.
For example, find advertisements for people who will earn:

more than £50 000 per year
between £30 000 and £50 000
between £20 000 and £30 000
between £15 000 and £20 000
between £10 000 and £15 000
between £7500 and £10 000
between £5000 and £7500

Describe how the working hours,
conditions and benefits (such as company
car, medical insurance, staff discount,
mortgage assistance) differ from one type of
work to another.
Choose examples of different types of jobs
and different types of payments (salaried,
wage-earning, part-time, etc.).
Compare the examples you have collected
by working out how much you think each
person earns per hour (taking into account
all the 'fringe benefits').
Write a report about what you discover.

2. Applicants must have a minimum of four GCSE's (Grade C or above) including English or English language, mathematics or a science subject and not more than one subject of a mainly artistic, commercial or domestic nature. Preference will be given to candidates with passes in English language, mathematics, physics and chemistry.

3. Assistant Scientific Officers are encouraged to take advantage of opportunities available, through day release, to obtain further qualifications such as HNC or equivalent.

4. Starting salary is dependant upon age, from £4,004 at age 16, £6,011 at age 19 and then by annual increments to a maximum of £8,284 plus Outer London Weighting of £544 per annum, up to age 18 and £725 per annum age 18 and over.

5. Flexible working hours are available. Annual leave is 22 days per annum minimum plus 10½ days for public holidays.

6. For further details and an application form, please write to: Personnel Office, RARDE, Powdermill Lane, Waltham Abbey, Essex EN9 1AX, or telephone ⁑ ⁑⁑2 713030, extension 291.

7. The closing date for receipt of comp⁑ Friday, July 14, 19⁑

8. The Civil Service is an Equal Op⁑

MOTORCYCLISTS!
The new Harlow office of the south's premier courier company needs owner or company bike riders.
If you are presentable, reliable and want £200 per week minimum, call Kevin on
79 4524

...all aspects of a substantial s...
...itment programme from mate...
...rough to response analysis. ...
...date will be a hard working, brig...
...cer with typing skills. Experience...
...eting and/or fund raising essenti...
...ot apply unless you have this exp...
...s is an exciting opportunity in a d...
...ronment.

£12,000 - £14,000pa. according to ...nce. Company pension scheme.

...iled job description and an applica-
...(no cvs) please write to: Alison ...Greenpeace, 30/31 Islington Green, ...1 8XE Closing date for the receipt of ...ns Friday 28th July. We regret we

Groom
Full-time or part-time person required for com-ing season with point-to-point horses. Capable rider, accommodation available.
TELEPHONE 0245   215/7
40 MWTSO 2

...TEL ...VOY LAUNDRY
Require experienced cook/supervisor, general assistant and washer up, references required. Catering for approximately 60 lunches per day, plus snack and tea breaks.
Rates of pay: Cook £8,000 per annum, 40 hour week, per arrangement. General Assistant by per hour, 27.5 hours, 9.30 am - 4 pm. Washer-up £2.77 per hour, 22.5 hours, 10 am - 2.30 pm. Fringe benefits include overalls, free lunches etc. chiropodist, dentist, free lunches etc.
Please apply Pers...
Savoy H...

...PRENEURIAL PROPERTY LAWYER
Circa £60,000   WEST

Full-time or Part-time Catering/Bar Staff Weekend Supervisors
Looking for a challenge?
Able to work hard with a smile?
The above positions are available in our 24-hour restaurant and bars ... Stansted Airpor...
We are looki...

TAKE NOTE

Overtime is often paid at 'time and a half'. For example, if the standard rate is £3.60 per hour the overtime rate is £5.40 per hour (£3.60 + ½ of £3.60).
Weekend (or Sunday) work might be paid at 'double time'.
When standard rate is £3.60 per hour the 'double-time' rate is £7.20 per hour (2 × £3.60).

A2

4   Read the *Take note*.

   a) Mary works
       6 hours for £3.60 an hour
       2 hours at time and a half
       and 1 hour at double time.

       How much does she earn?

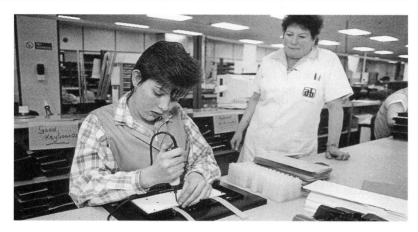

   b) Rula has a part-time job.
       The standard rate is £2.80
       per hour.

       This is her time card for the
       week.

       Calculate how much she
       earned.

	STANDARD (hours)	TIME AND A HALF (hours)	DOUBLE (hours)
Mon	5	–	–
Tues	4	2	–
Wed	–	–	–
Thurs	2	–	–
Fri	4	1	–
Sat	3	–	–
Sun	–	–	2

Tax and other deductions

1   All of us have to pay income tax on earnings over and above a certain limit. We all pay National Insurance
   and most people contribute to a company pension scheme.

   a) Gerald earns £247 per week before any deductions. This is called his *gross* pay. The first £53 is tax free.
      He pays 25% tax on the remainder. How much does he pay in tax each week?

   b) For National Insurance Gerald pays £22.23 per week. There are no other deductions from his wages.
      How much does he take home each week in his pay packet? (This is called his *net* pay.)

2   This is Helen's payslip for the 12th working week of the year.

   a) From the payslip you can
      see that she has earned
      gross pay of £816.00 (in the
      12 weeks). Check that this
      gives £68.00 per week.

   b) How much does she pay
      each week in National
      Insurance contributions?

   c) What percentage of her gross
      pay is take-home (net) pay?

Tax and pay year to date	Employee's contributions	Name: H Street Staff No. 7–0312 Period 12	
Code No.	National Insurance	Gross pay and additions	Deductions
203 L	73.44		
Gross pay	Pension	Gross pay 68.00	Tax 8.63
816.00	—		Insurance 6.12
Taxable pay			
470.64			
Tax		Gross pay 68.00	Total deductions 14.75
103.56		Net pay 53.25	Company name BLAKE ASSOCIATES

3 a) In 1989, your National Insurance contributions would have been 9% of your gross pay. How much would you have paid on a gross salary of £12 700 per year?

What is National Insurance?

Most people who are between 16 and state pension age (60 for women and 65 for men) and who work must pay contributions into the National Insurance (NI) scheme. These contributions enable you to get NI benefits such as Unemployment Benefit, Sickness Benefit, and state Retirement Pension.

You'll get your NI Numbercard in the post shortly before your 16th birthday. It has your personal number on it. Keep it in a safe place.

Your NI Numbercard

You should have received your NI Numbercard in the post shortly before your 16th birthday. It has your personal NI number printed on it. Keep it in a safe place. Your employer will need to know your number so that your NI contributions can be put on to your own contributions record.

Your Social Security office will also need to know your number if you need to claim benefits.

If you can't find your Numbercard or have never had one, ask your Social Security office for one straight away.

Your NI contributions

If you work for an employer

If you work for an employer and earn at least a set amount, you must pay **Class 1** NI contributions. The more you earn the more you pay. Your employer takes your contributions out of your pay and also has to pay employers' contributions for all employees who earn at least the set amount.

b) As a single person the income tax you pay normally increases in bands like this:

The tax bands and rates change year by year in the Budget so that the Government can collect more, or less, revenue for spending on roads, education, health, defence, etc. How much tax would you pay on a salary of £20 000, using these tax bands?

Band 1	Up to £3500	No tax
Band 2	Basic rate: Next £14 500	28%
Band 3	Higher rate: Next £10 000	35%
Band 4	Super rate: Over £28 000	40%

ENRICHMENT

1   These were the tax bands and the tax rates in 1986–87:

29% basic rate	First £17 200 of taxable income	50% rate	Next £7900
40% rate	Next £3000	55% rate	Next £7900
45% rate	Next £5200	60% rate	Anything more

How much income tax would a company director with a taxable income of £50 000 have paid in 1986–87?

ASSIGNMENT

2   Find out the present tax bands and rates.
Calculate how much tax a company director with £50 000 of taxable income would pay.
Would she/he pay more today than in 1986/87?
Explain why you think this is so.

REVIEW

- The *factors* of 48 are 1, 2, 3, 4, 6, 8, 12, 16, 24, 48.
- The *multiples* of 48 are 48, 96, 144, 192, ...
- The *prime factors* of 48 are 2 and 3.
- Every whole number can be expressed as a *product of prime numbers* or of itself and 1.

For example, $18 = 2 \times 3 \times 3 = 2 \times 3^2 = 18 \times 1$

$$46 = 2 \times 23 = 46 \times 1$$

$$405 = 3 \times 3 \times 3 \times 3 \times 5 = 3^4 \times 5 = 405 \times 1$$

■ Find a number which is both a multiple of 7 and a factor of 112.

CONSOLIDATION

A3

IN YOUR HEAD

1   a) Which factors of 240 are primes?

b) 36 and 27 share the same factor (other than 1). What is it?

c) What is the ninth multiple of 200?

d) Write 48 as a product of primes.

e) Write down all the factors of $2^3 \times 3^2$.

f) Which multiples of 4 are also factors of 24?

2   a) Copy and complete each 'factor tree'.

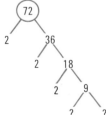
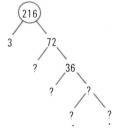
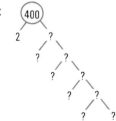

b) Use your 'factor trees' from a) to help you to write down each number as a product of primes.

CHALLENGE

3   Which number, smaller than 1000, has the greatest number of different prime factors?

4   One of the multiples of 12 which is less than 100 is also a multiple of 20. Which is it?

5   28, 42 and 91 have a factor (other than 1) in common. What is it?

━━━━━ EXPLORATION ━━━━━

6   12 has six factors: 1, 2, 3, 4, 6, 12.
    Four of these are even (2, 4, 6 and 12) and two are odd.

   a) Find some numbers which have all their factors, except 1, even. Describe the sequence of numbers to which they belong.

   b) Find some numbers which have exactly half their factors even. Describe the sequence of numbers to which they belong.

   c) Investigate some more combinations of odd and even numbers of factors.
      Record any interesting sequences you find.

A3

CORE

Common factors

1   a) List the factors of   (i) 24   (ii) 42.

    b) List the numbers which are factors of both 24 *and* 42. What is special about the number 6 with respect to 24 and 42?

    c) Find the largest number which divides into both 28 and 42.

2   Copy and complete this *Take note*.

━━━━━ TAKE NOTE ━━━━━

The factors of 30 are 1, 2, 3, □, □, 10, □, 30.
The factors of 45 are 1, □, 5, □, 15, 45.
The numbers which are factors of both 30 and 45 are 1, □, □ and □.
The *highest* common factor (HCF) of 30 and 45 (that is, the largest number which is a factor of both 30 and 45) is 15.

3   a) Write down the factors of   (i) 24   (ii) 60.

    b) What is the HCF of 24 and 60?

4   Find the HCF of

    a) 12 and 16   b) 40 and 100   c) 36 and 136.

5   a) Which factors are common to 12, 28 and 36?

    b) What is the HCF of 12, 28 and 36?

6   a) Write down two numbers which have 7 as their HCF.

   b) Write down three numbers which have 8 as their HCF.

7   If we choose any ten numbers *less* than 1000, their lowest possible common divisor (factor) is 1. What is their highest possible common divisor?

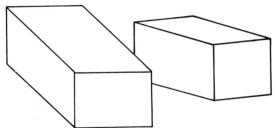

8   Two blocks are to be built out of 1 cm cubes. One block will have a volume of 36 cm^2, the other 60 cm^2.

   a) If the blocks are to have the same height, what is the tallest they can be?

   b) Explain what your result has to do with common factors.

CHALLENGE

A3

9   You want to tile a kitchen floor and a bathroom floor with the same style and size of tile. You do not want to cut any tiles, that is, you want to use only whole tiles.
The kitchen floor measures 3.0 m × 2.7 m and the bathroom floor 2.4 m × 2.8 m.

   a) What size tiles could you use? (Choose only sensible sizes. Give at least one possibility.)

   b) What is the largest size of tile you could use?

Common multiples

1   A fog-horn sounds every 20 seconds. Another fog-horn sounds every 25 seconds. They both sound together at midnight.

   a) After how many seconds do they next sound together?

   b) Write down the first five times after midnight when they sound together, like this:

     00:1:40, 00:3:20, ...

2   These are two fences on opposite sides of a road. The first posts in each fence are directly opposite each other.

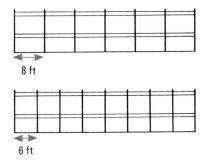

8 ft

6 ft

a) Which are the next two posts which are directly opposite each other?

b) Write down the distances from the first post, of the next five posts which are opposite each other, like this:

24 ft, 48 ft, ...

3   A number 7 bus leaves the bus station every 18 minutes. A number 12 bus leaves every hour. The first two buses of the day leave together at 6:30 a.m.

a) When do a number 7 and a number 12 bus next leave together again?

b) How many number 7 and number 12 buses leave the station together between 6:30 a.m and 11:30 p.m.?

4   a) List the first eight multiples of 9.

b) List the first eight multiples of 12.

c) List the first three numbers which are multiples of both 9 and 12.

5   These are the multiples of 8 and 12.

8,   16,   (24,)   32,   40,   (48,)   56,   64,   (72,) ...

12,   (24,)   36,   (48,)   60,   (72,)   84,   96,   108, ...

a) The numbers which are ringed are multiples of both 8 and 12. Write down the next two examples.

b) Copy and complete the *Take note.*

═══════════ TAKE NOTE ═══════════

The first 6 multiples of 12 are 12, 24, □, 48, 60, □.
The first 6 multiples of 16 are 16, □, □, 64, 80, □.
The first 4 multiples common to 12 and 16 are 48, □, □, 192.
The lowest (smallest) common multiple (LCM) of 12 and 16 is □.

6   Write down two numbers which have 16 as their lowest common multiple (LCM).

7   Write down three numbers which have 20 as their LCM.

A3

8   Find the LCM of

   a) 2 and 3   b) 5 and 9   c) 6 and 12   d) 9, 15 and 18.

9   In a factory, a chair is produced every 8 minutes and a table every 20 minutes.

   a) After how many minutes are the first chair and table finished together?

   b) In an eight hour day, working continuously, how many tables and chairs will be finished together?

   c) At the end of the day, how many chairs will have been produced for each table?

10   The largest collection of numbers less than 10 which have 10 as their LCM is

   1, 2, 5

   What is the largest collection of numbers less than 100 which share 100 as their LCM?

ENRICHMENT

CHALLENGES

1   These are instruction on how to add two fractions:

   To add $\dfrac{7}{8}+\dfrac{5}{12}$

   Find the LCM of 8 and 12:   24

   Write this as a common denominator: $\dfrac{\ldots+\ldots}{24}$

   24 is 3×8, so multiply 7 by 3.

   24 is 2×12, so multiply 5 by 2: $\dfrac{7\times3+5\times2}{24}$ The answer is $\dfrac{31}{24}$.

   a) Check that the result is correct.   b) Explain why the method works.

2   Write out a set of instructions like those in question 1 which explain how to do the calculation $\dfrac{5}{8}-\dfrac{3}{10}$.

   Your instructions should include the use of an LCM.

EXPLORATIONS

3   a) 12 represented as a product of primes is $2^2 \times 3$.
       18 represented as a product of primes is 2×3^2.
       The LCM of 12 and 18 is $2^2 \times 3^2$.
       The HCF of 12 and 18 is 2×3.
       Investigate some more pairs of numbers. Represent their HCFs and LCMs as products of primes.
       Find a rule which helps you to write down the HCF and LCM of two numbers when you know their
       representations as products of primes. (For example, what is the HCF and LCM of $2^3 \times 7 \times 5^2$ and
       $2^2 \times 7^2 \times 5$?)

   b) Use your rule in a) to find the LCM and HCF of
       a^2b^3c and ab^2c^2, where a, b and c are primes.

4   a) The HCF of two numbers is 4. Their LCM is 24.
        What are the two numbers?
        Is there more than one pair of numbers which match this HCF and LCM?

    b) Write down examples of pairs of numbers of your own choice which you consider to represent the HCF
       and LCM of two numbers, and try to find the two numbers. For example:

       HCF: 6

       LCM: 120   The two numbers are □ and □.

       Can you find a method which helps you to discover the two starting numbers?

REVIEW

Data can be represented using

- Frequency tables
- Bar charts
- Pictograms
- Pie charts
- Frequency polygons.

Number of children in families in High Street

Number of children	Number of families
0	3
1	4
2	5
3	2
4	1
5 or more	2
Total 17	

Frequency table

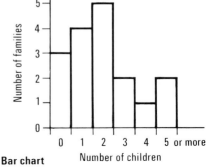

Bar chart

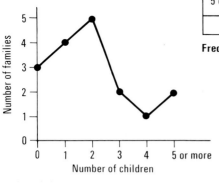

Frequency polygon

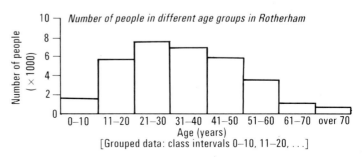

Pictogram

Pie chart

A4

The mass media (newspapers, TV, magazines) use a variety of types of charts, some much more sophisticated than others.

- Data is gathered through surveys and questionnaires.
  Sometimes it is grouped into *class intervals* to simplify the presentation.

Number of people in different age groups in Rotherham

[Grouped data: class intervals 0–10, 11–20, . . .]

CONSOLIDATION

1 a) Represent the information in the bar chart

   (i) in a frequency table
   (ii) as a pie chart.

   b) Design a questionnaire to gather data for a similar survey in your own town. Assume that the questionnaire is for police records and data is to be entered into a database at your local police station.

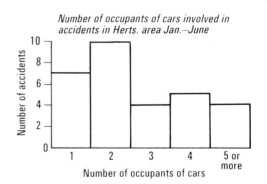

Number of occupants of cars involved in accidents in Herts. area Jan.–June

CORE

Histograms

WITH A FRIEND

1   The table and the two charts give information about the population of England and Wales in 1985. The charts display the information about the male population only.

Age (completed years)	Population (millions)	
	Males	Females
0–14	4.9	4.6
15–29	6.0	5.8
30–44	5.0	5.0
45–59	4.1	4.1
60–69	2.4	2.7
70–79	1.5	2.3
80–99	0.4	1.1
TOTALS	24.4	25.6

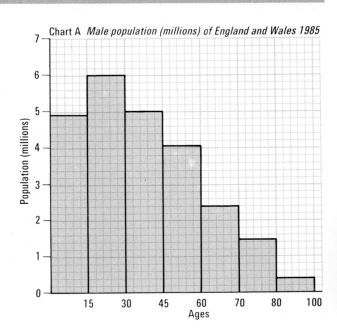

Chart A *Male population (millions) of England and Wales 1985*

a) Compare the two charts. Describe any differences you see.

b) Decide between you how accurately you think each chart represents the information in the table. Can the charts be improved in any way? If you think so, draw your own chart which you think gives a more accurate representation of the male population data.

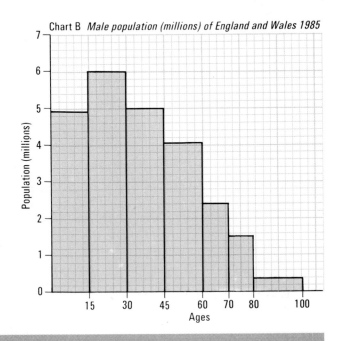

Chart B *Male population (millions) of England and Wales 1985*

A4

████████████████ TAKE NOTE ████████████████

Neither of the charts (A and B) on the previous page can be considered wholly satisfactory. Although the heights of the columns in chart A accurately represent the number of people in each age group, the widths of the columns do not accurately represent the age groups. (The widths of the columns are all the same, but the age group ranges are different from group to group.)

In chart B, again the heights of the columns accurately represent the number of people in each age group. This time the widths of the columns also accurately represent the age group ranges. However, the *areas* of the columns now give a misleading impression. For example, there are four times as many 15–29-year-olds as there are 70–79-year-olds. But the area of the column for 15–29-year-olds is 360 units (2 mm squares) and the area of the column for 70–79-year-olds is 48 units – suggesting six times more 15–29-year-olds than 70–79-year-olds.

You might have found a way in question 1 of producing a chart which gives a better representation of the data.

A4

2   This table shows the same population information for males as that in question 1. However a *frequency density* column has been added.

Age (in completed years)	Class width	Male population (millions)	Frequency density (2 DP)
0–14	15	4.9	0.33
15–29	15	6.0	0.40
30–44	15	5.0	0.33
		4.1	0.27
		2.4	0.24
			0.15
			0.02

a) Explain how the figures in the 'frequency density' column are obtained.

b) Compare the area of the column for 15–29-year-olds with the area of the the column for 70–79-year-olds. Which chart, chart B or chart C, do you think gives a better representation of the data?

Chart C   *Male population (millions) of England and Wales 1985*

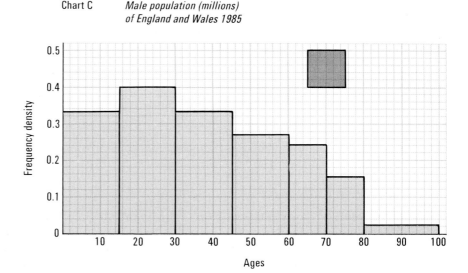

━━━━━━━━ WITH A FRIEND ━━━━━━━━

Chart C is called a *histogram*.

c) Draw a histogram for the female population figures in the table in question 1.

━━━━━━━━ THINK IT THROUGH ━━━━━━━━

d) What does each unit of area in chart C represent? (See, for example, the area marked).

3   The frequency table shows the marks for 60 students in an end-of-year English exam.

Percentage marks	1–20	21–30	31–40	41–50	51–60	61–70	71–80	81–100
Number	7	8	10	4	5	8	12	6

a) (i) Draw a histogram to represent the information.
   (ii) The students are in the same age group at school and are taught by the same teacher in two separate
         groups. Are there any features in the histogram which you consider to be unusual? Explain your
         answer.

b) The students' results were
graded for the end-of-year
reports. The table shows
the percentage marks for
each grade.

Estimate how many students
were awarded each grade.

Percentage	Grade
20 or less	E
>20–40	D
>40–60	C
>60–80	B
>80	A

4   The table shows the prices of 378 houses for sale in an area:

Price (£)	0–	30 000–	50 000–	60 000–	80 000–
Number	0	2	15	84	140

90 000–	100 000–	110 000–	120 000–	150 000–200 000
44	26	20	14	33

a) Draw a histogram to represent the information.

b) Sophia Konrad has saved £16 000 towards buying a house. She knows that she will have to use £2000 for
legal costs and removal expenses. A building society offers her a maximum loan of 90 per cent of the
purchase price, the other 10 per cent being the deposit which she will have to pay. Estimate how many of
the houses are within her price range with help from the building society loan.

A4

Scattered relationships

1   This scatter graph shows the heights and masses of 20 children in a hospital ward.

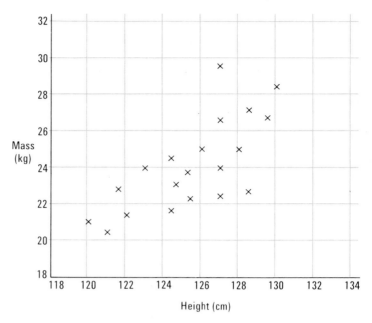

a) How tall (to the nearest cm) is
   (i) the shortest child   (ii) the tallest child?

b) How heavy (to the nearest kg) is
   (i) the lightest child   (ii) the heaviest child?

c) Roughly what would you guess to be the range of ages of the children?

d) (i) Find the cross which represents a child who has a mass of 25 kg and is 126 cm tall.
   (ii) There is another child with the same mass. How tall is this child?

e) There are four children who are about 127 cm tall. How heavy is each one?

f) Write down the heights and masses of five children which support this statement:

   The taller the child, the heavier she or he is.

g) Write down the heights and masses of three children which support this statement:

   The taller the child, the lighter she or he is

h) Which statement, that in f) or g), generally tends to be true for children in the ward?

━━━━━━━━━━━━━━━ TAKE NOTE ━━━━━━━━━━━━━━━

The crosses on the scatter graph tend to cluster around the dotted line. This suggests that (generally speaking) the taller the child, the heavier she or he is.

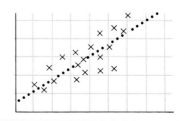

2   Here are two more scatter graphs. Three lines, a, b and c, have been drawn on each graph.

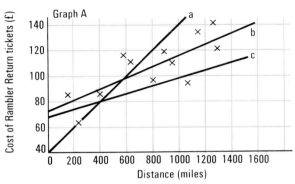

Graph of the relationship between the cost of a railway ticket and the number of miles travelled

Graph of the relationship between the average length of stride of athletes and their time for a 1000 m race.

a) Which line do you think gives the best idea of the relationship between the variables on each graph?

b) Estimate from graph A roughly how much you would expect to pay for a train journey 1600 miles long.

c) Which of these would you say is generally true for the athletes?
    (i) The greater is the mean length of stride, the shorter is the time for 1000 m.
    (ii) The greater is the mean length of stride, the greater is the time for 1000 m.

TAKE NOTE

The points on a scatter graph will sometimes lie in a narrow band so that it is possible to visualize a straight line which the points cluster around. The line is called the *line of best fit*. You can use the line of best fit to predict possible values in the data.

A4

Positive relationship. As one variable increases the other tends to increase.

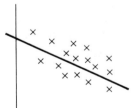

Negative relationship. As one variable increases the other tends to decrease.

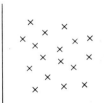

No relationship. The variables are not related.

THINK IT THROUGH

3   a) Think of an example of your own in which two variables (for example, height and age, length of stride and height, cost of secondhand car and age) are:

    (i) positively related
    (ii) negatively related
    (iii) unrelated.

b) Sketch what the scatter graph might look like for each of your examples. Label and calibrate the axes so that your graphs give a rough idea of how the values of the two variables might be related for individual items recorded on them.

4   For each scatter graph (i) to (iv), identify which of the situations lettered P to S it is most likely to represent.

P The total costs of buying a fixed number of articles and the prices per article.
Q The masses of a number of students and their heights.
R The times for each of a number of students to run 100 m and their marks in a mathematics exam.
S The numbers of goals scored against Stockport F.C. in a season and the number of matches they won.

ASSIGNMENT

5   Decide upon a pair of variables whose relationship you might like to study.

For example,   the heights and masses of your friends and relations
                the lengths and widths of oak leaves
                the amount of time people spend watching TV per week
                    and the amount of time they spend reading
                and so on

Choose a pair of variables for which you think an approximate relationship exists.
Collect the information, using a sample of at least 25 items or people.
Draw a scatter graph of your results.
Is there a line of best fit for your results? If so, can you give an approximate formula connecting the variables for your scatter graph?

[For example,   height (m) $\approx \frac{1}{60} \times$ mass (kg)
                length (cm) $\approx 2.5 \times$ width (cm)
                time watching TV (hhr) $\approx 16 \times$ time reading (hr).]

ENRICHMENT

1   'Slimline' enrolled ten new members. Details of their weights and average daily food consumption were measured and recorded.

   a) Use these figures to plot a scatter graph.

   b) Calculate

       (i) the mean weight of the ten people
       (ii) the mean daily consumption of the ten people.

   c) Plot the point which represents the mean weight and mean daily consumption on your graph.

Weight (kg)	Food consumption (hundreds of calories per day)
84	32
93	37
65	26
95	39
72	27
86	35
78	31
70	28
90	35
75	30

d) (i) On your scatter graph draw what you think is the line of best fit.
   (ii) Explain how you think the point for the mean weight and mean consumption helps in deciding the line of best fit.

e) From your graph estimate the weight of a person whose food consumption is 3300 calories per day.

f) Try to find a rough equation for your line of best fit. For example,
   Food consumption (calories per day) $\approx 3 \times$ weight (kg) $- 10$

2 The Department of Transport undertook a long term survey. The number of motorbikes on the roads on 1 January in each of eight years and the number of casualties in road accidents in each of the following twelve-month periods are shown in the table:

	1983	1984	1985	1986	1987	1988	1989	1990
Motorbikes on 1 January (millions)	1.8	2.1	2.6	3.0	3.4	3.7	4.0	4.2
Road casualties (thousands)	110	117	125	128	135	133	136	140

a) Plot a scatter graph from these figures, including also the point representing the means.

b) Draw a line of best fit on the scatter graph.

c) As a result of the survey a national road safety campaign is planned for 1991. The number of motorbikes at the start of the year is 4.5 million. The campaign should reduce accidents by 10%.
   Estimate the number of road casualties which could be anticipated in 1991.

A4

A5 POWERS, ROOTS AND RECIPROCALS

REVIEW

- The *square* of 5 is $5^2 = 5 \times 5 = 25$.

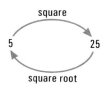

square

5   25

square root

- The *square root* of 25 is $\sqrt{25} = 5$.

- the *cube* of 5 is $5^3 = 5 \times 5 \times 5 = 125$.

- $a^b \times a^c \equiv a^{b+c}$ ∘∘∘ (for example, $2^7 \times 2^2 = 2^9$)

- $a^b \div a^c \equiv a^{b-c}$ ∘∘∘ (for example, $2^7 \div 2^2 = 2^5$)

- $\dfrac{1}{a}$ is written as a^{-1}; a^{-3} means $\dfrac{1}{a^3}$. ∘∘∘ ($4^{-3} = \dfrac{1}{4^3} = \dfrac{1}{64}$)

- [8] [x^y] [2] [=] gives the value of 8^2.

■ Find the value of

a) $4^{-1} \times \dfrac{4^5}{4^2}$ b) $3.1^{0.8}$ (correct to 1 DP).

CONSOLIDATION

1 Find the square roots of   a) 225   b) 729   c) 2.56   d) 0.0576.

2 a) Which numbers have a square root which is smaller than 1?

   b) Which numbers have a square which is smaller than 1?

   c) The cube of a number is smaller than 8. What can you say about the number?

3 a) In your head, estimate

      (i) $\sqrt{76}$ (ii) $\sqrt{1.3}$ (iii) $\sqrt{0.7}$ (iv) 0.61^2 (v) 0.61^3.

   b) Use your calculator to check your estimates in a).

4 Do not use the [√] key on your calculator.

   a) Find the square root of 138 correct to 1 DP. (Use trial and improvement – for example, try 12. Then $12 \times 12 = 144$. So 12 is too large; try 11.5. Then $11.5 \times 11.5 = \ldots$)

   b) Find the square root of 0.006 8 correct to 1 DP.

   c) Solve each equation correct to 1 DP   (i) $x^2 = 47$ (ii) $p^2 = 0.8$.

5 Write as a vulgar fraction or mixed number

   a) 2^{-1} b) 3^{-2} c) $(\frac{1}{2})^4$ d) $(\frac{2}{3})^{-2}$ e) $(\frac{3}{2})^{-3}$.

6 Use trial and improvement (you will need to use the [x^y] key) to solve the equation $3.1^x = 17$ correct to 1 DP.

7   Copy and complete each sentence:

a) $3^7 \times 3^4 = 3^?$ b) $8^6 \div 8^3 = 8^?$ c) $\dfrac{9^8}{9^3} = 9^?$ d) $\dfrac{1}{2^6} \times 2^8 = 2^?$ e) $3^{-5} \div 3^{-2} = 3^?$

f) $4^? \times 4^{-3} = \dfrac{1}{4^7}$ g) $2^? \div 2^{-3} = \dfrac{1}{2}$ h) $\dfrac{12^{-6}}{12^{-3}} = 12^?$.

CORE

Reciprocals and roots

TAKE NOTE

$2^{-1} = \frac{1}{2}$ is called the *reciprocal* of 2.

$\left(\frac{2}{3}\right)^{-1} = \dfrac{1}{\frac{2}{3}} = \frac{3}{2}$ is the reciprocal of $\frac{2}{3}$.

$4^{-1} = \frac{1}{4}$ is the reciprocal of 4.

$(0.2)^{-1} = \frac{1}{0.2} = 5$ is the reciprocal of 0.2.

1   What is the reciprocal of

a) 5   b) $\frac{1}{5}$ c) 0.1   d) $\frac{3}{10}$ e) 2.5?

2   a is the reciprocal of b.
Does this mean that b must be the reciprocal of a?
Give examples to explain your answer.

3   a) Write down   (i) the reciprocal of $\dfrac{p}{q}$ (ii) the reciprocal of $\dfrac{q}{p}$.

b) Is this a correct or incorrect
representation of the relationship between $\dfrac{p}{q}$ and $\dfrac{q}{p}$?

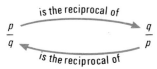

If you say 'incorrect', give an example to explain why.

4   a) Alan says that the reciprocal of the number $a + b$ is the reciprocal of a plus the reciprocal of b. Is he
correct? Give examples to explain your answer.

b) Meg says that the reciprocal of the number $a \times b$ is the reciprocal of a multiplied by the reciprocal of b. Is
she correct? Give examples to explain your answer.

c) Investigate relationships between reciprocals like those in a) and b) for subtraction and division. Give
examples to explain what you decide.

d) True or false?   (i) $\sqrt{\text{The reciprocal of } a} \equiv \text{The reciprocal of } \sqrt{a}$
(ii) $(\text{The reciprocal of } a)^2 \equiv \text{The reciprocal of } a^2$

Give examples to explain each of your answers.

A5

5   a) Find the reciprocal of the reciprocal of the reciprocal of 7.

    b) Find the value of

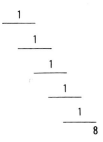

    c) Think of sentences like that in a), which include the phrase 'the reciprocal of' a number of times. Is there a rule connecting the number of times the phrase occurs and the final result? If so, explain what it is.

Powers and roots

━━━━━━━━━ TAKE NOTE ━━━━━━━━━

The *square* of 4 is 4^2 or 16.   The *square root* of 16 is 4.
The *cube* of 4 is 4^3 or 64.   The *cube root* of 64 is 4.
5 *raised to the power* 3 is 5^3 or 125. The *cube root* of 125 is 5.
3 *raised to the power* 4 is 3^4 or 81.   The *fourth root* of 81 is 3.

1   a) Copy and complete:

   (i) $2^? = 128$ (ii) $3^? = 243$ (iii) $5^? = 625$ (iv) $4^5 = ?$ (v) $3^5 = ?$
   (vi) $?^3 = 125$ (vii) $?^8 = 256$ (viii) $?^3 = 512$ (ix) $10^5 = ?$ (x) $?^5 = 3125$.

    b) Use your sentences from a) to find:

       (i) the fifth root of 1024   (ii) the cube root of 512
       (iii) the eighth root of 256   (iv) the cube root of 125
       (v) the fifth root of 243   (vi) the fifth root of 3125
       (vii) the fourth root of 625   (viii) the fifth root of 100 000.

2   What is

    a) the cube root of 1000   b) the sixth root of 1 million

    c) the square root of 1 million   d) the cube root of 1 million?

3   a) In your head estimate the cube root of 100.

    b) Using only the ⊠ key and the digit and ▭ keys on your calculator, find a better estimate for the cube root of 100.

    c) Continue to use your calculator to make better estimates. Find the cube root of 100 correct to 2 DP.

4   Find the fourth root of 1000 correct to 1 DP.

CHALLENGE

5   The cube root of a whole number is 13.7 correct to 1 DP.

a) Check that the number might be 2571.

b) Check that the number might be 2582.

c) List all the possibilities for the number (or write down the smallest and largest possible values).

THINK IT THROUGH

6   a) Study the number sentences:

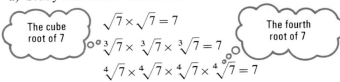

The cube root of 7

$\sqrt{7} \times \sqrt{7} = 7$

$\sqrt[3]{7} \times \sqrt[3]{7} \times \sqrt[3]{7} = 7$

$\sqrt[4]{7} \times \sqrt[4]{7} \times \sqrt[4]{7} \times \sqrt[4]{7} = 7$

The fourth root of 7

$7^{\frac{1}{2}} \times 7^{\frac{1}{2}} = 7^{1} = 7$ $\frac{1}{2} + \frac{1}{2} = 1$

$7^{\frac{1}{3}} \times 7^{\frac{1}{3}} \times 7^{\frac{1}{3}} = 7^{1} = 7$

$7^{\frac{1}{4}} \times 7^{\frac{1}{4}} \times 7^{\frac{1}{4}} \times 7^{\frac{1}{4}} = 7^{1} = 7$

Write two similar sentences which involve the fifth root of 7.

b) Find   (i) $512^{\frac{1}{9}}$ (ii) $243^{\frac{3}{5}}$ (iii) $2401^{\frac{1}{4}}$.

c) Write one or two sentences and give examples to explain what is meant by $a^{\frac{1}{n}}$.

ENRICHMENT

1   Write more simply, as a single power in the form a^{b}:

a) $8^{\frac{1}{2}} \times 8^{4}$ b) $3^{4} \times 3^{\frac{1}{3}}$ c) $2^{7} \times 16^{\frac{1}{4}}$ d) $27^{\frac{1}{3}} \times 9^{4}$.

2   Find the numerical value of:

a) $16^{-\frac{1}{4}}$ b) $25^{-\frac{1}{2}}$ c) $81^{-\frac{1}{4}}$ d) $9^{2} \times 27^{-\frac{1}{3}}$.

3   a) Find the numerical value of:

(i) $(9^{2})^{\frac{1}{4}}$ (ii) $(8^{\frac{1}{3}})^{4}$ (iii) $(10^{6})^{\frac{1}{3}}$.

b) True or false: $(a^{\frac{1}{p}})^{q} \equiv a^{\frac{q}{p}} \equiv (a^{q})^{\frac{1}{p}}$?

Give examples to explain your answer.

EXPLORATION

4   Which numbers have both whole number square roots and whole number cube roots?

5   a) The fourth root of the reciprocal of a number is $\frac{1}{5}$. What is the number?

b) The reciprocal of the fourth root of a number is $\frac{1}{5}$. What is the number?

c) True or false: $(a^{\frac{1}{n}})^{-1} \equiv (a^{-1})^{\frac{1}{n}}$?

Give examples to explain your answer.

A5

REVIEW

As objects move, points on them trace out paths in 2D or in 3D.

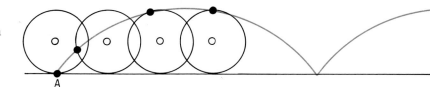

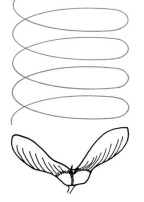

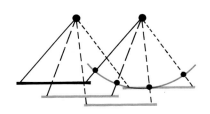

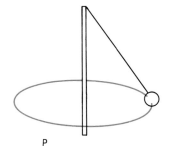

- The path which is formed when a point (P) moves so that it is always equidistant from two other points (A and B) is called the *perpendicular bisector* of AB. The path cuts AB in half and meets AB at 90°.

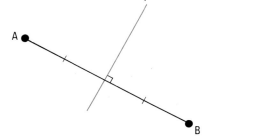

CONSOLIDATION

ACTIVITY

1 You need a sheet of tracing paper.

   a) Mark three points P, Q, and R anywhere on your tracing paper.

      By folding, construct the perpendicular bisectors of PQ, PR and RQ.

   b) Explain why the three perpendicular bisectors meet at one point.

   c) Draw a circle which passes through P, Q and R.

2 ABC is an equilateral triangle. As it rolls along the horizontal path, each point traces out a curve. Draw an equilateral triangle. Predict the curves which A, B and C trace out as the triangle rolls. Check your predictions by cutting out your triangle and rolling it.

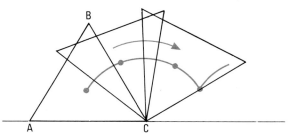

CORE

1 a) Point A is twice as far from line m as from line n. So is point B.

Draw a pair of straight lines like m and n.

Draw some points like A and B that are twice as far from m as from n.

Draw a line through all of your points.

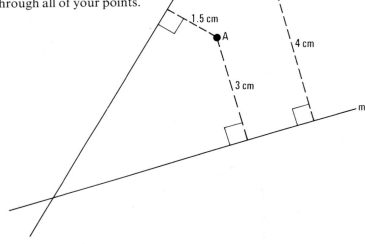

TAKE NOTE

We call the line through A and B the *locus* (path) of all the points which are twice as far from m as they are from n. (The plural of locus is loci (used here) or locuses.)

b) Draw some more pairs of lines like m and n. Sketch the locus of points that are:

(i) three times as far from m as from n
(ii) the same distance from m as from n
(iii) some distance ratios of your own choosing from m and n.

c) Mark two points, A and B (about 6 cm apart), on a sheet of paper. Sketch the locus of points that are:

(i) the same distance from the two points
(ii) twice as far from one point as from the other point
(iii) some distance ratios of your own choosing from the two points.

d) Explore the loci you get for various distance ratios of a point from:

(i) a point and a line
(ii) a point and a circle
(iii) two circles.

Write a report about what you discover.

A6

2   The circle is the locus of points that are 3.75 cm
     from O. However it is also the locus of points
     whose distances from A and B fit a particular
     rule.

     Make an accurate copy of the diagram and try to
     find the rule.

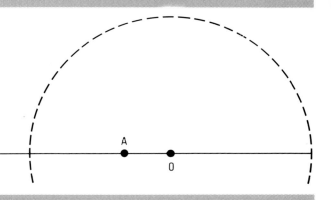

3   a) Study this construction. Describe the locus represented by the red line.

Mark two points, A and B.   Draw a circle, with centre at A.   Draw a circle with the same radius, centre B.   Draw a straight line through the points of intersection of the circles.

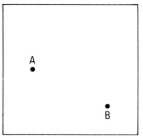 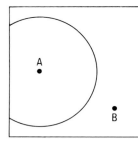 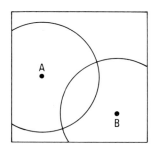 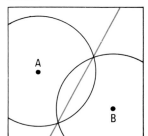

     b) This diagram shows the same construction as in a), but this time
         arcs have been drawn, rather than complete circles.
         Explain why the red line is the perpendicular bisector of line AB.

     c) (i)   Draw a line about 10 cm long on tracing paper.
         (ii) Use compasses to construct the perpendicular bisector of the
               line.
         (iii) Check the accuracy of your construction by folding.

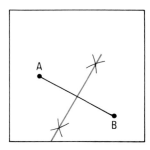

4   a) Draw a triangle on plain paper. Make the sides between 6 cm and 10 cm long.

     b) Use compasses to draw the perpendicular bisectors of two of the sides. Call their point of intersection O.

     c) Predict the path of the perpendicular bisector of the third side. Explain how you arrived at your
         prediction.

     d) Construct the third perpendicular bisector to check your prediction in c).

     e) What is special about the point O, the triangle, and a particular circle, centre O?

5   Draw a line m and mark a point P not on m.

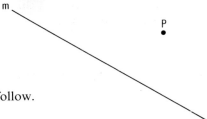

a) Using a compass (and a ruler for drawing straight lines), find a way of *dropping a perpendicular* from P to m (that is, of constructing a line through P perpendicular to m).

b) Write out a set of instructions for someone else to follow.

6   Study this diagram carefully. It shows the construction of the red line r, given the lines m and n.

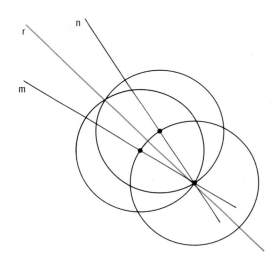

a) Draw two lines m and n, of your own, which intersect at an angle of about 40°. Carry out your own construction of the line r.

b) Describe the locus represented by the line you constructed in a).

This diagram shows the same construction as in a), but this time arcs have been drawn, rather than complete circles.

The red line is called the *angle bisector* of the angle between m and n.

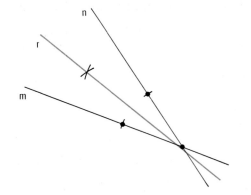

A6

c)   (i) Draw two lines intersecting at an angle of about 80° on tracing paper.
     (ii) Use a compass to construct the angle bisector.
     (iii) Check the accuracy of your construction by folding.

d) Construct the angle bisector of two lines which meet at an angle of about 140°.

7 a) Draw a triangle on plain paper. Make the sides between about 6 cm and 10 cm long.

   b) Use a compass to construct the angle bisector of two of the angles. Call their point of intersection O.

   c) Predict the locus of the third angle bisector. Explain how you arrived at your prediction.

   d) Construct the third angle bisector, and check your prediction in c).

   e) What is special about the point O, the triangle, and a particular circle, centre O?

THINK IT THROUGH

8 Starting from a single point, use a compass to construct the other three vertices of

   a) a rhombus   b) a kite.

TAKE NOTE

A compass and a ruler (used just as a straight edge) can be used to:

- draw the perpendicular bisector of a straight line

- draw a perpendicular from a point to a straight line

- draw the angle bisector of two intersecting lines

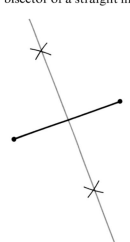
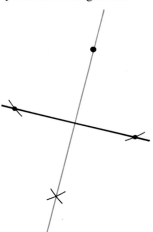
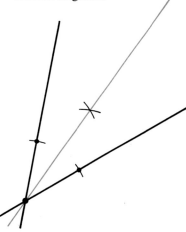

A6

CHALLENGE

9 a) Construct an angle of 45°. (Hint: construct perpendicular lines; construct the angle bisector.)

   b) Construct an angle of 15°. (Hint: start by constructing an equilateral triangle.)

   c) Choose an angle which you think can be constructed using just a compass and a straight edge. Try to construct it.

   d) Consider the angles between 0° and 90° (for example, 5°, 10°, 15°, 20°, …). Which can be constructed using just a compass and a straight edge? Explain your answer.

ENRICHMENT

Loci in 2D and 3D

1 a) ABCD is a thin metal plate, 8 cm square. Describe as fully as you can the locus (in 3D) of points 3 cm from the metal plate. Use words and sketches.

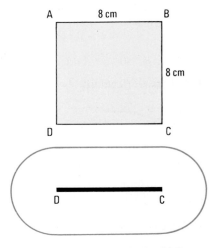

For example, you might produce sectional drawings like the one below, which shows the locus in a plane through DC perpendicular to the plane ABCD.

What, in particular, does the locus look like near the corners A, B, C, D? Is it part of a cylinder, or a sphere, or what?

b) Start with metal plates of different shapes, or solid objects such as a cylinder or cube. Again describe the loci in words and sketches.

WITH A FRIEND

2 Discuss these loci with a friend. Try to describe them to each other as fully as you can, but do not write or draw anything.
For each locus try to describe what it would look like:

(i) in two dimensions   (ii) in three dimensions.

a) Points 5 cm from a fixed point.

b) Points equidistant from two points, 10 cm apart.

c) Points 4 m away from a 10 m straight line.

d) Points 1 cm away from a 10 cm diameter circle.

e) Points equidistant from a plane and from a point 10 cm from the plane.

f) Think of some other locus examples. Describe them in words, and between you produce a small booklet which illustrates them in 2D and 3D.

A6

ASSIGNMENT

3 Draw two circles.
Imagine a set of circles that touch the original circles. Sketch the locus of their centres.
Explore what happens to the locus as the sizes of the original circles change. Write a report about what you discover.

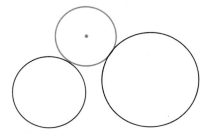

A7 ESTIMATING AND CALCULATING

REVIEW

- We often round measurements or amounts up or down.

4294 kg is
→ 4290 kg rounded to the nearest 10 kg
→ 4300 kg rounded to the nearest 100 kg
→ 4000 kg rounded to the nearest 1000 kg

175 kg is 180 kg rounded to the nearest 10 kg. (For 'halfway' numbers, we always round up.)

- We use rounded numbers to make estimations. We can round up or down.

5.7 km — About 6 km

About 4 km — 3.8 km

2.3 km — About 2 km

3.5 km — About 4 km

Total distance ≈ (6 + 4 + 2 + 4) km = 16 km

■ Estimate the total distance along the road by rounding each amount to the nearest $\frac{1}{2}$ kilometre.

- Numbers are also often rounded to a number of *decimal places* (DP) or *significant figures* (SF).

4.275 640 7 is:

4.3 rounded to 1 decimal place (1 DP)   4.276 rounded to 4 significant figures (4 SF)
4.28 rounded to 2 decimal places (2 DP)   4 rounded to 1 significant figure (1 SF)

- The first significant figure is the first digit which is not zero: 0.002 49

↑
1st significant figure

■ a) Round 4.275 640 7 to   (i) 4 DP   (ii) 2 SF   (iii) 5 SF   (iv) 3 DP.

b) Round 0.002 49 to   (i) 1 SF   (ii) 2 SF   (iii) 3 DP   (iv) 4 DP.

CONSOLIDATION

1   The length of a section of railway track is given as 2.1 m (to 1 DP). What do you think is:

a) the greatest length the section might actually be

b) the shortest length the section might be?

2   a) The heights of bridges are normally written with one figure after the decimal point. Do you think the height has been rounded to 1 DP? Why?

b) Sign posts on country walks are often written with one figure after the decimal point. Do you think the distance has been rounded to 1 DP? Why?

TITHE BARN
1.3 km

3   Which is the most significant figure in each of these numbers?

a) 17064   b) 0.4176   c) 10.47   d) 0.003 40.

4   Copy and complete:

$$0.000\,504\,7 \longrightarrow \begin{cases} \rightarrow 0.0005\ (1\ \text{SF}) \\ \ldots \quad (2\ \text{SF}) \\ \ldots \quad (3\ \text{SF}) \end{cases}$$

$$10.9999 \longrightarrow \begin{cases} \rightarrow 11.0\ (1\ \text{DP}) \\ \ldots \quad (2\ \text{DP}) \\ \ldots \quad (3\ \text{DP}) \end{cases}$$

5   Do each of these calculations. Write each result correct to   (i) 1 SF   (ii) 2 SF.

a) 3.76×0.04 b) $0.83 \div 17$ c) $6.71 + 14.06793$.

6   a) Calculate the area of a circle of radius 2.7 cm correct to   (i) 1 DP   (ii) 3 SF. (Area of a circle $= \pi r^2$; choose your own approximation for π. You can get one from your calculator.)

b) Explain why you chose the particular approximation you did for π in a).

IN YOUR HEAD

7   Estimate the result of each of these by first rounding each number to 1 SF.

a) 3.7×0.51 b) $8.3 \div 1.7$ c) $516 \times \frac{2.3}{98}$.   Check your estimates with your calculator.

8   Use rounding to 1 SF to estimate each of these:

a) the cost of 18 pens at £2.16 each

b) the average price of each egg in a box of twelve; total price £1.73

c) £7.64 + £113.72 + £57.60

d) 398.17 kg − 73.8 kg.

9   Which of these calculations must be incorrect?

A $72.16 \times 13.7 = 9885.92$ B $0.02 \times 14.76 = 29.52$ C $890.18 \div 0.47 = 1894$.

CORE

1   a) The drawing shows the ground plan of a house. Write down the length and width of the lounge to 1 SF.

b) Use your results from a) to estimate the area of the lounge.

c) Calculate the area of the lounge. Check that your estimate and calculation are roughly in agreement. If they are not, check both your estimate and your calculation.

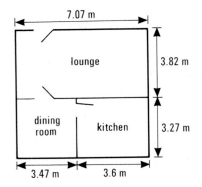

d) Estimate the areas of the dining room and the kitchen.

e) Calculate the areas of the dining room and the kitchen. Check that your estimate and calculation are roughly in agreement. If they are not, check both your estimate and your calculation.

A7

2 By first rounding each number correct to 1 SF, find an estimate for each calculation:

   a) 231×77 b) $231 \div 77$ c) 18.7×0.024 d) $1.76 \div 0.254$.

3 Use your calculator to find the result of each calculation in question 2, correct to 1 DP.
   Check that your calculations are roughly in agreement with your estimates in question 2. If they are not,
   check both your calculation and your estimate.

4 Why is it important to check both your estimates and your calculations in questions 1 to 3? Write one or
   two sentences to explain.

5 a) Below are three attempts at the calculation $\dfrac{276 \times 13}{76}$. In your head make an estimate and decide
      which calculations *cannot* be correct.

      A 432.7641   B 4.758491   C 47.21050

   b) Calculate $\dfrac{276 \times 13}{76}$. Were your choices in a) correct?

6 Each of you write down *five* calculations similar to that in question 5. You can use three whole numbers in
   each calculation, and use $\times$, $+$, $-$ or $\div$. For each calculation write down three alternative 'answers' A, B
   and C. One of them must be correct (to at least 3 DP).
   Your partner has to select the correct answer by making a mental calculation.
   Your three alternative 'answers' for each calculation must differ by a multiple of at least 10 (for example
   0.31476, 3.1476, 31.476).

7 Cornflake packs are packed into boxes with 288 packs in each box. Each pack weighs 0.23 kg (to 2 DP).
   Find the weight of cornflakes in a box. Write your result correct to 1 DP.
   Make sure you estimate the result before you calculate.

8 Calculate the area of the lawn (correct to 1 DP).
   Make sure you estimate the result before you calculate.

9 The radius of a circle is 3.67 m (2 DP). Take π as 3.14.
   Calculate the area of the circle. Write your result correct to 1 DP.
   Make sure you estimate the result before you calculate.

10 The area of the surface of a circular pond is 278 m^2 (3 SF).
    Take π as 3.14 (3 SF).
    Calculate the radius of the pond correct to 2 SF.
    Make sure you estimate the result before you calculate.

A7

ENRICHMENT

8.21 cm

11.57 cm

1   a) The capacity (C) of the can of lemonade is given by

$$C = \pi r^2 h$$

where C is in ml, r (the radius) is in cm and h (the height) is in cm.
In your head estimate how many millilitres of lemonade the can holds.

b) Calculate how much lemonade the can holds correct to the nearest millilitre. Use $\pi = 3.142$. Check that your estimate and your calculation roughly agree.

c) In your head, estimate the area of metal used to make the can (you can use pencil and paper to jot down partial estimates before you add).
(Area of the top of the can is given by $A = \pi r^2$; area of the curved surface is given by $A = 2\pi rh$.)

d) Calculate the area of metal used to make the can, giving your result correct to the nearest 1 cm². Check that your estimate and your calculation roughly agree.

CHALLENGE

e) You want to design a container about 20 cm tall which will hold half a litre of lemonade.

   (i) Assume the container is cylindrical. In your head, estimate the radius of the container.
   (ii) Calculate the radius correct to the nearest millimetre. Check that your estimate and your calculation roughly agree.
   (iii) Assume that the container has a square cross section. In your head, estimate the length of side of the cross-sectional square.
   (iv) Calculate the length of side of the cross-sectional square of the container. Check that your estimate and your calculation roughly agree.

2   Find the volumes of each of these solids. In each case use $\pi = 3.14$. Write each of your results to the nearest 1 cm³. Don't forget to make an estimate before you carry out the calculation.

a) *Sphere*

$V = \frac{4}{3}\pi r^3$
$r = 3.7$ cm

b) *Cone*

$V = \frac{1}{3}\pi r^2 h$
$r = 4.7$ cm, $h = 8.1$ cm

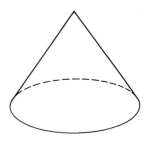

c) *Square-based pyramid*

$V = \frac{1}{3} \times$ Base area $\times$ Height
Height $= 18.6$ cm
Length of side of base $= 7.9$ cm

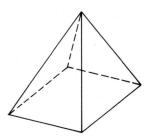

A7

ASSIGNMENT

3   Design a running track whose distance around the inside line of the inside lane is 500 m. Your track should have six lanes.

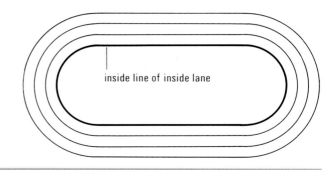

inside line of inside lane

Make a scale drawing of your track and mark on it the starting and finishing lines for all the major events. You might also like to mark areas for the field events.

Write a report about your work, which explains some of the decisions you had to take.

A7

REVIEW

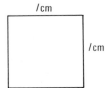

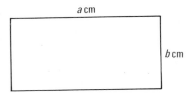

Area: $l \times l$ cm$^2 = l^2$ cm^2
Perimeter: $l+l+l+l$ cm $= 4l$ cm

Area: $a \times b$ cm$^2 = ab$ cm^2
Perimeter: $a+b+a+b$ cm $= 2(a+b)$ cm

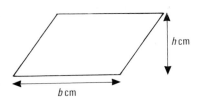

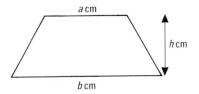

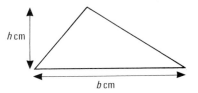

Area: $b \times h$ cm$^2 = bh$ cm^2

Area: $\frac{1}{2}(a+b)h$ cm^2

Area $= \frac{1}{2}b \times h$ cm$^2 = \frac{1}{2}bh$ cm^2

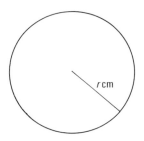

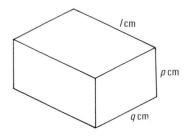

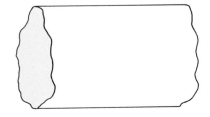

Area: πr^2 cm^2
Circumference: $2\pi r$ cm

Volume: $l \times p \times q$ cm$^3 = lpq$ cm^3

Volume:
Area of cross section $\times$ Length

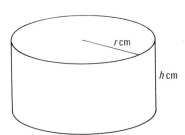

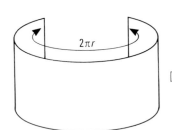

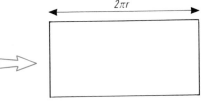

Volume: Area of cross section $\times$ Height
$= \pi r^2 \times h$ cm$^2 = \pi r^2 h$ cm^2

Area of curved surface: $2\pi r \times h$ cm$^2 = 2\pi rh$ cm^2

■ Find: a) the surface area of the cuboid in terms of l, p and q

          b) the total surface area of an oil drum of radius 0.5 m and height 2 m.

CONSOLIDATION

1   Find the area of each figure.

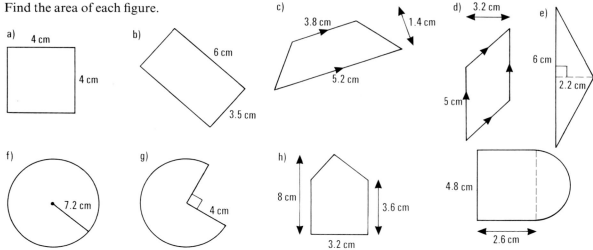

a)   4 cm

b)   6 cm   3.5 cm

c)   3.8 cm   1.4 cm   5.2 cm

d)   3.2 cm   5 cm

e)   6 cm   2.2 cm

f)   7.2 cm

g)   4 cm

h)   8 cm   3.6 cm   3.2 cm

4.8 cm   2.6 cm

(Give your result correct to 1 DP. Use $\pi = 3.14$.)

EXPLORATION

2   The rectangle is a sheet of cardboard which can be folded along its length or its width to make a cylinder.

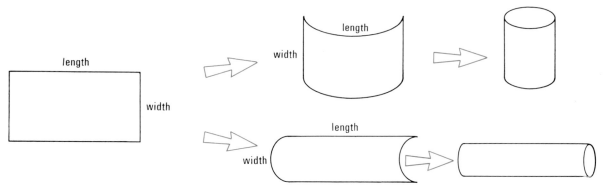

length   width   length   length   width

Notice that each cylinder has the same curved surface area.

a) For a length of 20 cm and a width of 10 cm, which cylinder contains the greater volume of air?

b) Investigate the relative volumes in a) for different lengths and widths which give the same area. Draw a graph or chart to show how the volumes compare.

3   The diagram shows an 'I' beam used to provide strength in structural work in buildings and bridges. What volume of steel is needed to produce the beam?

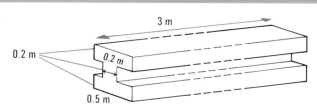

3 m   0.2 m   0.2 m   0.5 m

A8

4   The diagram shows plastic piping used for
    plumbing. The internal diameter is 8 cm and the
    external diameter is 10 cm. What volume of
    plastic is used in making each metre of pipe?

5   The volumes of the two blocks
    of wood are identical. What is
    the height h of the cuboid-
    shaped block?

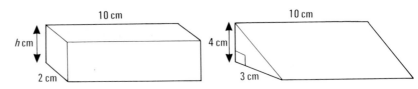

10 cm   10 cm
h cm   4 cm
2 cm   3 cm

▓▓▓▓ CHALLENGE ▓▓▓▓

6   Design your own prism with a trapezoidal cross
    section. Your prism should have a volume of 400 cm^3.
    On your sketch show all the lengths which would
    be needed to make the prism.

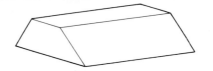

CORE

Units for length, area and volume

1   In the diagrams, the units
    attached to r are *centimetres*.
    r denotes a *length*.

    r cm r cm
    r^2 cm^2 r cm

    r cm r cm
    r^3 cm^3 r cm

    The units attached to r^2 are *square centimetres*.
    r^2 denotes an area.

    a) Write a similar statement for r^3.

    b) Is there a similar meaning for r^4?

2   In the diagrams, the units
    attached to a and b are cm.
    a and b denote *lengths*.

    a cm
    b cm

    b cm a cm ab cm^2

    b cm ab^2 cm^3 b cm
    a cm

    a) (i) What are the units attached to ab?
        (ii) What measure does ab denote –
             area, length or volume?

    b) (i) What are the units attached to ab^2?
        (ii) What measure does ab^2 denote – area, length or volume?

    c) What units should be attached to each of these expressions? Draw a diagram to illustrate your answer.
        (i) $a+b$ (ii) ba^2.

A8

▨▨▨▨▨▨▨ WITH A FRIEND ▨▨▨▨▨▨▨

3 a) p and q each denote a number of centimetres.
   Decide between you whether the expressions (i) to (vi) denote a
   number of cm, a number of cm^2 or a number of cm^3.
   For each expression draw a diagram to illustrate your answer.

   (i) pq (ii) p^2 (iii) p^3 (iv) pq^2 (v) $2pq$ (vi) $2(p^2+q^2)$.

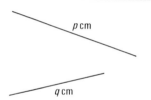

   b) Assume that a, b and c denote a number of centimetres.
   Each of you write down five expressions involving one or more of
   the variables a, b, c which you consider denote a length, an area or
   a volume (for example, abc or $2a^2b$). Challenge your friend to
   decide what each expression denotes. You must be able to draw a
   diagram to illustrate the meaning you intend for each of your
   expressions.

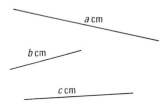

4 n and k each denote a number of centimetres.
   Match each of the expressions (i) to (x) with one of the diagrams a) to j) and with one of the quantities
   'length', 'area' and 'volume'. For example:

   (viii) ⟷ a) ⟷ Area   (that is, nk ⟷  ⟷ Area)

Expressions

(i) n^2 (ii) nk^2 (iii) $k+n$ (iv) k^2-n^2 (v) $2k$

(vi) $2(k+n)$ (vii) $n^2(2+n)$ (viii) nk (ix) $kn(n+2)$ (x) $2(k-n)$.

Diagrams

a)

b)
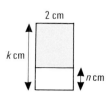

c)
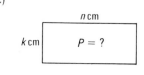

d)

e)
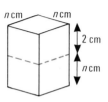

f)

g)
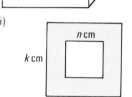

h)

i)

j)

Quantities

Length, area, volume.

5   r denotes a number of centimetres.

The expression $4r$ can denote a number of cm:

or a number of cm²:

4 cm

a) Draw a diagram and write an explanation to show how
    $4r$ can represent a number of cm³.

b) This diagram shows how $2r^2$ can denote a volume:

    Draw your own diagram to show how $2r^2$ can denote an area.

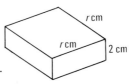

THINK IT THROUGH

6   Draw diagrams to help you to explain how $2(m+n)$ can denote:

a) a length   b) an area   c) a volume.

TAKE NOTE

$C = \pi r^2$, $V = \frac{1}{3}\pi r^2 h$, $S = 4\pi r^2$, are general formulas.
In general formulas, lower case letters ($r, h, l, \ldots$) normally denote lengths. Numbers ($\frac{1}{3}$, 4, π, $\ldots$) do not normally denote lengths. They are merely multipliers.

So if l denotes a length: l cm

then $2l$ denotes twice the length: $2l$ cm

If l^2 denotes an area: l cm   then $2l^2$ denotes twice the area:

l^2 cm² l cm

$2l^2$ cm² l cm

l cm l cm

We can normally decide, therefore, by studying a formula whether it denotes a length, an area or a volume.

For example: $V = \frac{1}{3}\pi r^2 h$ denotes a volume.

      number number length × length length

(Length × length × length gives volume (cm³, m³, $\ldots$))

And

    $S = 4\pi r^2$ denotes an area.

number number length × length

A8

7 a) These are all general formulas for area, length and volume. Decide whether each denotes a length, an area or a volume:

A $P = \frac{2}{3}\pi m^3$ B $L = 2(a+b)$ C $T = \frac{1}{2}(p+q)h$ D $M = \frac{1}{2}ab$
E $N = \frac{1}{2}abh$ F $C = 2\pi l$ G $F = \pi th$ H $G = 2\pi n^2$

b) By studying the formulas in a) and the diagrams below, you should be able to decide which formula matches which diagram. Try it.
For each formula explain what each letter denotes (for example, l in formula F denotes the radius of the circle).

(i) Area of the curved   (ii) Circumference of a   (iii) Perimeter of a rectangle
     surface of a hemisphere   circle

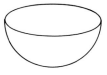   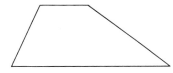   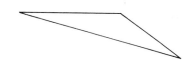

(iv) Volume of a   (v) Area of a trapezium   (vi) Area of a triangle
      hemisphere

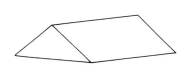

(vii) Volume of a   (viii) Area of the curved
       triangular prism   surface of a cone

THINK IT THROUGH

8 t denotes a number of seconds.
   n denotes a number of metres.
   k denotes a number of metres per second.

   a) Explain why kt is measured in metres.

   b) In what units is n/k measured? Explain your answer.

9 a) Each letter in each of these expressions denotes a length.
      Decide what each of the expressions denotes – a length, an area or a volume.

      A $\frac{1}{2}\pi t^2 + ta$ B $ab^2 + b^2a$ C $4a + 10b$

   b) Draw a diagram for each expression. On your diagrams show what length each letter in the formula denotes.

A8

CORE

TAKE NOTE

Network diagrams can help us solve many types of problem.
For example, how many handshakes are there if five people in a room all
shake hands with each other?
The answer is given by the number of lines joining A, B, C, D and E in
the network diagram. Each line represents a a handshake.

1   I spin a coin and then throw a die.

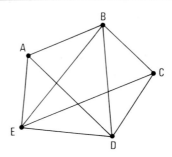

   a) Copy and complete the network (tree diagram) to show all the
      possible outcomes.

   b) What is the probability that I will get H and an even number?

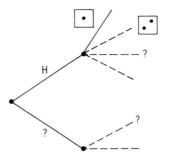

2   There are five people coming to dinner –
    Mr X, Mrs Y, Miss K, Mr N, Mrs L.
    Mrs Y is older than Mr X.
    Miss K is younger than Mr X.
    Mr N is younger than Mr X.
    Mrs L is younger than Mr N.

   a) Is it possible to write the names in order of age?
      Explain your answer.

   b) If you said 'No' in a), what is the minimum additional information you need?

3   How many 'hellos' are there if each of six people in a room say 'hello' to the other five?

4   There are five routes from town A to town B, three routes from town B to town C, and two routes from
    town C to town A.

   a) How many routes are there from town C to town B, via town A?

   b) Two of the roads from town A to town B are converted into one-way-only roads. How many routes are
      there now from town C to town B via town A,

      (i)   if the one-way roads are from A to B
      (ii) if the one-way roads are from B to A
      (iii) if one of the one-way roads is from A to B and the other from B to A?

Route matrices

1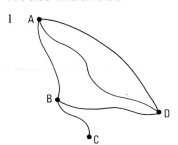

The network shows the roads between four towns, A, B, C and D:

The network can be represented by this route matrix:

Look at row D; the 2 tells us there are 2 roads from D to A; what does (i) the 1,   (ii) the first 0, tell us?

$$\begin{array}{c} & \text{To} \\ & \begin{array}{cccc} & A & B & C & D \end{array} \\ \text{From}\begin{array}{c} A \\ B \\ C \\ D \end{array} & \begin{pmatrix} 0 & 1 & 0 & 2 \\ 1 & 0 & 1 & 1 \\ 0 & 1 & 0 & 0 \\ 2 & 1 & 0 & 0 \end{pmatrix} \end{array}$$

2 Copy and complete the route matrices for these networks:

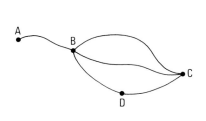

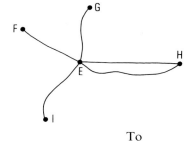

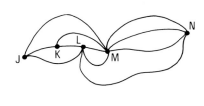

$$\begin{array}{c} & \text{To} \\ & \begin{array}{cccc} A & B & C & D \end{array} \\ \text{From}\begin{array}{c} A \\ B \\ C \\ D \end{array} & \begin{pmatrix} 0 & 1 & 0 & 0 \\ & & & \\ & & & \\ & & 1 & 0 \end{pmatrix} \end{array}$$

$$\begin{array}{c} & \text{To} \\ & \begin{array}{ccccc} E & F & G & H & I \end{array} \\ \text{From}\begin{array}{c} E \\ F \\ G \\ H \\ I \end{array} & \begin{pmatrix} 0 & 1 & & & \\ & & & & \\ 1 & 0 & & & 0 \\ & & & & \\ & & & & \end{pmatrix} \end{array}$$

$$\begin{array}{c} & \text{To} \\ & \begin{array}{ccccc} J & K & L & M & N \end{array} \\ \text{From}\begin{array}{c} J \\ K \\ L \\ M \\ N \end{array} & \begin{pmatrix} & & & & 1 \\ & & & & \\ & 1 & & & \\ & & & & \\ & & & & \end{pmatrix} \end{array}$$

3 Copy and complete the networks for these route matrices:

$$\begin{array}{c} & \text{To} \\ & \begin{array}{ccccc} A & B & C & D & E \end{array} \\ \text{From}\begin{array}{c} A \\ B \\ C \\ D \\ E \end{array} & \begin{pmatrix} 0 & 1 & 1 & 1 & 0 \\ 1 & 0 & 1 & 2 & 1 \\ 1 & 1 & 0 & 0 & 0 \\ 1 & 2 & 0 & 0 & 1 \\ 0 & 1 & 0 & 1 & 0 \end{pmatrix} \end{array}$$

$$\begin{array}{c} & \text{To} \\ & \begin{array}{cccc} F & G & H & I \end{array} \\ \text{From}\begin{array}{c} F \\ G \\ H \\ I \end{array} & \begin{pmatrix} 0 & 1 & 0 & 0 \\ 1 & 0 & 1 & 3 \\ 0 & 1 & 0 & 1 \\ 0 & 3 & 1 & 0 \end{pmatrix} \end{array}$$

$$\begin{array}{c} & \text{To} \\ & \begin{array}{cccc} J & K & L & M \end{array} \\ \text{From}\begin{array}{c} J \\ K \\ L \\ M \end{array} & \begin{pmatrix} 0 & 2 & 1 & 2 \\ 2 & 0 & 1 & 0 \\ 1 & 1 & 0 & 0 \\ 2 & 0 & 0 & 0 \end{pmatrix} \end{array}$$

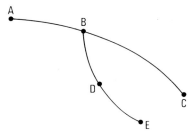

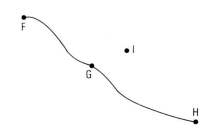

4   The matrix shows the direct bus routes
between five towns, A, B, C, D and E.
It shows, for example, that there is a direct
route from A to B but not from A to C.

To

A B C D E

$$\begin{array}{c} \\ \text{From} \end{array} \begin{array}{c} A \\ B \\ C \\ D \\ E \end{array} \begin{pmatrix} 0 & 1 & 0 & 1 & 0 \\ 1 & 0 & 1 & 0 & 1 \\ 0 & 1 & 0 & 0 & 0 \\ 1 & 0 & 0 & 0 & 1 \\ 0 & 1 & 0 & 1 & 0 \end{pmatrix}$$

Answer these questions without
drawing a network.

a) It is possible to go from A to E by this indirect route: A to B to E.
Use the matrix to find another indirect route from A to E.

b) Write down two indirect routes from C to E.

c) Write down a round trip from B that goes
through no town twice.

d) The rail routes between the five towns are shown by this matrix:

Write down the matrix that shows all the routes (bus or rail)
between the five towns.

To

A B C D E

$$\begin{array}{c} \\ \text{From} \end{array} \begin{array}{c} A \\ B \\ C \\ D \\ E \end{array} \begin{pmatrix} 0 & 1 & 0 & 0 & 1 \\ 1 & 0 & 1 & 0 & 0 \\ 0 & 1 & 0 & 0 & 1 \\ 0 & 0 & 0 & 0 & 0 \\ 1 & 0 & 1 & 0 & 0 \end{pmatrix}$$

A9

ENRICHMENT

Planning networks

1   Imagine the problem of ordering and erecting this
wooden shed. These are some of the factors you would
need to take into account.

Delivery dates:
- allow 10 days for
delivery after ordering

Erecting:
- allow 2 days for
erecting the shed once
foundations and floor
have been laid

Foundations and floor:
- digging and preparation:
allow 2 days
- concreting: allow 1 day
- drying: allow 4 days

Painting and drying:
- allow 3 days. Paint
before erecting.

a) What do you think is the minimum number of days between ordering the shed and completion?

b) The network diagram represents the activities which are involved. Notice that there are six activities, each of these has a number of days associated with it (just one of them is written in).

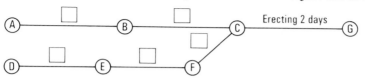

The diagram shows the order in which the activities can be carried out. Make a list of which activities are probably represented by the lines AB, BC, DE, EF and FC.

c) The path from D to C represents the activities involved in preparing the foundations and floor. AB represents the wait for delivery.
The diagram shows that the activities of DE, EF and FC can take place whilst waiting for delivery and for the paint to dry. How many 'spare days' are there in the path from D to C?

d) According to the diagram, what is the shortest possible completion time?

e) The digging and foundation preparation could be delayed by a day or more without adversely influencing the total completion time. However, there are three activities which, if delayed at all, will affect the total completion time. Which are they?

───── TAKE NOTE ─────

In question 1, ABCG is called the *critical path*.

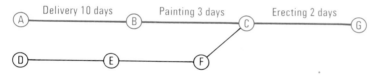

Any delay along this path will delay the completion date. The whole diagram is called a *critical-path diagram*. The minimum possible completion time is shown by the critical path: 15 days. In a critical-path diagram, the activities and the times for each should be shown along every path.

2   A café is to be built in a new shopping precinct. The table shows the major activities which need to be carried out.

		Estimated completion time (weeks)
1	Order/deliver café furniture	8
2	Order/deliver kitchen equipment	8
3	Order/deliver building materials	5
4	Clear the building site	4
5	Dig foundations	1
6	Lay foundations	2
7	Build café	8
8	Fit kitchen equipment	2
9	Fit café furniture	2
10	Decorate	2

Note: decoration should not begin until all other activities have been completed.

a) Draw a critical-path diagram for the project.

b) List the activities along the critical path(s).

c) What is the minimum time in which the project can be completed?

ASSIGNMENT

3   Think of a large project which you might want to carry out, which requires careful organization and time-planning.
Prepare details of your project, with times required for each activity, and draw a critical-path diagram.
Use your diagram to prepare a timetable of earliest and latest 'start dates' for each activity, assuming that the project starts on your birthday.

A9

A10 THINKING IN 2D AND 3D

REVIEW

The drawing shows a *3D view* of a house.

These drawings show the *plan* and *elevation* of the house from A.

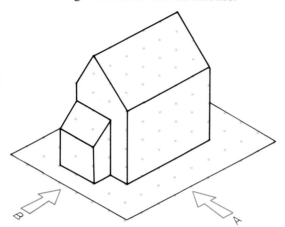

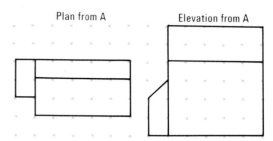

Plan from A   Elevation from A

■ Draw the plan and elevation of the house from B. (Use dotted squared paper.)

CONSOLIDATION

EXPLORATION

1   You need squared dotted paper.
    The drawings show a 3D view
    of a simple shed, and the plan
    view from A.

    a) Draw the elevation from A
       and from B.

    b) Imagine different sheds with
       the same plan as in a).
       Explore what the elevations
       from A and B could look like.

    c) Draw your own plan views of some simple sheds.
       Explore what the elevations from A and B could look like.

    d) The drawing shows the elevation from B of a simple shed.

       Explore what the elevation and plan from A
       could look like.

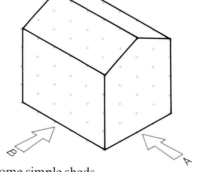

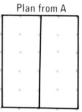

Plan from A

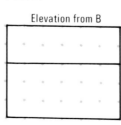

Elevation from B

CORE

Different views

A10

1   You need dotted squared and dotted isometric paper.

   a)   (i)   One of you draw an elevation which could be for a simple
             shed, like this:

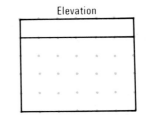
Elevation

       (ii)   The other should now draw another elevation that fits with
             the first elevation, for example:

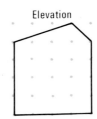
Elevation

       (iii) Both of you now draw
             a plan and a 3D view
             of the shed, which fit
             with the two
             elevations, for
             example:

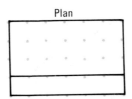
Plan

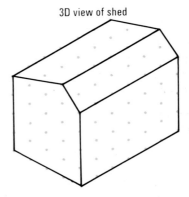
3D view of shed

   b)   Repeat a), but let the other person start. Change the order of the views if you want to, but leave the 3D
        view to last.
        Draw four sheds altogether.

We can usually describe a *simple* object sufficiently by drawing just two 'plain' views of the object (for example,
a plan and an elevation, or two elevations from directions at right angles to one another). The two plain views
allow us to draw 3D views of the object.

CHALLENGE

2   You need dotted squared paper.

The drawings show a plan
from A, and a 3D view, of a 'shed'.

Draw *two* possible elevations from C.

Plan from A

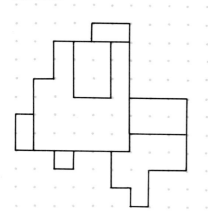

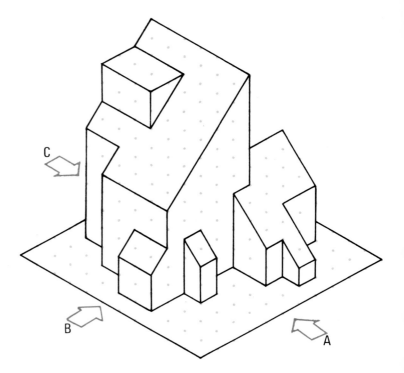

EXPLORATION

3   You need dotted squared and dotted isometric paper.
The diagram shows a 3D view of a simple hut. The roof forms a pyramid.

From just this diagram, it is not possible to tell the exact position of
V. The plan of the hut from A could, for example, look like one of these:

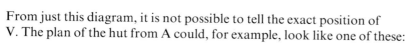

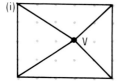

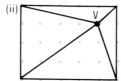

a) For each plan, draw the elevations of the hut from A and B.

b) Draw the elevations of the hut from A and B if the plan from A looks like this:

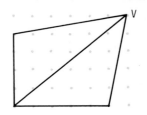

A10

c) Draw another possible plan for the hut. Also, draw the corresponding elevations from A and B.

d) Draw a 3D view of a hut with the same walls as the previous hut, but with V drawn in a different position. Explore the possible plan views of the hut, and the corresponding elevations.

TAKE NOTE

3D views are often ambiguous.
An additional plan or elevation may remove the ambiguity.

Oblique views

1   You need dotted squared and dotted isometric paper.
    Two towers, made from 1 cm cubes, are placed on a 6 cm square.
    This is the plan view.

a) This is the 3D view from K.

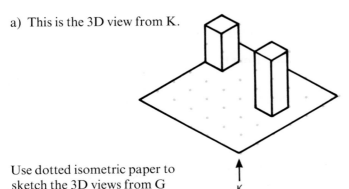

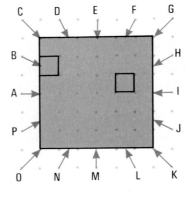

Use dotted isometric paper to
sketch the 3D views from G
and from C.

b) Choose another view (other than from O).
    Sketch the 3D view on plain paper.

c) Here is the elevation of the towers from M.

Use dotted squared paper to draw the elevations from E and from A.

▓▓▓▓▓▓▓▓ CHALLENGE ▓▓▓▓▓▓▓▓

d) Choose another view (other than from I). Sketch the elevation on plain paper.

e) Here are some more elevations. Which of the points A to P are the elevations from?

f) Make a rough sketch of the elevation of the towers from L. Use plain paper.

g) Study the sequence of drawings carefully. Use this method to produce an accurate, full-size drawing of the elevation of the towers from L.

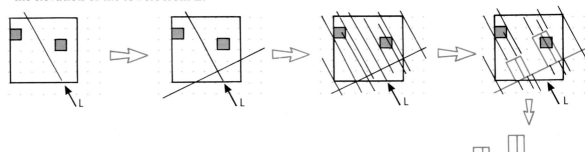

h) Use the method in g) to draw the elevation of the towers from P.

(i) Imagine an object (or objects) of your own, placed on a 6 cm square. Draw a 3D view like this:

(ii) Draw a plan view like this:

(iii) Now use your plan and the method in g) to draw an elevation from a point like B, C, D or F, etc.

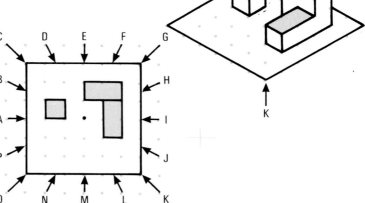

Chapter A10 THINKING IN 2D AND 3D 57

ENRICHMENT

1 Four 1 cm cubes are stuck together to make a cuboid. They are put on a slanting base.

a) Study this set of constructions. It shows how to construct the
    elevation of the cuboid from X.

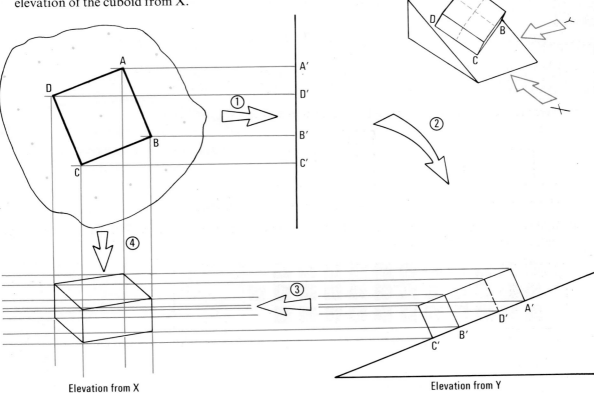

Elevation from X   Elevation from Y

b) Design your own cuboid. Imagine it placed on a wedge.
    Construct its elevation from X.

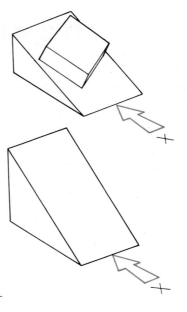

c) Imagine that the angle of the wedge gradually increases.
    Construct successive elevations from X.

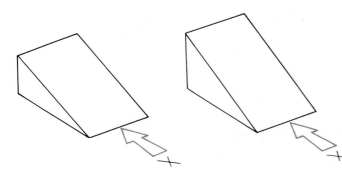

A10

CORE

Interest

1   When you put money into a savings account at a Building Society you receive *interest* on your savings.

For example, at the time the advertisement was produced the Surfleet Moneybox savings account offered interest of 7.75% per annum (per year).

**Everything
you pay in earns 7.75%***

Why leave cash lying around?
Put it into a Surfleet moneybox
and earn good interest on it
*Interest rate is variable

a) What is 1% of £1000?

b) What is 7% of £1000?

c) What is 7.75% of £1000?

d) Which of these gives the correct interest you
receive on £1000 after 1 year?

A [C] [.] [7] [7] [5] [×] [1] [0] [0] [0] [=]

B [C] [.] [0] [7] [7] [5] [×] [1] [0] [0] [0] [=]

C [C] [7] [.] [7] [5] [×] [1] [0] [0] [0] [=]

e) How much do you have in your Surfleet Moneybox savings account after 1 year if your initial saving is:

(i) £1000   (ii) £500   (iii) £5000?

f) Explain why this will give the total amount in your savings
account after 1 year if your initial saving is £800:

[C] [1] [.] [0] [7] [7] [5] [×] [8] [0] [0] [=]

g) Use the method suggested in f) to find the total amount after 1 year when the initial saving is £1750.

━━━━━━━━ WITH A FRIEND ━━━━━━━━

2   Imagine you invest £2000 in the Surfleet Moneybox savings account and you leave the money in the account for 2 years.

a) Each of you find how much will be in the account at the end of two years, using a calculator. Compare your results.

b) Here are the results obtained by two other pupils:

Pat £2310   Lesley £2322.01

Either could be correct.

Decide between you how the two results were calculated, and write down an explanation for each. Which method of calculation do you think Building Societies use, Pat's or Lesley's?

━━━━━━━━━━ TAKE NOTE ━━━━━━━━━━

There are two main methods of calculating interest.
Suppose you have £1000 invested for 2 years at 9% interest.

Method A

After 1 year, interest paid	=	£90
After 2 years, interest paid	=	£90 × 2
Total interest	=	£180

This is called *simple interest*.

Method B

After 1 year, interest paid	=	£90
Total in the account	=	£1090
Interest for year 2	=	£1090 × 0.09
	=	£98.10
Total interest = £90 + £98.10	=	£188.10

This is called *compound interest*.

3   When you borrow money, or 'take out a loan', you have to pay interest to the lender. You also pay interest on overdrafts at the bank and on money unpaid on credit card accounts. The interest you pay can vary a great deal. You should always check how much you will be paying before you take out a loan.

a) The table shows how much you pay back each month on different sized loans, when you take out a loan with a company called 'Moneymate'. Check that if you borrow £2000 for 60 months you pay £52.77 per month.

MONEYMATE
FAST PERSONAL LOANS!
TYPICAL MONTHLY REPAYMENTS

AMOUNT	36 MTHS	60 MTHS	120 MTHS	180 MTHS
£800	30.39	21.92	———	———
£2000	74.13	52.77	38.39	36.36
£3500	122.39	84.92	57.83	63.63
£7500	275.41	195.09	140.64	129.36

b) How much do you pay each month if you borrow £3500 and pay the money back over a 3 year period?

c) Calculate the total amount you pay back when you borrow:

   (i) £800 over a 5 year period
   (ii) £7500 over a 3 year period.

d) (i) How much do you pay in interest if you borrow £7500 and pay it back over a 5 year period?

   (ii) On average, how much interest is this per year?
   (iii) Use your result in (ii) to check that this represents a rate of simple interest of about 11.2% per year on £7500.

e) What rate of simple interest do the repayments on £2000 borrowed for 3 years represent?

Credit

1   a) When you buy an expensive article from a
       shop – say a television – you can either

       ● pay cash

       or ● pay in instalments (credit sale).

       This television costs £452
       if you pay cash.

       How much do you pay
       if you choose the
       credit sale?

CASH PRICE £452

Credit sale
Deposit: £50
then 10 monthly
instalments
of £45

   b) When you pay by instalments, you are really borrowing money from the store, and paying back over a
      period of time. For this service the store will charge you interest. That is why the cash price and credit
      sale price of the television are different.
      How much more do you pay for the television if you choose credit sale instead of paying cash?

   c) What is this difference in price as a percentage of the cash price?

2   The table shows the credit terms for buying second-hand cars from Blackbird Motors.

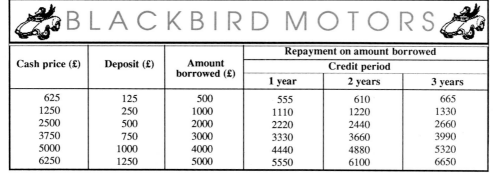

BLACKBIRD MOTORS

Cash price (£)	Deposit (£)	Amount borrowed (£)	Repayment on amount borrowed		
			Credit period		
			1 year	2 years	3 years
625	125	500	555	610	665
1250	250	1000	1110	1220	1330
2500	500	2000	2220	2440	2660
3750	750	3000	3330	3660	3990
5000	1000	4000	4440	4880	5320
6250	1250	5000	5550	6100	6650

   a) Why do you think you have to pay more if the payments are over 3 years rather than 2 years or 1 year?

   b) Imagine you want a car whose cash price is £6250.
      The total you pay on credit sale if you pay over 3 years is £1250 + £6650.
      How much more is this than the cash price?

   c) What is the difference between cash price and credit sale price, as a percentage of the cash price?

   d) How much more would you pay on credit sale than cash for a £2500 car bought over 3 years?

Hire purchase

1 Credit terms are sometimes also called 'hire purchase' terms (HP terms). Discuss between you why buying this way is sometimes called '*hire* purchase'. Write down what you decide.

2 a) Copy the HP calculation card, and use it to find the monthly instalments on the motor bike.

£

	800
Cash price	
Deposit (30%)	
Balance left to pay	
Interest to be paid on Balance (20%)	
Total repayments over 12 months (Interest and Balance)	
Monthly repayments	

MOTOR BIKE 100cc
Maximum speed 120 km / h
Tank capacity 7.8 litres

- Cash price £800
- HP terms available
Deposit 30%
12 monthly instalments. Interest rate 20%

b) How much more do you pay for the motor bike on HP than using cash?

3 The interest rate for hire purchase and credit schemes is usually called the *annual percentage rate* (APR). The table shows the repayment you make each month on each £100 you borrow at different APRs, over different loan periods.

You buy a music centre for £400 on HP, and pay back over 3 years. The APR is 22%.

a) How much do you pay per month?

b) How much do you pay altogether over the 3 year period?

c) How much more do you pay by this method than by paying cash?

Loan period		Monthly repayment				
		1 year	2 years	3 years	4 years	5 years
APR	20%	£9.19	£5.01	£3.63	£2.96	£2.56
	22%	£9.27	£5.09	£3.72	£3.05	£2.65
	24%	£9.35	£5.17	£3.80	£3.13	£2.75
	26%	£9.50	£5.33	£3.97	£3.31	£2.93

▬▬▬▬▬▬▬ ASSIGNMENT ▬▬▬▬▬▬▬

4   Investigate different ways of investing £1000 for 2 years.
Find the interest rates which are offered, and find out how the interest is calculated.
Write a report which compares the different amounts of interest you can receive from different forms of investment (such as Bank Accounts, Building Societies, Shares, Unit Trusts). Say which you think is the best investment and why.

ENRICHMENT

1   a) Imagine you put £P into a savings account which pays r% simple interest per annum. Write down a formula for the *total* amount of money (£T) you have in the account after (i) 1 year (ii) n years.

b) Now imagine that the savings account in a) pays r% compound interest, compounded once each year.

(i) Check that the amount in your account after 1 year is
$$£P \left(1 + \frac{r}{100}\right)$$

(ii) Explain why the amount after 2 years is
$$£P \left(1 + \frac{r}{100}\right)^2$$

(iii) Write down a formula for the amount you have in your account after n years.

(iv) Use your formula in (iii) to calculate how much you have in your account if you invest £1000 for 10 years at 8% compound interest per year.

2   You invest £10 000 in a savings plan which pays 7% compound interest per year. After how many years will your investment be worth more than £15 000?

REVIEW

- In mathematics we deal with sets of numbers, shapes, equations, ..., and we represent the relationship between sets on a Venn diagram.

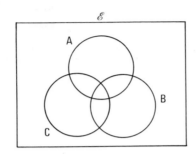

- $\mathscr{E}$ represents the Universal Set. The Universal Set contains all the elements which we are considering.

- $A \cap B$ is the intersection of A and B,

  for example, $\{1, 2, 3\} \cap \{1, 2, 4, 7\} = \{1, 2\}$

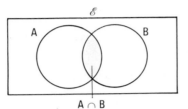

- $A \cup B$ is the union of A and B

  for example, $\{1, 2, 3\} \cup \{1, 2, 4, 7\} = \{1, 2, 3, 4, 7\}$

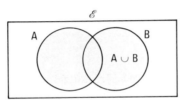

A12

CORE

Subsets

━━━━━━━ TAKE NOTE ━━━━━━━

The members of some sets belong also to larger sets. For example, each pupil in your mathematics classroom (set A) is also a pupil in your school year (set B).

We say that the first set is a *subset* of the second:

that is, 'A is a subset of B'
We write $A \subset B$, where $\subset$ means 'is a subset of'.

In a Venn diagram, subsets are drawn inside the sets of which they are a part.

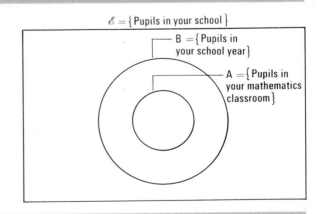

$\mathscr{E} = \{\text{Pupils in your school}\}$

$B = \{\text{Pupils in your school year}\}$

$A = \{\text{Pupils in your mathematics classroom}\}$

1   Check that {2, 9, 56} is a subset of A = {1, 2, 9, 24, 56}.
    Which of these are also subsets of A?

    a) {1, 2}   b) {1, 2, 3}   c) {9}   d) {1, 9, 24, 56, 57}

2   A = {a, b, c, d, e}   B = {a, b}   C = {c, d}

    a) Which Venn diagram best represents A, B and C?

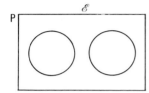 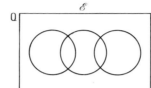 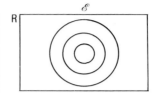 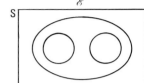

3   Draw a Venn diagram to represent this collection of sets.

    $\mathscr{E}$ = {Whole numbers from 1 to 15}

    A = {Multiples of 5 less than 15}

    B = {Prime numbers less than 15}

    C = {Divisors of 10}

4   Every square is a special type of rectangle, so

    {Squares} ⊂ {Rectangles}

    Write down some subset sentences about these shapes.

    {Squares}, {Rectangles}, {Rhombuses}, {Trapeziums}, {Kites}, {Parallelograms}

    How many sentences can you find?

5   Which of these diagrams
    shows the correct connection
    between rectangles,
    parallelograms and
    rhombuses? Explain why the
    other diagram is incorrect.

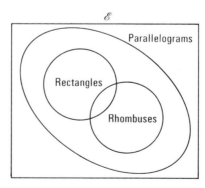 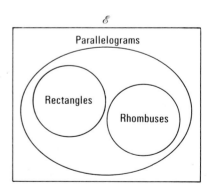

6   Every divisor of 12 is also a divisor of 24, so

    {Divisors of 12} ⊂ {Divisors of 24}

    Write down some subset sentences about these sets of numbers:

    {Odd numbers}, {Multiples of 4}, {Multiples of 3}, {Multiples of 12}, {Even numbers}.

    How many sentences can you find?

7   Which of these sentences are true for all possible sets P and Q?

(i) $(P \cap Q) \subset P$ (ii) $(P \cup Q) \subset P$ (iii) $P \subset (P \cup Q)$

8   $A \subset B$ and $B \subset A$. What can you say about A and B?

TAKE NOTE

A set is a subset of itself; for example, $\{1, 2\} \subset \{1, 2\}$.

Empty sets

1   $A = \{1, 3, 5, 7\}$ $B = \{2, 4, 8, 10\}$ $\mathscr{E} = \{1, 2, 3, 4, \ \ldots \ \}$.

a) Draw a Venn diagram to show A, B and $\mathscr{E}$.

b) What can you say about $A \cap B$?

TAKE NOTE

The sets $A = \{1, 2, 3\}$ and $B = \{4, 5\}$ have no intersection. We say that the intersection $A \cap B$ is *empty*, and we write $A \cap B = \varnothing$. The symbol $\varnothing$ represents an 'empty set', that is, a set with no elements.

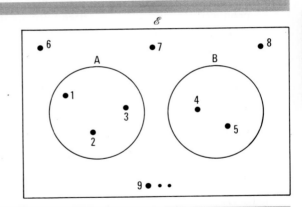

2   An example of an empty set is $\varnothing = \{\text{Birds with three legs}\}$.
Write down two examples of your own.

TAKE NOTE

The empty set, $\varnothing$, is a subset of all sets, for example, $\varnothing \subset \{1, 2\}$.

3   $A = \{1, 2, 3\}$ has 8 subsets. List them.

4   Which of these sets are empty?

A $\{\text{Numbers } x \text{ for which } x^{10} = {}^-1\}$ B $\{\text{Numbers } x \text{ for which } 10^x = {}^-1\}$

C $\{\text{Rectangles which are also parallelograms}\}$ D $\{\text{Parallelograms which are also rectangles}\}$

5   Draw a Venn diagram to represent the sets A, B and C which satisfy each of the conditions:

$A \subset B$ $A \cap C = \varnothing$ $C \subset B$

6   a) Drawings X and Y show two possible Venn diagrams
       for three sets C_1, C_2 and C_3. Check that each
       drawing satisfies these conditions:

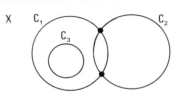

$$C_1 \cap C_2 \neq \varnothing$$
$$C_2 \cap C_3 = \varnothing$$

   b) Draw a third alternative arrangement of C_1, C_2
       and C_3 which also satisfies the conditions.

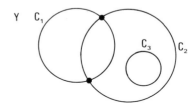

   c) To try to ensure that the arrangement in drawing X
       is produced, we can add this condition to the list:

$$C_3 \subset C_1$$

   Is this condition sufficient to ensure that the arrangement X will be produced? If not, what other
   conditions are necessary?

   d) Write a complete set of conditions which will ensure that your own arrangement in part b) will be
       produced. Try them out on a friend. Revise them if they can be interpreted in more than one way.

EXPLORATION

7   A line can be thought of as a set of points.
    This condition then tells us that lines l_2 and l_3 are parallel:

$$l_2 \cap l_3 = \varnothing$$

Investigate the sets of conditions which are needed to
specify the various ways in which three straight lines
can be arranged. For example, in the drawing we would
need the conditions

$$l_1 \cap l_2 \neq \varnothing$$
$$l_1 \cap l_3 \neq \varnothing$$
$$l_2 \cap l_3 = \varnothing$$

For each arrangement find the minimum number of conditions which is necessary.

Complements

TAKE NOTE

In this Venn diagram,
A represents the set of males at a party.
A′ (the shaded section) represents the set of
people at the party who are *not* males, that is,
A′ = {Females at the party}.
We call the set A′ (that is, the set of elements
which are *not* in A), the *complement* of A.

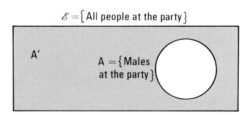

1   a) $\mathscr{E}$ = {Pupils in your school year}
      A = {Pupils in your mathematics class}

   Name two members of A′.

   b) $\mathscr{E}$ = {Letters of the alphabet}
      P′ = {Consonants}

   Describe the set P. How many members does it have?

   c) Give an example of your own of a Universal Set, a set A and its complement A′.

2   a) Check that the shaded section of the diagram represents (A ∪ B)′.
      Draw your own diagram to represent (A ∩ B)′.

   b) Draw diagrams to help you to decide if these are true or false:

      (i) (A ∪ B)′ = A′ ∪ B′   (ii) (A ∩ B)′ = A′ ∩ B′
      (iii) (A ∪ B)′ = A′ ∩ B′   (iv) (A ∩ B)′ = A′ ∪ B′

3   Copy and complete: a) A′ ∩ A = ...   b) A′ ∪ A = ...

4   Draw diagrams to represent each of these expressions:

   a) A′ ∩ (B ∪ C)   b) A ∩ (B′ ∪ C′)   c) A′ ∩ B′ ∩ C′

5   Match each expression with one of the diagrams A, B and C.

   a) (P′ ∩ Q) ∪ R   b) (P ∪ R)′ ∩ Q   c) (P ∪ Q′) ∩ R′

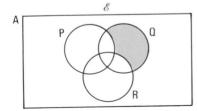
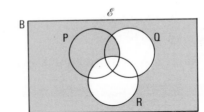
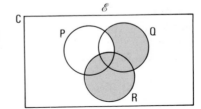

CHALLENGE

6   Think about all the different sections and combinations of sections which can be shaded on the Venn diagram. Find expressions (like those in question 2a)) for each section.

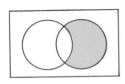
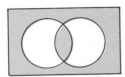
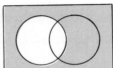
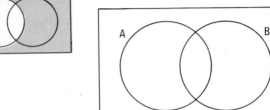

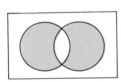

. . .

ASSIGNMENT

7　This is an identity for sets

$$(A \cap B)' \equiv A' \cup B'$$

You can check the two expressions
are always equal by studying
diagrams for each possible
arrangement of A and B.
Alternatively, you can study
different pairs of sets for A and B,
for example,

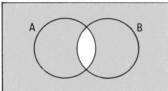
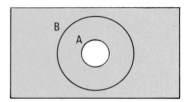

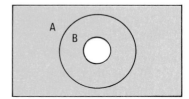

A = {1, 2, 3}　　B = {1, 2, 3, 4}

A = {1, 2, 3}　　B = {4, 5, 6}　etc.

Investigate some more expressions involving A and B. Find as many identities as you can (for example, is
there one for $A' \cup B$, $A' \cap B$, $(A \cup B)'$, etc?). Write about any patterns you find in your results.

Membership and number of elements

1　The number 2 is a member of the set of even numbers. We can write this in shorthand as

　　$2 \in \{$Even numbers$\}$　　　$\in$ means 'is a member of'

a) $x \in \{1, 2, 9, 11\} \cap \{3, 9, 12\}$

　　What can you say about x?

b) $x \in A$, and $x \in B$. Which of these must also be true:

　　(i) $x \in A \cap B$　(ii) $x \in A \cup B$　(iii) $x \in A' \cap B$　(iv) $x \in A' \cap B'$?

TAKE NOTE

To represent the *number* of elements in the set A, we write $n(A)$.
So if A = {Seasons of the year} then $n(A) = 4$.
For B = {Odd numbers}, $n(B) = \infty$ (that is, there is an infinite number of odd numbers).

2　$n(A) = 6$, $n(B) = 8$ and $n(A \cup B) = 12$.
　　What is $n(A \cap B)$? Draw a Venn diagram to explain your answer.

3　A = {Girls in your classroom}　　B = {Boys in your classroom}

　　What is　(i) $n(A)$　(ii) $n(B)$　(iii) $n(A \cup B)$　(iv) $n(A \cap B)$?

4　The number of elements in each set A and B is
shown in the diagram. You are given that
$n(A) = n(B)$.

　　What is　(i) x　(ii) $n(A \cup B)$?

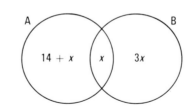

5 a) A is the set of subsets of {a, b}. Explain why $n(A) = 4$.

   b) P is the set of subsets of Q and $n(P) = 16$. What is $n(Q)$?

      Explain your answer.

6 $n(A \cup B) = n(A \cap B)$. What can you say about A and B?

━━━━━━━━ CHALLENGE ━━━━━━━━

7 A, B and C are three sets. The number of
   elements in the sets are shown in the Venn diagram.
   If $n(A \cup B \cup C) = 34$, find

   a) the value of x b) $n(A \cap B \cap C)$.

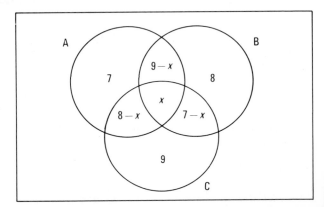

A12

ENRICHMENT

Sets, graphs and number lines

1 The graph of $y = x^2$ is a set of points. We can
   write

   $G_1 = \{(x, y): \ y = x^2\}$

   that is, G_1 is the set of points (x, y) which obey
   the rule $y = x^2$.
   Here are three more sets of points:

   $G_2 = \{(x, y): \ y = 4\}$

   $G_3 = \{(x, y): \ x = {}^-1\}$

   $G_4 = \{(x, y): \ x+y = 1\}$

   a) List the members of each of these sets:

      (i) $G_1 \cap G_2$ (ii) $G_1 \cap G_3$

   b) Make a sketch to show the members of $G_1 \cup G_4$.

   c) How many members of $G_1 \cap X$ are there when X is

      (i) $\{(x, y): \ x = 2\}$ (ii) $\{(x, y): \ y = 2\}$ (iii) $\{(x, y): \ y = {}^-1\}$?

2   The values of x which satisfy the inequality $^-1 < x \leqslant 4$, can be thought of as a set of numbers, P:

$P = \{x: \quad ^-1 < x \leqslant 4\}$ (that is, P is the set of numbers x, where x is greater than $^-1$ and less or equal to 4).

We can represent P on a number-line diagram:

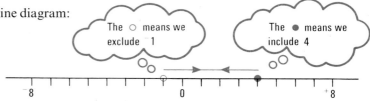

a) Represent these sets of numbers on a number line:

(i) $Q = \{x: \quad ^-4 \leqslant x < 3\}$ (ii) $R = \{x: \quad 2 < x < 10\}$.
(iii) $P \cap Q$ (iv) $Q \cup R$

b) Now assume that P, Q and R are sets of whole numbers only. How many members has

(i) $P \cap Q \cap R$ (ii) $P \cup Q \cup R$
(iii) $P' \cap R$ (iv) $P' \cap Q' \cap R'$

c) This number-line diagram represents a
set of numbers (not only whole numbers).

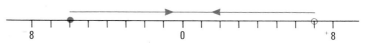

Write down two sets P and Q

(i) whose *intersection* is represented by the diagram
(ii) whose *union* is represented by the diagram.

CORE

- Statements like this are often seen in newspapers and on television. The statistics quoted are usually the end product of a lengthy survey.

DENTIST DISCLOSURE
statistics prove
"My patients have 50% fewer fillings- - - - - "

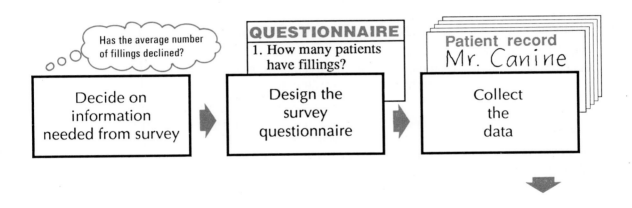

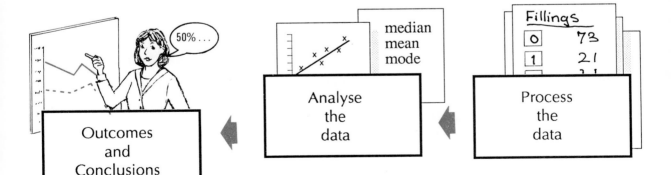

- There are two basic ways of collecting the data (called 'raw data' before it is processed and analysed):

  either   use records already in existence
  or   carry out your own survey.

Opinion surveys

1   A knitwear company is carrying out a staff opinion survey. There are ten statements in the survey booklet. The frequency table shows the pattern of responses to statement 1.

CONFIDENTIAL SURVEY

Ring one of the numbers for each statement

STATEMENT 1
Our firm is more efficient than it was 12 months ago

strongly agree	agree	don't know	disagree	strongly disagree
1	2	3	4	5

response	frequency
1	7
2	15
3	31
4	18
5	4
Total	

a) How many employees responded to statement 1?

b) How many employees feel strongly that the firm is more efficient now than it was 12 months ago?

c) Generally speaking, do you think the employees feel that the firm is more efficient or less efficient than it was twelve months ago? Explain how you arrived at your conclusion.

d) Design an alternative 'range of possible responses' to statement 1 which would give you an immediate indication as to whether employees consider the firm to be more efficient or less efficient than twelve months ago.

e) The questionnaire might have used this range of responses:

Tick one box	Agree	Don't know	Disagree
	☐	☐	☐

Imagine this was used for statement 1.
Make out a frequency table to show what you think the response pattern would look like for the same group of employees.

ASSIGNMENT

2   Think of an opinion survey you would like to carry out which needs a set of statements like those in question 1.

It might be survey about politics
    or bands
    or sport
    or poetry ...

Include at least three statements in your survey, and decide upon your own range of possible responses (for example, 'Very interesting, Interesting ... Very boring').
Ask a group of people (at least fifteen) to complete your questionnaire. Make out frequency tables and bar charts to represent the pattern of responses to each statement.
Write a short report about the opinions which are expressed in your survey.

3   Fifty people were asked to list five perfumes in order, from 'most liked' to 'least liked'.

> **Perfume questionnaire**
> *Decide your order of preference*
> *for the samples. Put the numbers*
> *1 (most liked) to 5 (least liked)*
> *in the boxes to show your order*
> *of preference.*
>
> Perfume
>
> A ☐
> B ☐
> C ☐
> D ☐
> E ☐

These were the results:

Perfume	People									
	1	2	3	4	5	6	7	8	9	10
A	1	5	3	1	5	3	2	4	2	3
B	3	4	4	3	4	5	5	3	4	5
C	4	2	1	2	3	2	1	5	3	4
D	5	1	5	5	2	1	4	1	1	2
E	2	3	2	4	1	4	3	2	2	1

a) Together, discuss how you might use the results to decide which perfume is liked most.

b) Imagine you are responsible for launching new perfumes. You have five new perfumes which you need to test on the market. Discuss how you would collect the data you need and how you would analyse the results to decide which perfume to launch. If you decide that a questionnaire is needed, design it together.

A13

4   A, B and C are three different surveys you could do.
Choose *one* of them, or think of a survey of your own which you would like to do. (Your survey should involve you in asking members of your class to pick a collection of items or events in order of preference.) Carry out the survey, and use the information to decide an answer to the question which is set, or the question you set yourself. Present all the data you collected, using charts and diagrams, and explain how you arrived at your decision.

A   Your class has been offered a day out. Use a questionnaire to help you to decide where you should go.

B   You can invite a famous person into your classroom for a day. Use a questionnaire to help you to decide whom you would invite.

C   Your class can decide what the main meal menu should be for tomorrow. Use a questionnaire to help you to decide what it should be.

Choosing a sample

1. a) Ask three people for their favourite colour, or favourite number from 1 to 10, or favourite band.
        Write down the most favoured choice.

    b) Ask three more people the same question.
       Write down the most favoured choice for all six people you have asked.

    c) Ask three more people.
       Write down the most favoured choice for all nine people you have asked.

    d) Continue asking three more people, then three more, ...
       Describe what is happening to your 'most favoured' result.

    e) Imagine you wanted to find out the most favoured colour of all the people in Coventry. It is clearly
       impossible to ask every person.
       How would you decide?
       How would you ensure your result was 'representative', that is, not biased?

2. To decide the most likely outcome of a National (General) Election, a company asked 3000 people in
    Blackpool which party they would vote for.

    a) Why is this not a sensible way of predicting the outcome?

    b) How could the company obtain a more representative (that is, less biased) estimate of the result?

TAKE NOTE

A *population* is the total number of individuals or items in a group/class/category that is being examined.
A *sample* is a selection from the population.
A *representative* sample is a sample which (within certain acceptable limits) accurately reflects the result which
would be obtained if the whole population were included in the survey. The results from a representative
sample are considered to be unbiased.

A13

EXPLORATION: WITH A FRIEND

3. You need ten counters, beads, marbles, ..., of two different colours – or you can use strips of paper marked
    with a colour.

    a) One of you choose a selection of five of the counters (beads, ...). Put them in a bag and hide the rest.
       This is your 'population'.
       The other chooses one counter at a time from the bag, replacing it each time.
       Investigate how many choices of a counter you need to make a reasonable estimate of the make-up of
       colours in the bag (that is, of the 'population').

    b) Repeat the experiment in a). This time however, choose *two* counters at a time from the bag.
       About how many trials do you need now to decide the make-up of colours?

    c) Repeat the experiment for other numbers of choices (three counters at a time, four counters
       at a time, ...).
       Record how many choices appear to be needed.

    d) Write a report to explain how the size of the sample (that is, one counter, or two counters, ...) influences
       the number of samples you have to take to obtain a good estimate of the make-up of a population.

4   Here are two samples of information from newspapers. Each is the outcome of a survey.

Choose one of them and decide how you think the data might have been collected and prepared. Assume that every attempt was made to ensure that the resulting data were not biased.

Write down your main decisions, for example, what constituted the total population? What kind of sample was probably used? How were the data collected (by postal questionnaire, by visiting houses with a questionnaire, ...)? and so on.

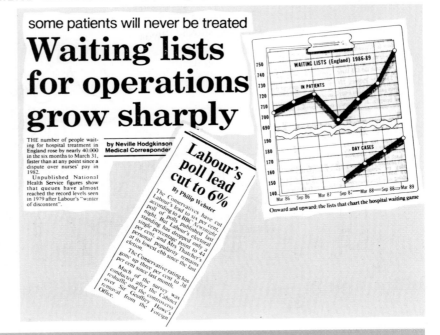

some patients will never be treated

Waiting lists for operations grow sharply

by Neville Hodgkinson
Medical Correspondent

THE number of people waiting for hospital treatment in England rose by nearly 40,000 in the six months to March 31, faster than at any point since a dispute over nurses' pay in 1982.

Unpublished National Health Service figures show that queues have almost reached the record levels seen in 1979 after Labour's "winter of discontent".

Labour's poll lead cut to 6%

By Philip Webster

The Conservatives have cut Labour's lead to six per cent, according to a BBC Newsnight poll of polls published last night. But Labour's electoral standing has dropped only a single percentage point to 44 per cent, and Mrs Thatcher's personal popularity remains at its lowest ebb since the last election.

The Conservative rating has gone up three per cent to 38 per cent since last month. Much of the survey was conducted after the Cabinet reshuffle and the controversy over Sir Geoffrey Howe's removal from the Foreign Office.

Onward and upward: the lists that chart the hospital waiting game

5   A customer information research company wishes to know how often households in a city bake their own bread.

The following methods of collecting the data are suggested by members of the survey team:

A   A pre-paid reply slip printed on all packets of McKnees plain flour

B   A random sample of 500 address – pre-paid reply slips sent

C   A random sample of 500 telephone numbers. Researchers to telephone and ask questions

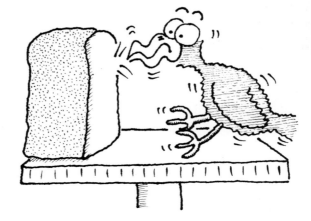

Work together to:

a) Suggest an alternative method of obtaining a sample and collecting the data.

b) List the advantages and disadvantages of using each type of data collection (including your own suggestion).

c) Decide what questions you would ask in your own survey.

d) Explain how you would analyse and present the results.

A13

6   Imagine you work for an advertising agency. Your next task is to produce an advertising video for 'Morning crunch' breakfast cereal.

To decide what 'angle' your video should take, you decide to carry out a survey. Design a questionnaire which would give you useful information. Explain how you would collect the information, and from whom.
The *Take note* will help you organize your thoughts.

TAKE NOTE

When collecting data

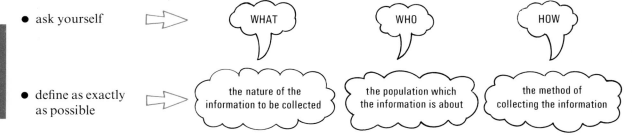

- ask yourself   WHAT   WHO   HOW

- define as exactly   the nature of the   the population which   the method of
  as possible   information to be collected   the information is about   collecting the information

- the questions need to be *simple* and *unambiguous*.

ENRICHMENT

1   900 pupils attend a school in Brighton. There are six forms in each of the five year groups. Some of the pupils have school lunches, some have packed lunches and the rest go home.
The Headmistress wishes to find out how many pupils are in each of these three categories at the various age levels in the school. For this purpose she plans to use a 10% sample of the school population.

a) Describe a method of choosing an appropriate sample of the pupils for this survey.

b) Design a questionnaire which will obtain the relevant information for this survey.

c) Design a chart for presenting the information obtained from the questionnaire.

2   There are many numerical methods for selecting a
    sample so that every member of the population has
    an equal chance of being chosen.
    Find out about the following sampling methods:

    Random numbers
    Stratified sampling
    Sampling bottles
    Quota sampling

    Write a brief report on each method.

3   You are asked to make a statistical survey of the TV viewing habits and preferences of the pupils in your
    school. In order to carry this out, it is planned to distribute a questionnaire to a 5% representative sample
    covering the whole age range in your school.

    a) State four aims of your survey.

    b) Describe how the sample should be chosen from your school.

    c) Prepare four questions to be included in the questionnaire in the precise form in which they would be
       stated to obtain the required information for your survey.

    d) Design a chart for presenting the information obtained from your questionnaire.

A13

REVIEW

- Two shapes are *similar* when one is an enlargement (or reduction) of the other.

Similar shapes have corresponding angles equal, and pairs of corresponding sides in the same ratio. For example:

$$\frac{AB}{A'B'} = \frac{BC}{B'C'} = \frac{1}{2}$$

$$\frac{AB}{BC} = \frac{A'B'}{B'C'}$$

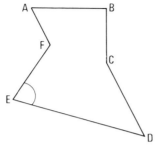
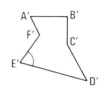
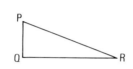

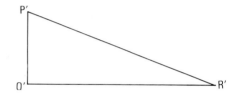

- Two shapes are *congruent* when they are identical in shape *and* size (the scale factor for enlargement is $\times 1$ or $\times^{-}1$).

Two triangles are congruent if they have:

1) all three sides equal (SSS)

2) two sides and the included angle (the angle between the two sides) equal (SAS)

3) a corresponding side and two corresponding angles equal (AAS).

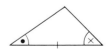

- If we know two sides and a non-included angle, we can usually draw two different triangles.

    a) Draw two different triangles which have sides of 4 cm and 6 cm and a 60° angle.

    b) Draw two different triangles which have a 6 cm side and angles of 90° and 30°.

CORE

B1

Calculations for similar triangles

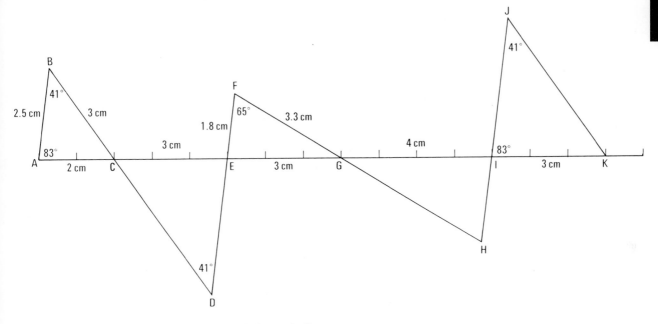

1 a) Explain why triangles ABC and EDC are similar.

   b) Write down (i) another pair of similar triangles   (ii) a pair of congruent triangles.

   c) Use properties of similar triangles to work out the length of side DE. (Check your answer by measuring.)

   d) Here are two methods for working out the length GH. Copy and complete each one.

   (i) *Ratios method*

   Triangles EFG and IHG are similar so corresponding pairs of sides are in the same ratio.
   Form a pair of ratios involving GH,
   e.g. $\dfrac{GH}{GI} = \dfrac{GF}{\Box}$

   i.e. $\dfrac{GH}{4} = \dfrac{3.3}{\Box}$

   × 4: so GH = $\dfrac{3.3}{\Box}$ × 4

   = $\Box$

   The length of GH is $\Box$ cm.

   (ii) *Scale factor method*

   Triangles EFG and IHG are similar and the length of GI is $\frac{4}{3}$ times the length of the corresponding side GE.
   So all lengths in triangle IHG are $\frac{4}{3}$ times the corresponding lengths in triangle EFG.

   So GH is $\frac{4}{3}$ times side $\Box$

   i.e. $GH = \frac{4}{3} × \Box$

   = $\Box$

   The length of GH is $\Box$ cm.

   e) Choose one of the methods in d). Use it to work out the lengths of

   (i) IH   (ii) CD. (Check your answers by measuring.)

████████ TAKE NOTE ████████

We can find lengths in similar shapes by

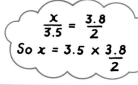

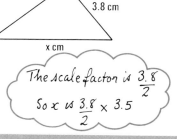

(i) constructing
equal ratios

$$\frac{x}{3.5} = \frac{3.8}{2}$$

So $x = 3.5 \times \dfrac{3.8}{2}$

or   (ii) using the
scale factor

The scale factor is $\dfrac{3.8}{2}$

So x is $\dfrac{3.8}{2} \times 3.5$

2   a) The marked angles in the diagram are equal.
       Which triangle is similar to ABD?

    b) Find the length of CD.

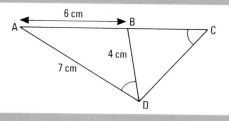

████████ THINK IT THROUGH ████████

    c) Which is larger, a or b? Explain your answer.

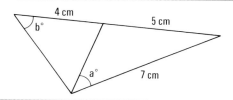

3   This is a spiral made from similar triangles (for example,
    OAB is similar to OBC).

    a) How many triangles are needed to produce a complete turn?

    b) Find the longest side of the last triangle.

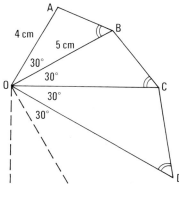

4   a) There are three triangles in the diagram:
       ABD, ACD and BCD.

       (i) Explain why they are all similar.
       (ii) List the three triangles, with the letters of
            corresponding vertices in the same order.

    b) (i) Use the two smaller triangles to find the
            length of CD.
       (ii) Use the smallest and largest triangle to
            find the length of CD.

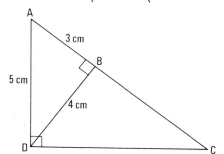

Congruent figures

1 In a triangle ABC, AB = 4 cm, ∠ABC = 60° and ∠BCA = 20°.
   In a triangle PQR, PQ = 4 cm, ∠PRQ = 60° and ∠QPR = 20°.
   Are the triangles congruent? Make a sketch to illustrate your answer.

2 The opposite sides of parallelograms are parallel
   and equal. ABCD is a parallelogram.

   Use the properties of parallelograms to explain why:

   a) triangles ACD and ACB are congruent

   b) triangles AXB and DXC are congruent.

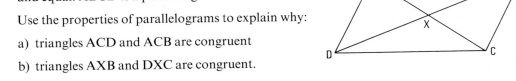

3 a) In the diagram, PQ is parallel to AC and
      PR is parallel to BC. P is the midpoint of AB.

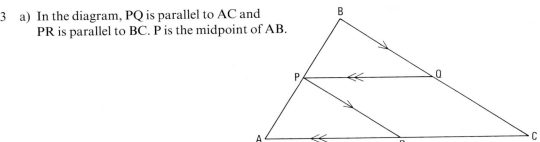

   Use the properties of parallel lines and the fact that P
   is the midpoint of AB, to help you to complete this
   proof that triangles PBQ and APR
   are congruent:

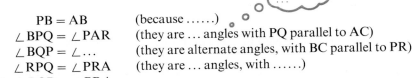

   corresponding?
   alternate?
   ...

   PB = AB   (because ......)
   ∠BPQ = ∠PAR   (they are ... angles with PQ parallel to AC)
   ∠BQP = ∠...   (they are alternate angles, with BC parallel to PR)
   ∠RPQ = ∠PRA   (they are ... angles, with ......)
   So ∠BQP = ∠PRA

   Therefore the triangles BPQ and APR are congruent (two angles and a corresponding side are equal).

   b) Write out a proof like that in a) to show that triangles QRC and PAR are congruent.

4 In the diagram, DC = CB = xcm.

   Imagine that C can move (along with A, B, D
   and E) providing always that DC = CB. Under what
   circumstances are triangles ABC and DEC
   (i) congruent (ii) similar? Explain your answers.

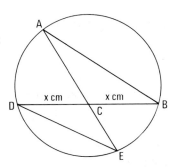

B1

5 a) In the diagram, $\angle CAB = 30°$.

Explain why, if $\angle ACD$ is also 30°, the triangles ABC and ACD must be congruent.

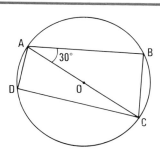

b) If instead, $\angle DAC$ is 30°, are triangles ABC and ACD still congruent? Why?

6 In the diagram, BA is parallel to CE, CB = BE and CD = BA.

Explain why triangles CBD and BAE must be congruent.

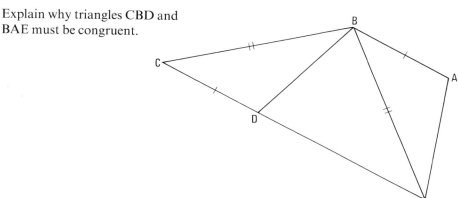

7 a) Here are four pairs of statements. Decide which of the statements in each pair is true (only one might be, or both might be).

A 1 If triangles X and Y are congruent, then at least one side of triangle X and one side of triangle Y are the same length.
   2 If a side of triangle X and a side of triangle Y are the same length, then the two triangles are congruent.

B 1 If triangles X and Y are congruent, then at least two pairs of corresponding sides are equal.
   2 If two pairs of sides of triangles X and Y are equal, then the triangles are congruent.

C 1 If triangles X and Y are congruent, then the triangles have three pairs of corresponding sides equal.
   2 If triangles X and Y have three pairs of corresponding sides equal, then the triangles are congruent.

D 1 If triangles X and Y are congruent, then the two triangles have three pairs of corresponding angles equal.
   2 If triangles X and Y have three pairs of corresponding angles equal, then the two triangles are congruent.

b) Write down a pair of statements of your own like those in a). Make one statement in the pair true and the other false. Your statements should make reference to two sides and an angle of each of two triangles.

c) Two sides and an angle of triangle ABC are equal to two sides and an angle of triangle PQR. Draw a diagram to explain why this is not sufficient to ensure that triangles ABC and PQR are congruent.

B1

TAKE NOTE

If two triangles are congruent, then (at least) two angles and a side in one triangle will be equal to two angles and a side of the other triangle.

But as you can see from triangles ABC and PQR, the fact that two angles and a side are equal is not sufficient to ensure that the triangles are congruent. For the triangles to be congruent, the side must be a *corresponding* side as in triangles LMN and XYZ.

We say that for two triangles to be congruent, it is *necessary* that two angles and a side are equal, but that this requirement is not *sufficient* to ensure that the triangles are congruent.

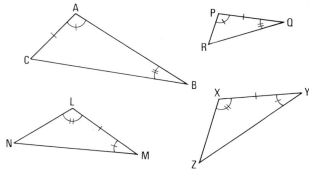

For two triangles to be congruent they must have two angles and a *corresponding* side equal. This is a *necessary* and *sufficient* condition.

8   Read the *Take note*, then write your own *Take note* for the triangles in question 7 c).

WITH A FRIEND: CONGRUENT QUADRILATERALS

9   You may need dotted squared paper.
   a) There are many kinds of quadrilateral: trapezium, kite, parallelogram, rhombus, …

   (i) Together choose one type, say a kite.
   (ii) Each of you draw a kite, as accurately as you can (dotted paper might help).
   (iii) Now each of you give your partner just enough information to draw your kite.

   You could do this by writing measurements on a sketch, for example:
   Try to draw each other's kite.
   (iv) Discuss all the different ways in which you could define a specific kite. Each way should use as little information as possible. Record your conclusions.
   (v) Write down a set of equalities of sides, angles or lengths of diagonals in two kites which is sufficient to ensure that the two kites are congruent.

   b) Repeat a) for another type of quadrilateral.

ENRICHMENT

1   In the diagram, 0 is the the centre of the circle, ∠ RPQ = 20° and ∠ CAB = 70°.

   Use the properties of circles and the information above to prove that triangles ABC and PQR are congruent.

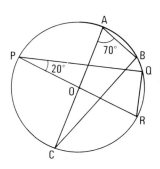

B1

2 a) Express BD in terms of a, b and c by:

   (i) using the similar triangles ABC and DBA
   (ii) using the similar triangles ABC and DAC.

   b) Use your expressions to prove that, for a right-angled triangle,
   $a^2 + b^2 = c^2$.

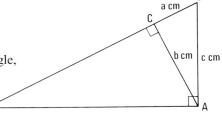

3 In the diagram, SP = PT.

   a) Triangles PRS and PTQ appear to be congruent.
   But this is not necessarily the case. Explain why not.

   b) What else needs to be true before we can be
   sure that the two triangles are congruent?
   (You might find more than one
   possible condition.)

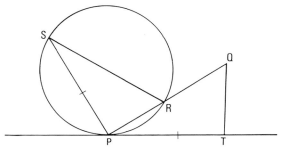

REVIEW

You have met these six transformations of the plane:

- translation   • rotation   • reflection   • enlargement   • stretch   • shear.

Under a transformation, those points which do not change their positions are called *invariant* points. The diagrams show the effect of each of the above types of transformation on a point A.

◼ Copy each diagram and draw the image of the rectangle ABCD in the plane.

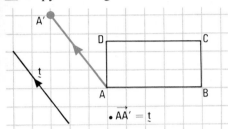

- *Translation* with displacement $\underset{\sim}{t}$

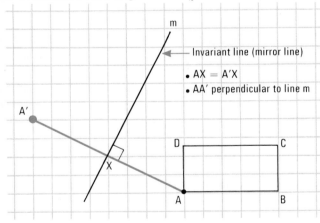

- *Reflection* in mirror line m

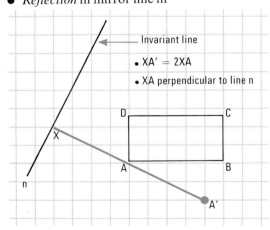

- *Stretch*, scale factor $\times 2$, invariant line n

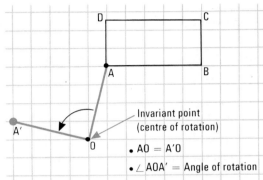

- *Rotation* of 90° anticlockwise about O

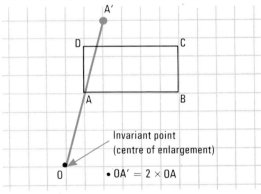

- *Enlargement*, scale factor $\times 2$, centre O

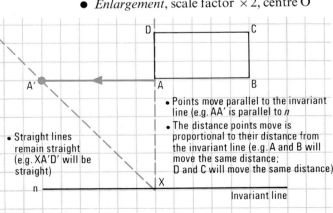

- *Shear*, with invariant line n

CONSOLIDATION

Invariance

1 Which types of transformation have:

   a) no invariant points

   b) one invariant point

   c) a line of invariant points?

   List the types of transformation in each case.

2 Which types of transformation:

   a) preserve shape (but not necessarily size)

   b) preserve shape *and* size

   c) preserve area

   d) keep straight lines straight and parallel lines parallel?

   List the types of transformation in each case.

TAKE NOTE

- Transformations of the plane which preserve all distances (that is, preserve shape *and* size) are called *isometries*.
  Translations, rotations and reflections are isometries.

- Transformations which preserve straightness *and* parallelism are called *affine* transformations.
  Translations, rotations, reflections, enlargements, stretches and shears are all affine transformations.

WITH A FRIEND

3 You will remember that we can use position vectors to represent transformations. For example, a rotation of 90° anticlockwise about the origin is given by this position-vector rule:

$$\begin{pmatrix} x \\ y \end{pmatrix} \longrightarrow \begin{pmatrix} {}^-y \\ x \end{pmatrix}$$

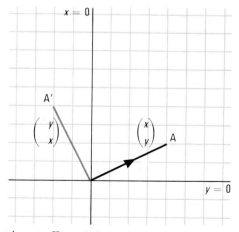

Invent a rule that represents a transformation that is *not* affine. Ask your friend to show the effect of your transformation on a rectangle in the (x, y) plane.

CORE

Combining transformations and finding invariant points

1   The diagram shows the effect
on points in the (x, y) plane, of

- an enlargement scale factor
  $\times 2$, centre the origin, followed by

- a translation given
  by the displacement vector $\begin{pmatrix} 4 \\ 2 \end{pmatrix}$.

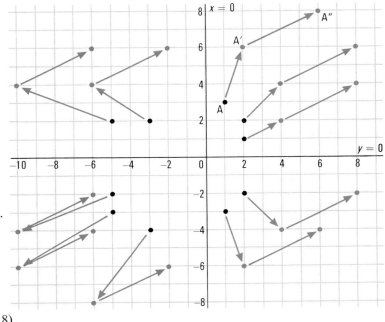

There is a single enlargement, scale
factor $\times 2$, which has the same
overall effect. Its centre is the point
that remains invariant (that is,
returns to its original position)
under the combined transformation.
Look at the diagram. Try to
visualize the position of the
invariant point.
When you have found the invariant
point, check that an enlargement,
scale factor $\times 2$, with that point as
centre, takes point A $(1, 3)$ to A″ $(6, 8)$.

B2

════════ EXPLORATION ════════

2   a) Here is another way of finding the invariant point in question 1:

Draw a simple object.	Enlarge it, scale factor $\times 2$, centre the origin.	Translate the new object by $\begin{pmatrix} 4 \\ 2 \end{pmatrix}$.	Join corresponding points of the original and final object.

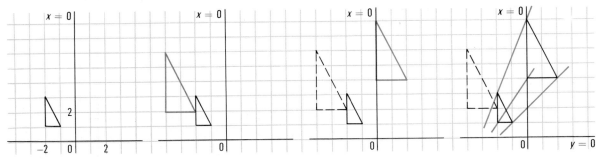

Copy and complete the fourth drawing. Find out where the three lines meet.

b) Explore the combination of other enlargements with the translation $\begin{pmatrix} 4 \\ 2 \end{pmatrix}$.

(For example, try an enlargement, scale factor $\times 3$, centre the origin, followed by the translation $\begin{pmatrix} 4 \\ 2 \end{pmatrix}$).
Find the equivalent enlargement. Use the method of question 1 or part a) of this question.
Write about any rule that you find.

B2

3   For each diagram, find the single transformation equivalent to the pair of transformations described. Use the 'invariant points' method of question 1 or draw objects and images as in question 2. Before you begin, try to predict what kind of transformation you are looking for each time.

a) A rotation of 90° anticlockwise about the origin, followed by a translation of $\begin{pmatrix} 2 \\ 2 \end{pmatrix}$.

b) A rotation of 90° anticlockwise about the origin, followed by a translation of $\begin{pmatrix} 4 \\ 0 \end{pmatrix}$.

c) A reflection in $y = 0$ followed by a translation of $\begin{pmatrix} 0 \\ 4 \end{pmatrix}$.

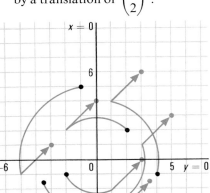
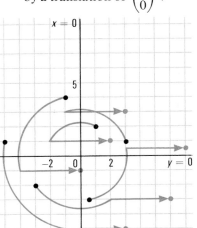
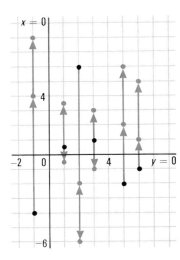

CHALLENGE

4   Explain why none of the single transformations which you have met so far (that is, no translation, rotation, reflection, enlargement, stretch or shear) is equivalent to the pair of transformations shown in this diagram.
(Hint: think of invariant points.)

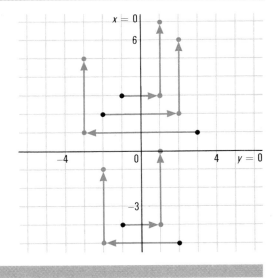

A reflection in $x = 0$ followed by a translation of $\begin{pmatrix} 0 \\ 4 \end{pmatrix}$.

THINK IT THROUGH

5   A shear is followed by a translation. In what direction (compared to the direction of the invariant line of the shear) must the translation be, if the two transformations are equivalent to a single shear?

6   a) Read these arguments. Take your time.

> An enlargement followed by a translation is equivalent to another enlargement because any transformed object will have the same shape as before. (from the enlargement) and the sides of the shape will stay parallel to their original orientation (from the translation).

> An enlargement followed by a rotation is not usually equivalent to another enlargement (or any other single transformation) because any transformed object will not usually have its sides parallel to their original orientation (from the rotation) even though it will be the same shape as before (because the enlargement preserves shape and the rotation preserves size and shape).

> But, if the rotation is a half-turn, an enlargement followed by a rotation will be equivalent to another enlargement because the sides of any transformed object will stay parallel to their original orientation.

> A reflection followed by a translation is sometimes equivalent to a single reflection, because any transformed object is the same size and shape as before, but 'turned over'. However, if the translation is not perpendicular to the mirror line, there will be no invariant points and so the pair of transformations will not be equivalent to a reflection (or any other single transformation).

b) Use the same kind of reasoning to decide on the outcome of combining other pairs of transformations. (For example, a rotation followed by a translation; a rotation followed by a rotation.) Are some pairs always equivalent to a single transformation? Are there exceptions?

Write about what you decide. Consider all the kinds of transformations we have met in this chapter.

ENRICHMENT

The isometries

1 a) Explain why a reflection followed by a reflection in a parallel mirror is equivalent to a translation (think about the shape, size and orientation of any transformed object, and think about invariant points).

   b) Explain why a reflection followed by a reflection in a non-parallel mirror is equivalent to a rotation (think about the shape, size and orientation of any transformed object, and think about invariant points).

CHALLENGE

   c) For a pair of parallel mirrors, the resultant translation of an object is related to the direction of the parallel mirrors and the distance between them. Find out what the relationship is.

   d) For a pair of intersecting mirrors, the resultant rotation of the object is related to the angle between the mirrors and their point of intersection. Find out what the relationship is.

2 Because any translation is equivalent to two reflections, and any rotation is equivalent to two reflections (in parallel and intersecting mirrors, respectively), we can 'convert' any combination of translations, rotations, and reflections into a combination of reflections. For example, you can use diagram X to help you to see that a 90° anticlockwise rotation about A, followed by a translation $\begin{pmatrix} 4 \\ 0 \end{pmatrix}$ is equivalent to a reflection in m_1, then m_2, then m_3, then m_4:

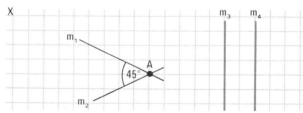

   a) Now look at diagrams Y and Z.

      (i) Explain why diagram Y is equivalent to diagram X.
      (ii) Explain why diagram Z is equivalent to diagram Y.
      (iii) Explain why the original rotation and translation is equivalent to a 90° anticlockwise rotation about B (diagram Z).

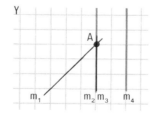
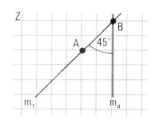

THINK IT THROUGH

   b) Use the method of a) to find the transformation equivalent to a half turn about A followed by a quarter turn anticlockwise about B.

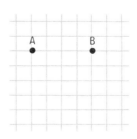

3 A rotation of 90° anticlockwise about a point A, followed by a reflection, is equivalent to a single reflection. What can you say about:

a) the position of the original mirror line

b) the direction of the resultant mirror line?
(Hint: think about the ideas in question 2.)

4 A translation $\begin{pmatrix} 2 \\ 6 \end{pmatrix}$ followed by a reflection in a mirror line that passes through the origin is equivalent to a single reflection. Find the new mirror line.

B2

──────── ACTIVITY ────────

5 You need tracing paper.

a) Draw a diagram to show the effect of rotating flag F through 90° anticlockwise about A, and then rotating the image through 90° anticlockwise about B, and then rotating the new image through 180° about C.

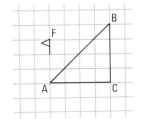

b) On plain paper draw any triangle ABC and a flag F. Use tracing paper to help you rotate flag F through $2\alpha°$ anticlockwise about A, and then rotate the image through $2\beta°$ anticlockwise about B, and then rotate the new image through $2\gamma°$ about C.

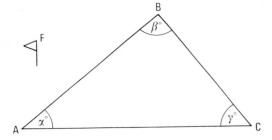

c) Explain your findings in a) and b). (Hint: think about the ideas in question 2.)

B3 BRACKETS AND FACTORS

CORE

1 These are all the ways of writing $2a^2b$ using only '$\times$' and whole numbers. (We ignore the use of 1, as in $1 \times 2a^2 \times b$, $1 \times 2 \times a^2 \times b$, etc.)

Using one $\times$: $2a^2 \times b$ $2a \times ab$ $2ab \times a$ $2b \times a^2$ $2 \times a^2b$
Using two $\times$s: $2 \times a^2 \times b$ $2b \times a \times a$ $2 \times ab \times a$
Using three $\times$s: $2 \times a \times a \times b$

a) Each of you complete this list of factors of $2a^2b$:

$2, a, a^2, ab, \ldots$

Compare your results.

b) Each of you, independently write down all the factors of $6a^2 \times b^2$.
After five minutes compare your results. Make sure you have listed all the possibilities.

2 $a(b+2)$ can be written also as $ab+2a$.
a is a factor of $ab+2a$, and so is $(b+2)$.

a) Write each of these expressions using brackets:

   (i) $pk-4k$ (ii) a^2+2a (iii) pk^2+pk.

b) Write down the factors of each expression in a).

3 Here are three ways of writing km^2-km using brackets:

$k(m^2-m)$, $km(m-1)$, $m(km-k)$.

We say that k, (m^2-m), km and m are *algebraic factors* of km^2-km.

a) Write $pq+pq^2$ in three different ways using brackets.

b) List the algebraic factors of $pq+pq^2$.

c) List the algebraic factors of a^2n-n^2a.

When we write $4n^2-2an$ (for example) as a product of factors, such as $2n(2n-a)$, we say we have *factorized* $4n^2-2an$.

4   The diagram shows that

$(a+b)(c+d) \equiv ac+ad+bc+bd$

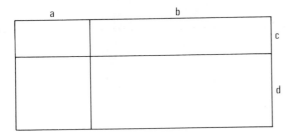

Total area: $(a+b)(c+d)$
Area of each part: ac, bc, ad, bd
Total area: $ac+ad+bc+bd.$

a) Use the diagram below to help you to explain why these are true:

   (i) $(a+b)(c-d) \equiv (a+b)c-(a+b)d$
   (ii) $(a+b)(c-d) \equiv a(c-d)+b(c-d)$
   (iii) $(a+b)(c-d) \equiv ac-ad+bc-bd.$

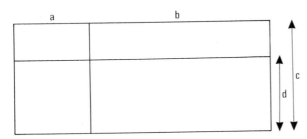

b) Draw a diagram which helps you to explain why these are true:

   (i) $(a-b)(c-d) \equiv a(c-d)-b(c-d)$
   (ii) $(a-b)(c-d) \equiv (a-b)c-(a-b)d$
   (iii) $(a-b)(c-d) \equiv ac-ad-bc+bd.$

5   Copy and complete:

a) $(4+b)(c+3) \equiv 4(\quad)+b(\quad) \equiv 4c+\square+bc+3\square$

b) $(t+n)(2-c) \equiv t(\quad)+\square(2-c) \equiv \square-\square+\square-\square$

c) $(p-q)(3-k) \equiv p(\quad)-q(\quad) \equiv \square-\square-\square+\square$

▬▬▬▬▬▬ TAKE NOTE ▬▬▬▬▬▬

$(a+b)(c+d) \equiv a(c+d)+b(c+d) \equiv ac+ad+bc+bd$
$(a+b)(c-d) \equiv a(c-d)+b(c-d) \equiv ac-ad+bc-bd$
$(a-b)(c-d) \equiv a(c-d)-b(c-d) \equiv ac-ad-bc+bd$

Quadratic expressions

1 a) Begin with a square   Add a section

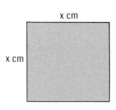 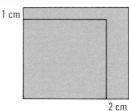

Explain why the area of the complete figure can be represented by:

(i) $(x+1)(x+2)$ cm²   (ii) $(x^2+2x+x+2)$ cm²   (iii) (x^2+3x+2) cm².

b) Begin again with a square   Remove a section

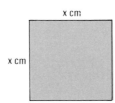 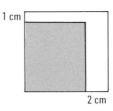

Explain why the area remaining can be represented by:

(i) $(x-1)(x-2)$ cm²   (ii) $(x^2-2x-x+2)$ cm²   (iii) (x^2-3x+2) cm².

c) Begin with the square again   Add a section, then remove a section

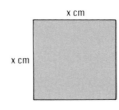 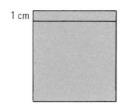 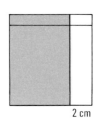

Explain why the final area is:

(i) $(x+1)(x-2)$ cm²   (ii) $(x^2-2x+x-2)$ cm²   (iii) (x^2-x-2) cm².

2 Copy and complete:

a) $(x-4)(x-1) = x(x-1)-4(x-1) = \square^2-\square x+\square$

b) $(2-x)(x-1) = 2(x-1)-x(x-1) = -\square^2+\square x-\square$

c) $(x+3)(x-2) = x(\quad)+3(\quad) = \square^2+\square x-\square$

d) $(x-2)(x+6) = x(\quad)-2(\quad) = \square^2+\square x-\square.$

CHALLENGE

3 Write each of these using two pairs of brackets:

a) x^2+3x+2 b) x^2-3x+2 c) x^2-3x-4.

Expression of the form ax^2+bx+c, for example, $2x^2+5x-3$, are called *quadratic expressions*.
They can sometimes be represented as a product of two 'brackets', for example:

$x^2+3x+2 \equiv (x+2)(x+1)$
$2x^2+5x-3 \equiv (2x-1)(x+3)$

4   Factorize each of these quadratic expressions, that is, write them in the form $(\square+\square)(\square+\square)$.
    You should find the values in the brackets by trial and error. Eventually you will begin to find a method of
    your own for dealing with them.

a) x^2+5x+4 b) x^2+7x+6 c) $x^2+8x+16$ d) $x^2+7x+10$

e) $x^2+8x+12$ f) $x^2+7x+12$ g) $x^2+13x+12$ h) x^2+2x+1.

5   Write each of these expressions in the form $(x+\square)(x-\square)$:

a) $x^2+2x-15$ b) x^2+2x-8 c) $x^2+3x-10$ d) $x^2+4x-12$ e) $x^2+11x-12$

f) $x^2-4x-12$ g) $x^2-11x-12$ h) $x^2-6x-16$ i) $x^2+6x-16$ j) x^2+x-20

k) x^2-x-20 l) $x^2+10x-24$ m) $x^2+8x-20$ n) $x^2-8x-20$ o) $x^2-10x-24$

p) $x^2-2x-24$ q) $x^2+2x-24$ r) x^2-16 s) $x^2+5x-24$ t) x^2-9.

6   Write each of these expressions in the form $(x-\square)(x-\square)$:

a) x^2-4x+4 b) x^2-9x+8 c) x^2-6x+8 d) $x^2-7x+10$

e) $x^2-11x+10$ f) $x^2-8x+16$ g) $x^2-10x+16$ h) $x^2-17x+16$.

7   Together, discuss and then write out a set of instructions to explain the best way of deciding upon the
    factors of various quadratic expressions. For example, how can we arrive most quickly at the result

$x^2+7x+12 \equiv (x+3)(x+4)$
or $x^2-x-12 \equiv (x+3)(x-4)$?

Deal with each of these types of expressions in turn:

a) Expressions with two '+'s, such as $x^2+9x+20$

b) Expressions with a '−' and a '+', such as x^2-4x+3

c) Expressions with a '+' and a '−', such as x^2+2x-8

d) Expressions with two '−'s, such as x^2-x-3.

8   Match each expression A to E with a factorized expression J to N:

A $3x^2+11x-4$ J $(2x+1)(x-1)$
B $2x^2-x-1$ K $(x+2)(3x-2)$
C $3x^2+4x-4$ L $(3x-1)(x+4)$
D $^-2x^2+3x-1$ M $(1-2x)(x-1)$
E $^-2x^2+x+1$ N $(1+2x)(1-x)$

B3

9 Investigate the factorization of expressions of the form $bx^2 - a^2$, for example,

$x^2 - 4, \quad x^2 - 3, \quad \ldots, \quad 4x^2 - 9, \quad 3x^2 - 16, \ldots$

Explain how they can be factorized.

10 Factorize each expression:

a) $2x^2 - 7x + 3$ b) $2x^2 + 5x - 3$ c) $9x^2 + 9x + 2$ d) $9x^2 + 3x - 2$

e) $6x^2 + x - 1$ f) $6x^2 + 5x + 1$ g) $6x^2 - x - 1$ h) $6x^2 - 5x + 1$

To factorize an expression, for example,

$6x^2 + 10x - 4$

- Write down two brackets $(\square \quad)(\square \quad)$

- Choose these two expressions to give $6x^2$,

  for example, $(6x \quad)(x \quad)$ or $(3x \quad)(2x \quad)$

- Choose these $(\quad \square)(\quad \square)$ to give $^-4$ when multiplied,

  for example, $(6x + 2)(x - 2)$ or $(6x + 4)(x - 1)$ or $(3x - 4)(2x + 1)$ or $\ldots$

- Test each possibility until you find the correct result for the x term.

11 Find the factors of the expression in the *Take note*.

12 Factorize: a) $9x^2 - 27x$ b) $4x^2 - 25y^2$ c) $6x^2 + 16x - 6$.

ENRICHMENT

1 Multiply out: a) $(x + 2)(x + 3)$ b) $(x + 2)(x + 3)(x + 1)$.

2 Show that $(x - 1)(x + 2)(x + 1)(x - 2) \equiv x^4 - 5x^2 + 4$.

3 a) By replacing x by 4, show that $x = 4$ is a solution of the equation

$x^3 - x^2 - 10x - 8 = 0$.

b) By trial and testing, find the other two solutions of the equation.

c) Use your result in b) to help you to write $x^3 - x^2 - 10x - 8$ in the form

$(x \ldots \square)(x \ldots \square)(x \ldots \square)$.

d) By trial and testing (or any other method), find the three solutions to the equation

$x^3 - x^2 - 6x = 0$.

e) Use your result in d) to factorize $x^3 - x^2 - 6x$.

4 a) Explain why the value of the expression $x^2 + 5$ is never smaller than 5.

b) Explain why the value of the expression $5 - x^2$ is never greater than 5.

c) Write down an expression of your own whose value is:

(i) always larger than or equal to $^-5$
(ii) always smaller than or equal to $^-5$.

5 a) Check that this is the graph of $y = x^2 + 5$.

Explain how the graph illustrates the
answer to question 4 a).

b) Draw the graph of $y = 5 - x^2$.

Explain how your graph illustrates the
answer to question 4 b).

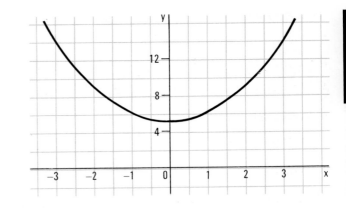

6 a) Show that $x^2 - 2x + 1 \equiv (x - 1)^2$.

b) Find the value of $x^2 - 2x + 1$ when x is: (i) 4   (ii) $^-3$ (iii) 0   (iv) $^-10$.

c) Use the identity in a) to explain why the value of $x^2 - 2x + 1$ is never less than 0.

d) Draw the graph of $y = x^2 - 2x + 1$. Explain how your graph illustrates the answer to c).

 CHALLENGE

7 Write down an expression of the form $ax^2 + bx + c$, where a, b and c are not 0, whose value is:

(i) never greater than 0   (ii) never greater than 10
(iii) never less than $^-4$ (iv) never greater than $^-4$.

REVIEW

- To calculate the median of a set of data, it helps to add a *cumulative frequency* column to a frequency table. The cumulative frequency column gives a 'running total' of the frequencies.

- From the frequency table we can produce a *cumulative frequency* graph:

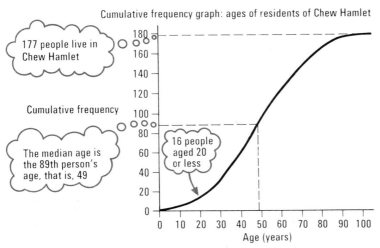

Frequency table: Ages of residents of Chew Hamlet

Age (years)	Frequency	Cumulative frequency
1	0	0
2	1	1
3	1	2
4	0	2
5	2	4
.	.	.
.	.	.
20	1	16
21	1	17
.	.	.
.	.	.
40	2	60
41	4	64
.	.	.
.	.	.
98	0	176
99	1	177

The cumulative frequency graph shows a 'picture' of the cumulative frequencies when (in the example) the ages are arranged in order. From the graph the median age can be found as shown.

■ Approximately how many people in Chew Hamlet are in their 50s?

- For *grouped data* the upper limits of intervals are used for plotting points on a cumulative frequency graph.

Cumulative frequency table (grouped data): ages of residents of Chew Hamlet

Age (years)	Frequency	Cumulative frequency
1–10	6	6
11–20	10	16
21–30	15	31
31–40	17	48
41–50	33	81
51–60	40	121
61–70	28	149
71–80	15	164
81–90	11	175
91–100	2	177

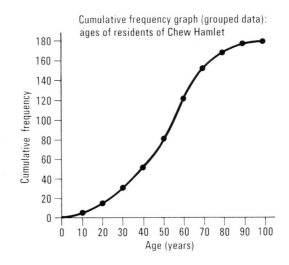

■ The two cumulative frequency graphs appear to be very similar – but how are they different, and why?

The age axes on the graphs represent different things. In what way?

● We can *estimate* the mean from a grouped-data cumulative frequency table, using *midpoints*:

$$\text{Mean} = \frac{\text{Total of (Midpoint} \times \text{Frequency)}}{\text{Total frequency}}$$

■ Complete the calculation of the estimated mean from the grouped frequency table.

Cumulative frequency table (grouped data): ages of residents of Chew Hamlet

Age (years)	Frequency	Midpt × Freq.	Cumulative frequency
1–10	6	33.0	6
11–20	10	155	16
21–30	15	397.5	31
31–40	17	.	48
.	.	.	.
.	.	.	.
.	.	.	.
91–100	2	191.0	.
Totals	177	.	

● The grouped data can also be represented on a bar chart to help us to compare numbers between groups.

■ What is the modal class for the distribution of ages in Chew Hamlet?

● The *range* of a set of data is the difference between the largest and smallest values recorded. The range gives a measure of the spread of the data. The range of the ages of residents of Chew Hamlet is $99 - 2 = 97$ (years).

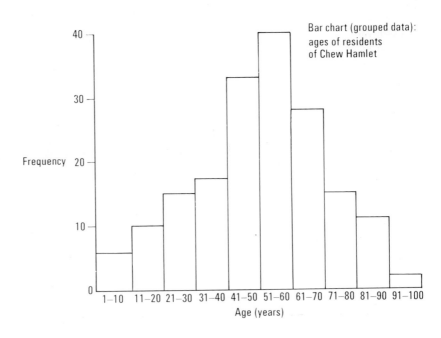

Bar chart (grouped data): ages of residents of Chew Hamlet

CONSOLIDATION

1   The data give the masses in grams, rounded down to the nearest 5 g, of a sample of 200 potatoes from an experimental growth plot. The sample was taken during early spring.

a) Using the class intervals 1 − 20, 21 − 40, 41 − 50, ..., make out a cumulative frequency table for the data and draw a cumulative frequency graph.

b) From your graph estimate the median mass of the sample of potatoes.

c) Because the masses of potatoes were rounded down, it is possible only to estimate the range. Write down an estimate for the range.

15	25	40	55	65	75	80	85	15	25
35	35	55	70	75	85	90	95	75	60
60	65	65	55	45	65	55	60	85	85
80	80	70	70	55	55	35	15	20	45
65	70	90	100	95	40	35	75	75	65
20	35	30	45	75	75	75	60	80	85
35	70	70	65	35	80	80	100	95	105
70	75	65	60	70	70	95	110	75	80
50	45	35	35	70	40	75	60	60	60
20	40	40	40	35	40	55	70	75	85
90	25	30	30	75	70	65	65	70	75
65	70	75	75	75	80	40	70	40	40
105	100	75	30	15	45	75	80	60	65
50	55	55	50	35	35	70	60	60	65
75	75	70	80	90	95	95	35	35	35
25	25	75	70	60	60	75	80	80	95
100	20	40	40	40	75	85	95	25	35
40	70	70	60	60	55	40	65	70	85
90	40	35	75	60	50	50	45	50	75
30	40	50	70	75	95	40	25	30	75

B4

CORE

Interquartile range and dispersion

1   The three frequency dot diagrams show the ages (in completed years) of three groups of students in an education survey.

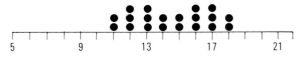

Sample A

Sample B

Sample C

a) Calculate the mean and the range for each sample.

b) Calculate the mean and the range for samples D and E.

Sample D

Ages (years)	6	10	10	12	15	15	15	15	15	21

Sample E

c) Which of the five samples has the greatest range?

Ages (years)	5	10	13	14	15	17	18	18	20	20

TAKE NOTE

The range is a very crude measure of 'spread' or 'dispersion'. It has two main disadvantages:

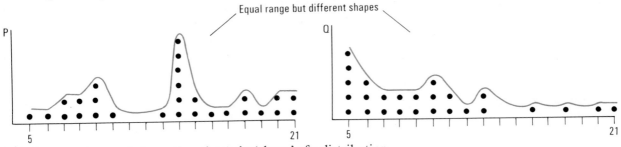

- it does not give any information about the 'shape' of a distribution
- it can give a misleading impression because it uses the extreme values of the data. These may be atypical or isolated.

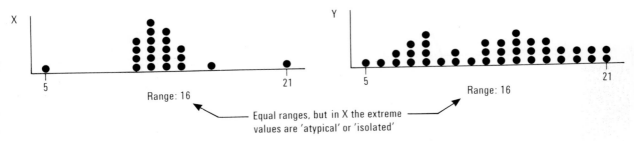

An alternative method of indicating the spread of data, which is not so influenced by extreme values as is the range, is to use the middle 50% of the values.

For example, there are 28 values in the diagram. 25% of 28 is 7. The values in the loop are representative of the 'middle 50%' (25% of the values to the left and right, that is, 7 each side, have been left out).

The range of the middle 50% in the diagram is $15-8 = 7$.

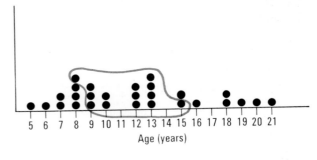

CHALLENGE

2　a)　The measure of spread which uses the 'middle 50%' of the data values is called the *interquartile range*. Give your own explanation as to why you think it is called this.

b)　For this set of data, find　(i) the range　(ii) the interquartile range:

Number of children in 64 families in a village

0	1	2	3	4	5	6 or more
6	13	28	5	8	4	0

3   The two cumulative frequency graphs record the same information – the heights of 160 saplings after two months growth.

a) Check that the range for the distribution is about 5.4 cm. (The graphs suggests that one or more saplings are 0.6 cm tall, and the tallest is 6 cm.)

b) Estimate the interquartile range (the range of heights of the middle 50% of saplings) to the nearest millimetre.

c) Roughly, what percentage of saplings are taller than 3 cm?

d) Roughly, what percentage of saplings are shorter than 5 cm?

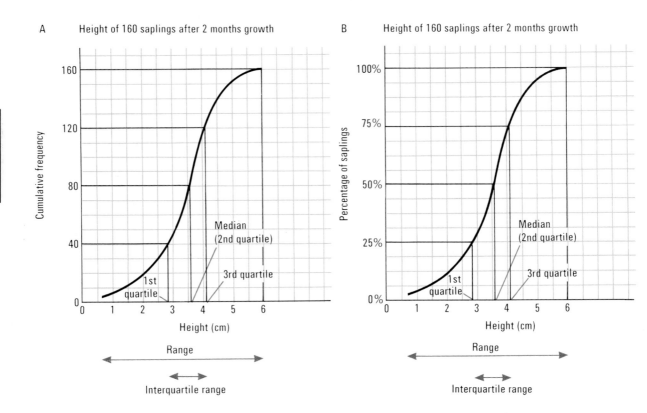

TAKE NOTE

Graph A represents the *number* of saplings which are less than a given height.
Graph B represents the *percentage* of saplings which are less than a given height.
40 saplings (25% of saplings) are less than about 2.8 cm tall.
We say that the *25th percentile* is 2.8 cm.
The 25th percentile is also called the *first quartile*.
The 50th percentile is called the *second quartile* (or median). The median in the example is about 3.6 cm.
The 75th percentile is called the *third quartile*.
The *interquartile range* (about 1.3 cm) is the range from the first quartile to the third quartile values.

4   The graph shows the distribution of the lengths of two different populations of eels from an eel farm.

a) Roughly, what percentage of the eels in each population are between 15 and 30 cm long?

b) From the graph estimate:

   (i) the range for each population
   (ii) the median length in each population
   (iii) the interquartile range for each population.

c) Imagine a bar chart drawn to represent each population, using class intervals of 5 cm (0 – 5 cm, > 5 cm – 10 cm, > 10 cm – 15 cm, …). *Predict* and *sketch* the shape of each chart.

d) Use the information you have obtained for b) to draw a bar chart for each population, using class intervals of 5 cm, and so check your predictions in c).

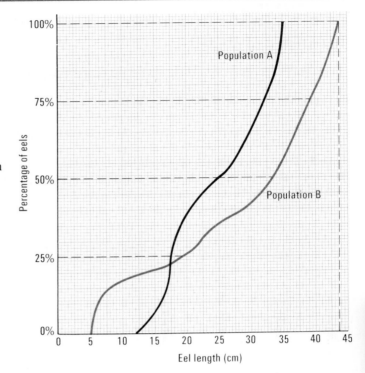

e) Write one or two sentences to explain the main differences in the distribution of the lengths of eels in the two populations.

f) The two populations were started at approximately the same time, with the same number of males and females. One of the populations now has twice as many eels as the other. Which do you think this is, A or B? Explain what information you used to arrive at your conclusion.

5   *Best buy* magazine collected information about two different makes of car, A and B. One question asked owners to indicate how many miles they travelled before the car developed its first serious fault. The graph shows the results for the survey question. (200 owners of each make of car answered the questionnaire.)

Which make of car do you think is more reliable? Why?

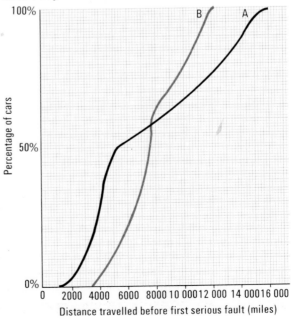

ENRICHMENT

Deviation and dispersion

████████████████ TAKE NOTE ██

The 'spread' of data can be indicated by either

- the range

or - the interquartile range.

Neither of these measures of spread, however, takes all of the items of data into account.
The range takes simply the highest and lowest values into account. The interquartile range takes the range
from the middle 50% of the population into account. Both of them can therefore give a misleading
impression about the similarity or lack of similarity of two distributions.

For example, the two age distributions in the frequency dot diagrams have the same range and
interquartile range – but the distributions are very different.

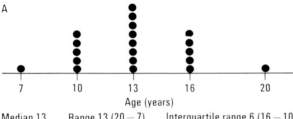

A

Median 13   Range 13 (20 − 7)   Interquartile range 6 (16 − 10)

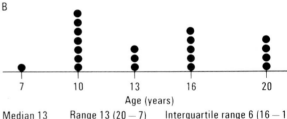

B

Median 13   Range 13 (20 − 7)   Interquartile range 6 (16 − 10)

████████████████ WITH A FRIEND ██

1 An alternative way of giving information about the 'spread' or 'dispersion' of a distribution is to give an
indication of how the distribution clusters around, say, the median value. For example, you can see that the
ages in chart A in the *Take note* cluster more closely around the median than the ages in chart B.

a) Discuss and explain the meaning of this calculation in respect of the data for chart A in the *Take note*:

$$\frac{(1 \times 6) + (5 \times 3) + (8 \times 0) + (5 \times 3) + (1 \times 7)}{20} = 2.15$$

(Think about the median, and the 'distance' of each item of data from the median.)

b) Check that this same calculation fits chart B:

$$\frac{(1 \times 6) + (7 \times 3) + (3 \times 0) + (5 \times 3) + (4 \times 7)}{20} = 3.5$$

c) What do the numbers 2.15 and 3.5 indicate about the 'spread' or 'dispersion' of the data in charts A and
B? Write one or two sentences to explain.

d) Decide between you how a set of twenty ages might be distributed if the calculation above gave the result
(i) 6 (ii) 0. Draw a frequency dot diagram to illustrate each of your answers.

We call the result of a calculation like that in question 1 the 'mean of the absolute deviations of the data from the median', or 'absolute mean deviation from the median'. The result gives us an idea of how widely the data is spread from the median.

For example, the result 2.15 for chart A in the *Take note* tells us that the data is not so widely spread as that for chart B (mean deviation from the median = 3.5).

('Absolute' means that the sign of the deviation is ignored.)

2   a) Check that the following statistics are correct for each age chart.

	X	Y
Mean	10	10
Median	12	10
Mean deviation from the median	3.0	1.6

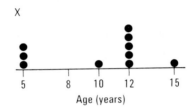

   b) Are the results for the mean deviation from the median as you would have expected? Explain why.

   c) Study each of these calculations carefully. Explain what information they give you about the spread of the data in charts X and Y.

$$\text{(i)} \quad \frac{(3 \times 5)+(1 \times 0)+(5 \times 2)+(1 \times 5)}{10} = 3.4$$

$$\text{(ii)} \quad \frac{(4 \times 2)+(2 \times 0)+(4 \times 2)}{10} = 1.6$$

The calculations in question 2 c) give the 'means of the absolute deviations from the mean' of each distribution, or the 'absolute mean deviation from the mean'. This is a measure of spread similar to the 'absolute mean deviation from the median'. The larger is the mean deviation, then generally the more 'spread out' is the data from the mean.

3   This is a formula for the absolute mean deviation from the mean, for a frequency distribution with n items of data.

$$M = \frac{\Sigma |f(x_i - \bar{x})|}{\Sigma f_i} \qquad i = 1, \ 2, \ \dots, n$$

   a) Study and explain the meaning of each element in the formula. (That is, what does $\bar{x}$ represent, x_i represent, $x_i - \bar{x}$ represent, $f(x_i - \bar{x})$ represent, …)

   b) Write a similar formula for the absolute mean deviation from the median.

4   The table shows the annual profits made by a small firm.

Year	1975	1976	1977	1978	1979	1980	1981	1982	1983
Profit £	2300	3720	5780	1140	⁻480	2640	5840	7320	10980

a) What is the range covered by the profits?

b) Calculate the mean annual profit.

c) Draw a line graph to show the profit trend over the period.

d) Calculate the mean deviation from the mean.

e) Prepare a report for the firm's directors describing the progress of the business from 1975 to 1983.

TAKE NOTE

The mean deviation from the mean is often used in economic and social statistics. The lower its value, the smaller the spread of the data.

5   In a school there are 30 classes. One morning a check was made on the number of absentees in each class. It gave this information:

No. of absentees	No. of classes
0	2
1	7
2	9
3	5
4	3
5	3
6	1

a) (i) Find the median of the distribution of the number of absentees.
    (ii) Calculate the mean deviation from the median for the distribution.

b)   Compare your result in a) (ii) with a day when each of the classes had three absentees. Explain what the relative value of the mean deviation from the median tells you about the distribution of absentees.

ENRICHMENT

Distribution shapes

1 a) A scientist carried out the experiment on the percentage of oxygen in a gas mixture. The frequency table
shows the results:

Experiment: to measure the percentage of oxygen in a gas mixture obtained as a bubble in a capillary tube.
Note: errors may arise from variations in temperature, irregularities in the diameter of the tube and small variations in bubble size during measurement. To judge the extent to which random errors are affecting the result, perform 25 trials.

% Oxygen	Frequency	f
17 –	/	/
18 –	/HH	5
19 –	HH //	7
20 –	HH ///	8
21 –	///	3
22 –	/	/
23 –		
	TOTAL	25

The dotted outline of the tally marks gives a rough picture of the pattern of the distribution of the results.
Calculate the absolute deviation from the mean for the distribution.

b) The shape of a distribution can also be seen by investigating the histogram displaying the data:

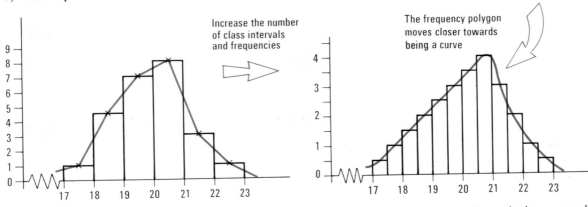

Increase the number of class intervals and frequencies

The frequency polygon moves closer towards being a curve

In a *symmetrical* frequency distribution, the mean, median and mode coincide. This results in a *normal*
or bell-shaped distribution (graph A). If the frequency distribution is not symmetrical, the mean, median
and mode may not coincide; two possible arrangements are shown in graphs B and C.

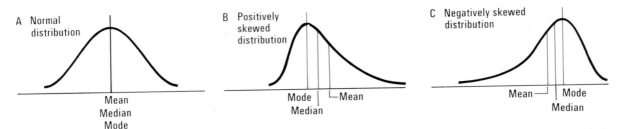

A Normal distribution
Mean
Median
Mode

B Positively skewed distribution
Mode
Median
Mean

C Negatively skewed distribution
Mean
Mode
Median

Would you say that the distribution of oxygen in the trials is normal, positively skewed or negatively skewed?

2 a) If we drew a frequency curve for people's heights in the UK, we would find that the result is very close to a normal curve. Roughly, what would you expect the mean height to be?

   b) (i) A frequency curve for the distribution of wages in the UK would show a positive skew. What does this tell you about the distribution of wages? Write one or two sentences to explain.

      (ii) Give another example of a distribution you would expect to be positively skewed.

   c) Age-related data is sometimes negatively skewed. In which country or countries would you expect to see this? Why?

CHALLENGE

3 Here are some more types of frequency curve. For each one describe a population which might give rise to the shape.

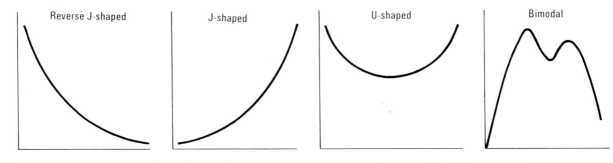

Reverse J-shaped   J-shaped   U-shaped   Bimodal

Standard deviation

TAKE NOTE

An important statistic, different from the mean deviation, from the mean or median, and which is also used to indicate how the data in a population is distributed, is called the *standard deviation* (SD).

It can be shown that for a normal distribution nearly all data values (*i.e.* about 99.8%) lie within a range of $3 \times$ the standard deviation either side of the mean.

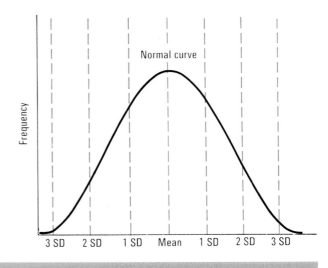

1 The flow chart shows how the standard deviation (SD) can be calculated.

a) Follow the flow chart, and complete the calculation of the standard deviation for the ages in chart A. For chart A:

$$\text{Mean} = \frac{(3 \times 5)+(1 \times 10)+(5 \times 12)+(1 \times 15)}{10} = \square$$

Deviations from the mean: 5, 5, 5, 0, 2, ...
Squares of deviations from the mean: 25, 25, 25, 0, 4, ...
Sum of the squares of deviations from the mean: 120

Mean of the sum of the squares of the deviation from the mean: $\dfrac{120}{10} = \square$

Standard deviation (SD) = $\sqrt{12} = \square$ (2 DP)

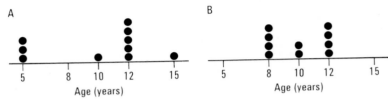

A   B

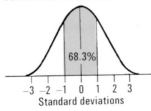   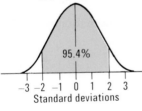

Flow chart (right side, top to bottom):

| Calculate the mean |

| Find the deviation of each data value from the mean |

| Square each deviation value |

| Add the squares of the deviations together and find the sum of the squares of the deviations |

| Divide by the number of data items, that is, find the mean of the sum of the squares |

| Find the square root of the mean of the sum of the squares |

b) Calculate the standard deviation of the ages in chart B.

c) Which standard deviation is greater, that for chart A or that for chart B? What does this suggest about the distribution of ages in the two charts?

d) Check that all of the data for each chart lies within about three standard deviations either side of the mean (see the *Take note* at the beginning of this section).

TAKE NOTE

A *normal distribution* has the following properties:

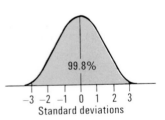

- it is symmetrical about the mean
- the mean ±1 standard deviation will give you the middle 68% of the data
- the mean ±2 standard deviations will give you the middle 95% of the data
- the mean ±3 standard deviations will give you almost all the data (the middle 99.8%).
- the mean ±$\frac{2}{3}$ standard deviations will give you the middle 50% of the data.

2 An accountant discovered that the wages paid by a particular firm were normally distributed, with a mean of £160 and standard deviation £15.

a) Roughly, what is the highest wage earned in the firm?

b) Approximately, how many employees of the firm earn between £130 and £190 per week?

c) Approximately, what percentage of the employees of the firm earn more than £145 per week?

3   Researchers have attempted to measure intelligence in units called Intelligence Quotients (IQ). IQs are normally distributed with a mean score of 100 and standard deviation of 15.

a) Approximately, what percentage of the population has an IQ of 145 and over?

b) Approximately, what is the interquartile range of IQ?

c) Approximately, what is the chance of having an IQ of 130 or more?

CHALLENGE

4   The distribution of test marks is normal, mean 25, standard deviation 5. What will happen to the distribution if:

a) five extra marks are awarded to every pupil

b) the marks awarded are doubled?

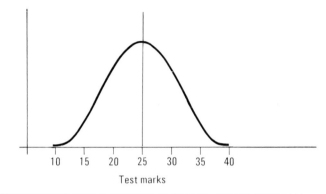

Test marks

B4

5   For an entry in a song contest, a total of 60 marks were awarded by 10 judges. They were:

4, 8, 6, 4, 7, 9, 4, 6, 5, 7.

a) For these marks, calculate: (i) the mean deviation from the mean   (ii) the standard deviation.

b) How would the statistics in a) have changed had there been four extra judges and each had awarded six marks?

6   The tables show data concerning the weekly earnings of men and women (aged 18 and over) in Britain in April 1970.

Men

Percentage with weekly earnings less than				
£20	£24	£30	£36	£45
7.7	35.3	60.2	76.4	91.0

Women

Percentage with weekly earnings less then				
£10	£12	£16	£20	£30
11.9	28.0	60.0	79.6	94.7

Calculate the mean and standard deviation of each distribution.
Use your statistics to compare the two distributions. Write a short report to explain the differences.

7   The frequency of individuals with different lengths of shell in a population of limpets was recorded as follows:

Shell length (mm)	No of individuals
8	3
9	2
10	4
11	7
12	6
13	8
14	10
15	8
16	12
17	10
18	12
19	14
20	12
21	13
22	15
23	19
24	20
25	18
26	12
27	10
28	8
29	3
30	3
31	2

B4

Represent the information on a histogram and prepare statistics so that you can compare it with other populations.

B5 EXPONENTIAL GROWTH AND DECAY

REVIEW

- calculates 7^2.

■ Calculate $3^{2.1}$.

- 146.214 written in *standard form* is $1.462\,14 \times 10^2$.
  0.006 93 in standard form is 6.93×10^{-3}.

To express a number in standard form, we write it in the form $A \times 10^n$, where $1 \leqslant A < 10$, and n is any integer.

■ Write these in standard form: a) 0.1   b) 173.01.

- $a^n \times a^m = a^{n+m}$, for example, $2^{10} \times 2^{12} = 2^{22}$.

- $a^n \div a^m = a^{n-m}$, for example, $2^{10} \div 2^{12} = 2^{-2}$.

- $a^0 = 1$.

■ Simplify $\dfrac{3^{10} \times 3^2}{3^{-5} \times 9^2}$.

CONSOLIDATION

1   Write each number in standard form:

   a) 11.12   b) 0.000416   c) 14.1×10^8 d) 176×10^{-4}.

2   a) Write $4^8 \times 2^3 \times 8^6$ in the form 2^n.

   b) Write $12^8 \times 6^{-4}$ in the form $2^n \times 3^m$.

   c) Write $\dfrac{25^8}{125^{-3}}$ in the form 5^k.

About zero

3   a) Estimate $\dfrac{10^8(10^{-4} + 10^3)}{(10^{-7} + 10^2) \times 10^8}$.

   b) Check your estimate in a) with your calculator.

4   The distance apart (d m) of two space ships is given by the formula:

   $d = 4000 - 2^{t+9}$

   where t is the time in seconds since the first measurement was made.

   a) Are the ships moving towards each other or away from each other?

   b) How far apart were the two space ships when the first measurement was recorded?

   c) How far apart are the space ships ten seconds after the first measurement was recorded?

   d) Check that when t is 4, d is $^-4192$. What does this information tell you about the ships?

CORE

1 a) Estimate the value of $2^{3.5}$. Try to give the result to the nearest whole number.

   b) Check your result in a) with a calculator.

   c) (i) Explain how we know that $2 < \sqrt{5} < 3$.
      (ii) Copy and complete: $\square < \sqrt{19} < \square$.

   d) $2^x \times 2^x = 2$.
      What is x?

   e) $8^y \times 8^y \times 8^y = 8$.
      What is y?

TAKE NOTE

$\sqrt{2} \times \sqrt{2} = 2$, and $2^{\frac{1}{2}} \times 2^{\frac{1}{2}} = 2^1 = 2$.
$2^{\frac{1}{2}}$ is another way of writing $\sqrt{2}$.

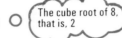
The cube root of 8, that is, 2

$8^{\frac{1}{3}} \times 8^{\frac{1}{3}} \times 8^{\frac{1}{3}} = 8^1 = 8$ $\sqrt[3]{8} \times \sqrt[3]{8} \times \sqrt[3]{8} = 8$

$8^{\frac{1}{3}}$ is another way of writing $\sqrt[3]{8}$, that is, 2.

$8^{\frac{1}{3}}$ is the *cube root* of 8.

2 a) Find $\sqrt[3]{64}$.

   b) What is $64^{\frac{1}{3}}$?

   c) The fourth root of 81 is 3, because $3 \times 3 \times 3 \times 3 = 81$.

      Copy and complete:

      $\sqrt[4]{81} = 81^{\square} = 3$.

3 Calculate: a) $25^{\frac{1}{2}}$ b) $100^{\frac{1}{2}}$ c) $27^{\frac{1}{3}}$ d) $216^{\frac{1}{3}}$ e) $1^{\frac{1}{4}}$.

4 a) $(8^{\frac{1}{3}})^4$ is $8^{\frac{1}{3}} \times 8^{\frac{1}{3}} \times 8^{\frac{1}{3}} \times 8^{\frac{1}{3}}$, which is $8^{\frac{4}{3}}$.

      Write $8^{\frac{4}{3}}$ as a single whole number.

   b) Write each of these as single whole numbers:

      (i) $64^{\frac{2}{3}}$ (ii) $125^{\frac{2}{3}}$ (iii) $81^{\frac{3}{4}}$.

5 $49^{-\frac{1}{2}}$ is $\dfrac{1}{49^{\frac{1}{2}}}$, which is $\frac{1}{7}$.

   Write each of these as a fraction:

   a) $64^{-\frac{1}{2}}$ b) $125^{-\frac{1}{3}}$ c) $27^{-\frac{2}{3}}$ d) $10000^{-\frac{3}{4}}$.

6 a) Estimate the value of $10^{0.6} \times 10^{0.4}$.

   b) Check your result with a calculator.

B5

7　Write each of these as a whole number or a fraction:

a) $3^{\frac{1}{2}} \times 9^{\frac{1}{3}} \times 3^{\frac{1}{2}} \times 9^{\frac{2}{3}}$　　　　b) $4^{\frac{1}{2}} \times 36^{-1} \times 216^{\frac{2}{3}}$　　　　c) $44^{\frac{1}{2}} \times 22^{\frac{1}{3}} \times 44^{-\frac{1}{2}} \times 22^{\frac{2}{3}}$　　　d) $\dfrac{8^{\frac{1}{3}} + 16^{\frac{1}{2}}}{16^{\frac{1}{2}} - 8^{\frac{1}{3}}}$.

8　For what values of t is:　(i) 2^t equal to t^2　(ii) 2^t greater than t^2　(iii) 2^t less than t^2?

▓▓▓▓▓▓▓▓▓▓ EXPLORATION ▓▓▓▓▓▓▓▓▓▓

9　Explore values of a^n and n^a, for whole number values of a and n.
For what values of a and n is $a^n > n^a$? (That is, for what values of n is $2^n > n^2$, $3^n > n^3$, …?)

Write a report about what you discover.

Exponential growth

1　Imagine that an amoeba divides into two, and the two new amoeba each divide into two more, and so on every hour.

The graph shows the total number of amoeba at the end of each hour.

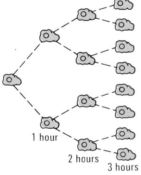

1 hour
2 hours
3 hours

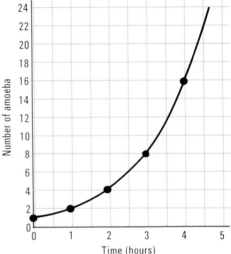

a)　How many amoeba will there be after six hours?

b)　Guess how long it will be before there are more than one million amoeba.

c)　Check your guess in b) by calculation.

d)　This formula tells us how many amoeba (N) there will be after t hours. Copy and complete it:　$N = \square^t$

▓▓▓▓▓▓▓▓▓▓ TAKE NOTE ▓▓▓▓▓▓▓▓▓▓

We say that the number of amoeba in question 1 increases *exponentially*.

Functions such as　$y = 2^x$　　(or $n \rightarrow 2^n$)
　　　　　　　　　　$y = 10^x$　　(or $n \rightarrow 10^n$)
　　　　　　　　　　etc.　　　　　　　　　　　　are called *exponential functions*.

2　a)　Which increases most rapidly, as n increases:　4^n, n^2 or $4n$?
　　　　Explain your answer.

　　b)　For what values of n is each of the expressions in a) greater than one million?

3　Draw the graph of the exponential function:　$t \rightarrow 3^t$ for $-5 \leqslant t \leqslant 5$
From your graph estimate the value of $3^{3.5}$.

Exponential decay

1 a) Use your calculator to find the value of 0.9^t for values of t from 0 to 5.

b) As t increases, does 0.9^t increase, decrease, or increase and decrease?

c) You need 1 mm square graph paper.

Draw the graph of the function

$t \rightarrow 0.9^t$ for $0 \leqslant t \leqslant 5$.

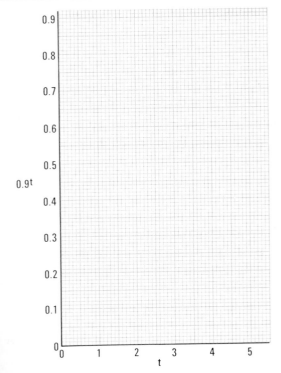

2 In 1988 a disease killed many seals in the North Sea. It was estimated at one time that the population was decreasing by 8% each month.

a) Assuming there were 10000 seals in the North Sea at the beginning of June, make a table to show how many there would have been at the end of each month, from June to December.

b) Copy and complete the graph to represent your results.

c) If the rate of death due to the disease continued, after how many months would there be less than   (i) 4000 seals
(ii) 1000 seals?

d) Copy and complete the formula to show the number of seals (N) left in the North Sea after n months:

$N = \square \times (\ \ )^n$.

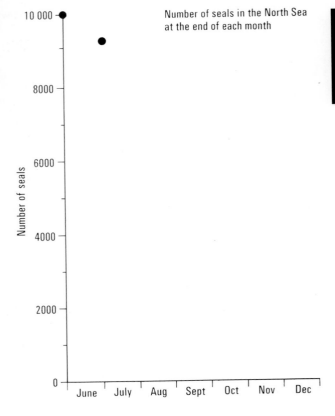

Number of seals in the North Sea at the end of each month

B5

- When m is greater than 1, the values of m^t increase as t increases.
- When m is less than 1, the values of m^t decrease as t increases.

The way in which 2^t behaves is called *exponential growth*.
The way in which 0.2^t behaves is called *exponential decay*.

The number of seals left in the North Sea (question 2) follows a curve of exponential decay.

3   a) A millionaire puts £2 million into an investment account which pays 12% interest at the end of each year. The following year the interest is paid on the total amount in the account, and so on.
      (i) How much is in the account after 1 year?
      (ii) How much is in the account after 2 years?
      (iii) Copy and complete this expression to show how much is in the account after 10 years: $\square \times \square^{\square}$
         Write down how much this is, correct to the nearest £1.

   b) *Sketch* a graph for years 1 to 10 to show how the amount in the account increases (the graph will not be smooth: you can assume the interest is added – suddenly – at the end of each year).

   c) The millionaire also buys a yacht for £2 million. It is estimated that its value will decrease by 12% of its previous year's value, each year. Find how much the yacht is worth after 10 years (to the nearest £1) and *sketch* a graph to show the decreasing value. (Use the same axes as in b).)

4   a) These functions represent either exponential growth or exponential decay. Say which is the case for each one: (i) $y = 0.8^x$ (ii) $y = 0.8^{-x}$ (iii) $y = 1.2^{-x}$ (iv) $y = 1.2^x$.

   b) On the same axes, sketch each function for values of x from 0 to 6.

B5

5   Radioactive isotopes decay to lighter isotopes or elements with the emission of α, β and γ-rays. The amount of radioactive material decreases and the time for the amount to halve is called the *half-life* of the isotope.

   a) Radium-226 has a half-life of 1600 years. How many years will it take for the amount of radium-226 in a sample to become less than: (i) 50%   (ii) 25%   (iii) 1% of its present value?

   b) Radiocarbon dating is often used to date archaeological finds of organic materials. Living organisms take in carbon (as carbon dioxide) from the atmosphere. This carbon contains a tiny proportion of radioactive carbon-14. The proportion is kept constant in the atmosphere by the action of cosmic rays. Once an organism dies, it stops taking in carbon and the proportion of carbon-14 it contains decays. The half-life of carbon-14 is 5730 years and the age of an object can be estimated from its carbon-14 content, using a Geiger counter to measure the level of radioactivity. The number of counts per second is proportional to the amount of radioactive isotope.
   A sample of roof from a roof beam is found to produce 7.5 counts per second. An identical amount of wood just removed from the same type of tree had an activity of 15 counts per second. How old is the roof beam?

6   Sketch a graph to show how the amount of a radioactive isotope varies with time.

REVIEW

A compass and a straight edge can be used to:

- draw the *perpendicular bisector* of a straight line
- *drop a perpendicular* from a point to a straight line
- draw the *angle bisector* of two intersecting lines

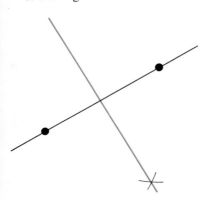
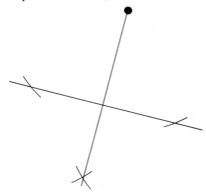
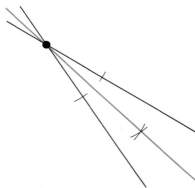

■ Construct an angle of $22\frac{1}{2}°$.

- the path which a point traces out is called the *locus* of the point.

■ Describe the locus of a point in a plane which moves so that it is

a) always 3 cm from a point A

b) always 3 cm or more from a point A.

What is the locus in each case if the point can move in three-dimensional space?

CONSOLIDATION

ACTIVITY

1 In this activity you may only use a compass and a straight edge.

a) Draw a dot on a plain sheet of paper. Let it represent the point of intersection of the diagonals of a kite. *Construct* the diagonals and so draw the kite.

b) In your mind, try to decide which other quadrilaterals can be *constructed* starting from a dot.
Make a list.

c) Test your ideas in b) by constructing quadrilaterals.

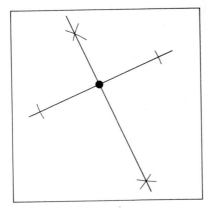

TAKE NOTE

Do you remember these constructions?

Here is a way of constructing
the centre of the circle
that goes through
the vertices of a
triangle.

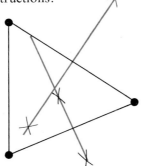

Here is a way of constructing
the centre of the circle
that touches the sides
of a triangle.

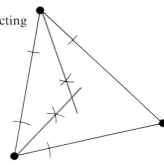

2   Explain why each of the constructions in the *Take note* works. (That is, why the 1st produces the centre of a
circle which passes through each vertex, and the 2nd produces the centre of a circle which touches each side.)

EXPLORATION

3   Draw some quadrilaterals (for example, kites, rhombuses, trapeziums, etc.). (You can construct them or use
measurement or use dotted paper.) Investigate whether it is possible to draw circles that

a) go through each vertex   b) touch each side.

CORE

Loci in the (*x, y*) plane

EXPLORATION: MOVING ROD

B6

1   You need 1 cm squared or dotted paper.

a) XY is a rigid 10 cm rod. The points X and Y travel along
the sides of a 10 cm square. Sketch the locus of Z,
the midpoint of XY.

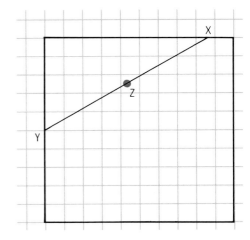

b) This time, X and Y respectively travel along the horizontal and vertical limbs of this cross. Again, sketch the locus of Z. What kind of shape is it?

c) Investigate other paths for X and Y (for example, along the sides of: an equilateral triangle; a 15 cm square; a rhombus with 10 cm sides; an X). Try different positions for Z. Draw examples of the shapes you produce.

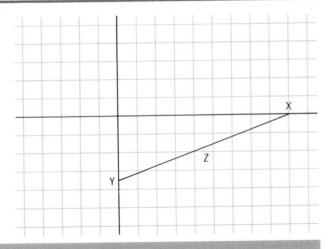

EXPLORATION: TURNING RODS

2   r and s are infinitely long rods, turning about points A and B. Investigate the locus of their point of intersection. (The rods can rotate at the same or different speed, in the same or opposite direction, from the same or different initial orientation.)

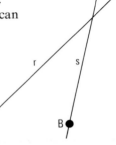

3   Line A is the locus of points which satisfy the rule:

$y = x^2$ (or, $x \rightarrow x^2$)

a) (i) What rule do the points for line B satisfy?
    (ii) Which points in the plane do the two loci have in common?

b) (i) Sketch the locus of points which satisfy these rules:
        A $y + x = 10$
        B $y^2 - x = 0$
    (ii) Which points in the plane do the two loci have in common?

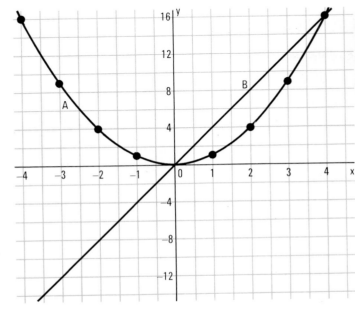

B6

4   A point moves so that it is equidistant from the lines $x = 5$ and $x = 10$.

What is the equation of the locus of the point?

5   A point moves so that it is equidistant from the lines $x = 10$ and $y = 10$.
Sketch the locus of the point and write down its equation.

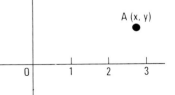

6   A point A moves so that its distance from the origin 0 is always 3 units.

a) Sketch the locus of A.

b) Explain why the equation of the locus is $x^2 + y^2 = 9$.
(Hint: use Pythagoras' rule.)

7   Find the equation of the locus
of the point which moves at right
angles to the line $2y = x$ and:

(i) through the origin
(ii) through the point (2, 1).

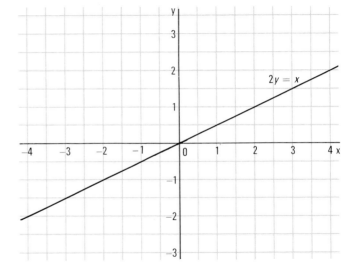

8   Find the equation of the locus of a point which moves so that it is equidistant from the points:

(i) (0, 0) and (24, 0)   (ii) (0, 2) and (0, 12)   (iii) (1, ⁻1) and (1, 9)
(iv) (⁻3, 0) and (0, 3)   (v) (8, 8) and (0, 0)   (vi) (3, 0) and (0, ⁻2).

============ CHALLENGE ============

9   a) Sketch the locus of the point which moves so that its distance
from the point (0, ⁻2) is always equal to the distance from the line
$y = 2$.

b) List the coordinates of four positions on the locus.

c) What is the equation of the locus?

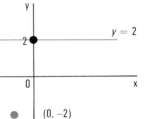

ENRICHMENT

Constructions and proofs

1 a) Draw a parallelogram (construct Extend the sides Construct the exterior
it or draw it on dotted paper) angle bisectors (the red lines)

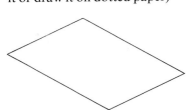 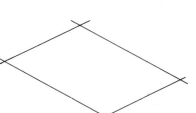 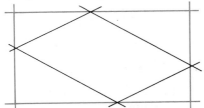

b) Complete this proof to show that the resulting
quadrilateral is a rectangle.

Let $\angle$ BAD $= a°$
and $\angle$ ABC $= b°$
Then $\angle$ XAB $= \ldots$ (Because ...)
So $\angle$ QAB $= \ldots$ (Because ...)
Similarly $\angle$ ABY $= \ldots$
and $\angle$ ABQ $= \ldots$
Hence $\angle$ QAB $+ \angle$ ABQ $= \square$ $(a° + b°)$
But $\angle$ BAD $+ \angle$ ABC $= a° + b° = \square°$ (ABCD is a parallelogram)
Hence $\angle$ QAB $+ \angle$ ABQ $= \square°$
Hence $\angle$ AQB $= \square°$ (Angle sum of a triangle)

A similar argument is true for the angles at P, S and R.

2 Draw a rectangle Draw a line cutting two Try to construct a parallelogram
adjacent sides inside the rectangle, like this (you
might think back to question 1).

 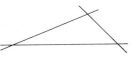 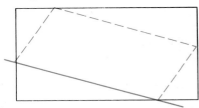

3 Draw a triangle Extend the sides Draw this
new triangle
XYZ by
constructing
exterior angle
bisectors

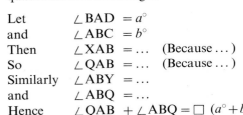 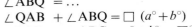 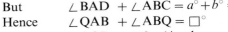 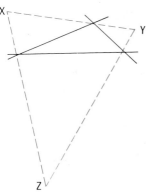

Try to find a relationship between the angles of the two triangles.

B6

4 Repeat question 3 for quadrilaterals.
Prove that the resultant quadrilateral is always cyclic (that is, a circle can be drawn through each vertex).

5 A point P moves in the (x, y) plane so that its distance from the point A $(2, 0)$ is always 2 units.

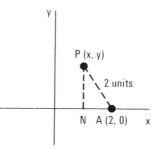

a) Describe in words the locus of the point P.

b) Check that the distance PN in the diagram is y units.

c) Write the distance NA in terms of x.

d) Copy and complete

$$PA^2 = y^2 + (\Box - \Box)^2$$

e) Show that the locus of the point P has the equation

$$x^2 + y^2 - 4x = 0$$

(Use your result in c) and the fact that PA is two units.)

CHALLENGE

6 Use the same kind of argument as in question 5 to show that the equation of the locus of a point which moves so that it is always 3 units from the point $(0, 2)$ is $x^2 + y^2 - 4y = 5$.

7 a) Check that the equation of the locus of a point P, which moves so that its distance from the x axis is always equal to its distance from the y axis, is $x = y$.

b) Check that the equation of the locus of a point P, which moves so that its distance above the x axis is always 10 units, is $y = 10$.

c) What is the equation of a point P which moves in a straight line so that:

(i) its distance below the y axis is always 10 units
(ii) it passes through the points $(0, 0)$ and $(2, 3)$
(iii) it passes through the points $(1, 0)$ and $(2, 1)$?

B6

REVIEW

● We should always *estimate* a result before using a calculator.

For example, $2.71 \times 19.6 = ?$

Estimate: $3 \times 20 = 60$ *Calculator result*: 53.116

If the estimate and the calculator result are not of the same order, we should check both the estimate and the calculation.

For example, $17.7 \div 0.6 = ?$

Estimate: $20 \div \frac{1}{2} = 40$ *Calculator result*: 10.62

If the estimate and the calculation are not sufficiently close, both should be checked.

■ Check the estimate and the calculator result above. Write down your own estimate and calculator result.

CORE

Calculating from measurements

TAKE NOTE

When we make a measurement, the result is always an approximation to the 'true' result.
2.3 m (correct to 1 DP) means that the actual length satisfies the inequality

$2.25 \text{ m} \leqslant \text{Actual length} < 2.35 \text{ m}$
or $2.25 \text{ m} < \text{Actual length} \leqslant 2.35 \text{ m}$.

We can choose whichever interpretation we wish, but we should make clear which alternative we are using.

1 a) The length of a room is given as 4.7 m (correct to 1 DP).
Copy and complete the inequality:

$\square \text{ m} < \text{Actual length} \leqslant \square \text{ m}$

b) The height of a room is given as 3.94 m (correct to 2 DP).
Copy and complete the inequality:

$\square \text{ m} \leqslant \text{Actual length} < \square \text{ m}$

2 a) The times for a 100 m race are rounded up to the next one hundredth of a second. The time recorded for the winner is 10.17 seconds. What is the minimum time in which the race might have been won?

b) The distances thrown in a javelin-throwing competition are rounded down to the next centimetre. The distance recorded for the winner is 89.76 m. What is the maximum distance the winner might have thrown?

3   The same country road runs through three villages A, B and C. The distance between the village crosses of A and B is given as 8 km (to the nearest km), and between B and C as 11 km (to the nearest km).

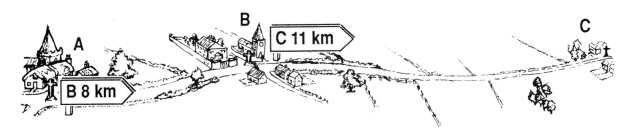

a) What is the maximum distance between the crosses for villages: (i) A and B (ii) B and C (iii) A and C?

b) What is the minimum distance between the crosses for villages: (i) A and B (ii) B and C (iii) A and C?

CHALLENGE

4   The perimeter of a square is given as 8.4 m (correct to 2 SF). The perimeter was calculated by measuring one side of the square correct to 3 SF, multiplying by 4 and then rounding the result to 2 SF.
What is a) the maximum possible perimeter, b) the minimum possible perimeter, of the square?

WITH A FRIEND

5   An architect uses the value of 3.1 for π to calculate the perimeter of a circular room. The diameter of the room is measured as 6.5 m (1 DP).
Discuss the accuracy of the final calculation.
(The value of π correct to 10 DP is 3.141 592 653 5.)
Write a short report to explain what you decided.

6   The length of side of a cube is measured as 3.7 cm (1DP).

a) What is   (i) the maximum volume,   (ii) the minimum volume, the cube might have?

b) What is   (i) the maximum surface area,   (ii) the minimum surface area, the cube might have?

7   a) A firm makes ball-bearings which it packs in boxes of 100. The weight of each ball-bearing can vary from 27.5 g to 28.5 g. What is:

   (i) the maximum possible weight of a pack
   (ii) the minimum possible weight of a pack?

b) You need to estimate the total weight of a load of 10 000 bricks. You can weigh individual bricks or a small number together.

   (i) Your friend suggests that you should weigh one of the bricks to the nearest kg and multiply by 10 000.
   Do you think this is a reasonable and sensible method? Why?
   (ii) How would you make the estimate?

8   500 sheets of card weigh 12.75 kg (2 DP). Assuming each sheet is identical and weighs the same, what is a) the maximum weight, b) the minimum weight, of each sheet?

━━━━━━━━━━ CHALLENGE ━━━━━━━━━━

9   The fourth root of a whole number is 10.8 (correct to 1 DP). Write down the range of possibilities for the number.

ENRICHMENT

Maximum and minimum values from calculations

1   a) Check that if the dimensions of the triangle shown in the diagram are *exact*, then the area of the triangle is exactly 5.76 cm².

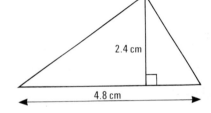

2.4 cm

4.8 cm

   b) Assuming that the lengths shown in the diagram are given to the nearest 0.1 cm, write down the maximum and minimum base length and height in the form

   ☐ cm ⩽ Base length < ☐ cm

   ☐ cm ⩽ Height < ☐ cm.

   c) Use your relationships in b) to complete

   ☐ cm² ⩽ Actual area < ☐ cm².

2   The time taken for a car travelling at a steady speed of s km/h to travel d km is given by the formula $t = \dfrac{d}{s}$. The speed is read from a speedometer as 62 km/h correct to the nearest 1 km/h. The distance is measured as 10 km to the nearest km.

   a) Explain why the maximum time for the journey is given by the calculation $\dfrac{10.5}{61.5}$ hours.

   b) Find the maximum time correct to the nearest minute.

   c) Show that the minimum time correct to the nearest minute is 9 minutes.

3   The values of a, b and c below are given correct to 1 DP:

   $a = 9.2$ $b = 7.4$ $c = 0.6$

   a) Explain why the maximum value of $\dfrac{ab}{c}$ is $\dfrac{9.25 \times 7.45}{0.55}$.

   b) Write a similar calculation to that in a) for the minimum value of $\dfrac{ab}{c}$.

   c) Work out the maximum and minimum values of $\dfrac{ab}{c}$ in a) and b) as accurately as your calculator will allow.

   d) Show that when the minimum value is rounded down to the nearest whole number and the maximum value is rounded up to the nearest whole number, this gives the range of possible values of $\dfrac{ab}{c}$ as

   $103 \leqslant \dfrac{ab}{c} \leqslant 126$

B7

4   A train accelerates steadily from 10 km/h to 90 km/h in 0.20 hours. (Each of the figures is given correct to 2 SF.)
Acceleration (a km/h^2) is given by the formula

$$a = \frac{v - u}{t}$$

where u is the initial speed, v is the final speed and t is the time taken.
Show that if the maximum and minimum values of the acceleration are calculated, and if the maximum value is rounded up to the nearest 1 km/h^2 and the minimum is rounded down to the nearest 1 km/h^2, then
$$385 \leqslant a \leqslant 416$$

EXPLORATIONS

5   Investigate the difference in maximum and minimum values of $\dfrac{a - b}{c}$ for different values of a, b and c, when each is given correct to 1 DP.
For what values of a, b and c does the calculation produce a very large difference? For what values does it produce a very small difference?

6   a) The square root of a whole number is given as 15.4 correct to 1 DP. Find the range of possible values for the number.

b) Investigate how accurately (to how many significant figures) the square root of a whole number needs to be given to ensure that you can identify the number uniquely from the approximate square root. Explain how the required accuracy changes with the size of the number.

B8 CALCULATIONS WITH SOLIDS

REVIEW

Cross section

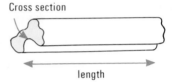

- The volume of a prism = cross-sectional area × length.

length

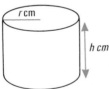

r cm

h cm

- The volume of a cylinder = $\pi r^2 h$.

■ Find the volume of a cylinder of radius 5 cm and length 10 cm. Give your result correct to 1 DP.

- Pythagoras' rule states that in a right-angled triangle, $a^2 + b^2 = c^2$.

We can use Pythagoras' rule to calculate the lengths of edges of solids.
For example, in the square-based pyramid ABCDE,

$$DB^2 = 4^2 + 4^2$$
$$= 32$$
$$DB = \sqrt{32} \text{ cm (5.7 cm to 1 DP)}$$

■ Calculate (i) 0B (ii) OA.
Give your results correct to 1 DP.

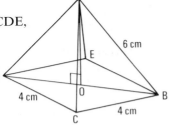

6 cm

4 cm

4 cm

- In the right-angled triangle,

$$\sin \theta = \frac{AB}{AC} \quad \cos \theta = \frac{CB}{AC} \quad \tan \theta = \frac{AB}{BC}$$

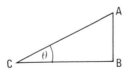

■ In the square-based pyramid PQRST,

a) explain why
$$PX = \sqrt{27} \text{ cm}$$

b) use sin to calculate the size of ∠PRS.

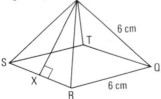

6 cm

6 cm

CONSOLIDATION

1 a) Prisms A and B have the same volume. What is the cross-sectional area of the prism on the right?

b) The triangular prism and the cylinder have the same volume. Find the height of the cylinder correct to 1 DP.

c) The cube of modelling clay is rolled into a cylinder of length 6 cm. Find (correct to 1 DP):

   (i) the area of the circular cross section of the cylinder
   (ii) the radius of the cylinder.

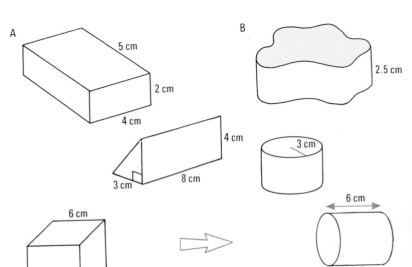

A

5 cm

2 cm

4 cm

B

2.5 cm

4 cm

3 cm

8 cm

3 cm

6 cm

6 cm

2   For the cuboid ABCDEFGH, calculate:

   a) the volume   b) the surface area

   c) CH   d) FH

   e) BH   f) ∠CHG

   g) ∠BHF.

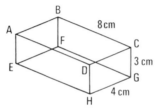

3   For the cube ABCDEFGH, calculate:

   a) the volume   b) the surface area

   c) AG   d) ∠AGH

   e) ∠AGE   f) ∠AGF

   g) ∠AGC.

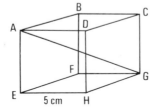

CHALLENGE

4   For the cuboid ABCDEFGH, calculate the angle
     at which the diagonals AG and CE meet (give the
     size of the larger angle).

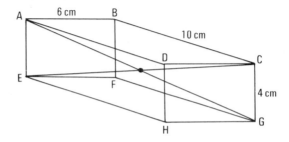

5   PQRST is a square-based pyramid. ∠PQS = 45°.

     What is the height of the pyramid?
     (Leave √ in your result.)

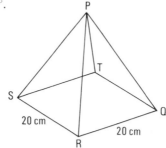

CHALLENGE: MAKING PYRAMIDS

6   Make a square-based pyramid in which the
     'angle of pitch' is 45°.

     First, sketch a net of your pyramid.
     Explain how you made the necessary
     calculations.

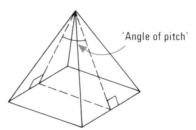

B8

CORE

Volumes of pyramids and cones

1 a) How many of the pyramids are needed
        to make the cube?

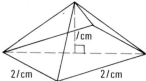
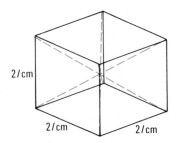

   b) Check that the volume of the cube is $8l^3$ cm³.

   c) Explain why the volume of the pyramid is $\frac{4}{3}l^3$ cm³.

   d) Copy and complete this formula for the volume (V) of the pyramid: $V = \square \times$ Base area $\times$ Height

   e) Assume that the cube has sides of length 10 cm.

        (i) What is l?
        (ii) What is the volume of the cube?
        (iii) What is the volume of the pyramid?

   f) Check that when l is 5, the base area of the pyramid is 100 cm², and its height is 5 cm.
       Substitute these values in your formula in d) and check that the result is the same as that you
       obtained in e) (iii).

2 Imagine that this square-
   based pyramid is made from
   thin slices of a special polymer
   stuck together.

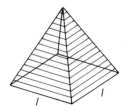
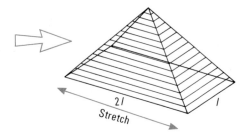

   a) Imagine that the base is stretched to twice the length but that the pyramid retains the same width and
       height (so each slice of polymer remains the same thickness).

        (i) What happens to the volume of each slice of polymer?
        (ii) What does this suggest about the volume of the new pyramid?

   b) Now imagine the the original pyramid is
       stretched to twice its height.

        (i) What happens to the volume
             of each slice of polymer?
             (Assume each doubles its thickness.)
        (ii) How are the volumes of the
             two pyramids connected?

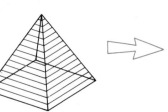
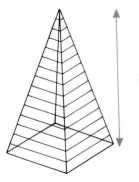

B8

3   The pyramid has been
     stretched to three times its
     base length and twice its
     height.

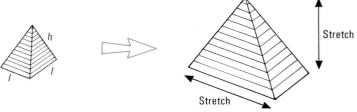

a) Explain why the volume of the new pyramid is six times the volume of the original.

b) The volume of the original pyramid is $\frac{1}{3} l^2 h$.
   Copy and complete this formula for the volume of the new pyramid: $V = \frac{1}{3} \ldots$

TAKE NOTE

The volume of a pyramid is $\frac{1}{3} \times$ Base area $\times$ Height.

4   The square-based pyramid
     made from modelling clay is
     reshaped into the rectangular-
     based pyramid.

     What is the height of the
     rectangular-based pyramid?

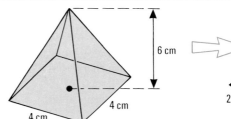
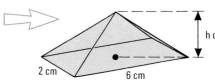

5   Sketch a pyramid which has a volume of 30 cm³.

WITH A FRIEND

6   The square-based pyramid
     made from modelling clay is
     reshaped into a cone of the same height.

     a) What is the volume of the cone?

     b) What do you think is the area of the base
        of the cone? Decide between you what
        you think it is, and why. Explain how
        you arrived at your conclusion.

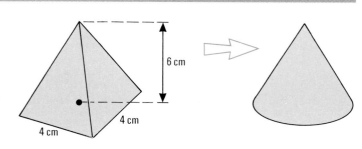

7   This square-based pyramid of
     modelling clay is reshaped
     into a cone of the same height.
     Use your conclusions from
     question 6 to find a rough
     estimate for the radius of the
     base of the cone.

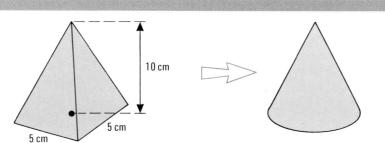

The volume of a cone is $\frac{1}{3} \times$ Base area $\times$ Height

$$= \tfrac{1}{3} \pi r^2 h$$

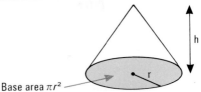

Base area πr^2

8   Calculate the volume of a cone of base radius 5 cm and height   (i) 5 cm   (ii) 10 cm   (iii) 15 cm. Give each of your results correct to 1 DP.

9   a) Design a cone with volume 60 cm³.

— slant height

b) The curved surface area of a cone is $\pi r l$, where r is the radius and l is the slant height.

Check that this formula is correct for *your* cone.

10 a) The volume of a cone is 50 cm³. What is the volume of a cone with:

(i) the same radius but three times the height
(ii) twice the radius and twice the height
(iii) one third of the radius and six times the height?

b) Look again at part a). Explain how these expressions relate to the question:

(i) $\frac{1}{3}\pi r^2 h$ (ii) $\frac{1}{3}\pi r^2 \cdot 3h$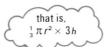

(iii) $\frac{1}{3}\pi (2r)^2 \cdot 2h$ (iv) $\frac{1}{3}\pi (\frac{1}{3}r)^2 \cdot 6h$.

that is,
$\frac{1}{3}\pi r^2 \times 3h$

c) Match each of the expressions in b) with one of the expressions:

(i) $\pi r^2 h$ (ii) $\frac{1}{3}\pi r^2 h$ (iii) $\frac{8}{3}\pi r^2 h$ (iv) $\frac{2}{9}\pi r^2 h$.

d) Explain how parts b) and c) help you to answer part a).

11 a) The volume of a cone is 100 cm³. Its height is 8 cm. What is its radius (correct to 1 DP)?

b) Find the height of a cone of volume 18 cm³ and base radius 4 cm.

Spheres

The volume of a sphere is $\frac{4}{3}\pi r^3$, where r is the radius.

The surface area of a sphere is $4\pi r^2$.

r cm

B8

1   This is a hemisphere of radius r cm.

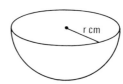

a) Write down a formula for   (i) its volume   (ii) its surface area.

b) Calculate the volume and surface area of a hemisphere of radius 3 cm.

2   The radius of a tennis ball is 3.2 cm. What volume of space does a tennis ball occupy?

3   Find   (i) the volume,   (ii) the surface area, of a sphere of radius:

a) 2 cm   b) 4 cm   c) 6 cm   d) 10 cm.

4   a) The volume of a sphere is 20 cm^3. What is the volume of a sphere with:

(i) twice the radius   (ii) three times the radius?

b) The surface area of a sphere is 30 cm^2. What is the surface area of a sphere with:

(i) twice the radius   (ii) half the radius?

5   Look at question 4 a) again.

a) Explain how these expressions relate to the question:

$\frac{4}{3}\pi r^3$ $\frac{4}{3}\pi(2r)^3$ $\frac{4}{3}\pi(3r)^3$.

b) Match each of the expressions in a) with one of the expressions:

$\frac{32}{3}\pi r^3$ $\frac{4}{3}\pi r^3$ $36\pi r^3$.

c) Explain how parts a) and b) help you to answer each part of question 4 a).

6   Design a ball whose volume and surface area have the same numerical value. (For example, is there a sphere with volume 20 cm^3 and surface area 20 cm^2?)

═══════════ CHALLENGE ═══════════

7   A beach ball of radius 20 cm falls vertically through 1 m. What is the total volume of space which the ball has occupied during its descent?

ENRICHMENT

1 a) Design and make a cone whose curved surface area has the same numerical value as its volume.

   b) Is there more than one such cone? If so, what is special about the dimensions of all cones which obey the rule (that is, numerical value of curved surface area = numerical value of volume)?

2 The volume of a cannon ball is 3600 cm^3. What is its surface area? Give your result to the nearest 1 cm^2.

3 A swing ball travels in a horizontal circle at an angle of 60° to the vertical. The string is 2 m long, and the swing ball has a radius of 5 cm.

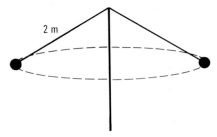

   a) What is the radius of the horizontal circle which the centre of the ball describes?

   b) How far does the centre of the ball travel in one complete revolution?

   c) Estimate the total volume of space which the swing ball occupies in one complete revolution.

4 Calculate the volume of a metal bar of length 10 m whose cross section is a regular hexagon of side 10 cm. Give your result correct to the nearest 1 cm^3.

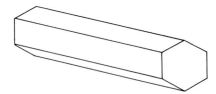

CHALLENGE

5 The road cone has a *total* height of 45 cm, the radius of the conical part is 17 cm, and the sides of the hexagonal base are 20 cm long. The hexagonal base is 5 cm tall. The cone is made from 1 cm thick plastic. What volume of plastic is needed to make the cone?

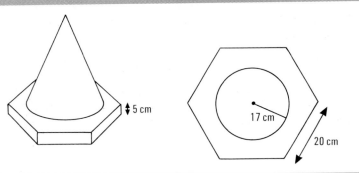

B9 | **CORE**

1 a) Look at these networks.
       Write down ways in which network D is the odd one out.

 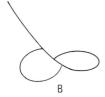  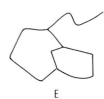

A   B   C   D   E

   b) There is the same kind of odd one out in each of these sets of networks. Write down which network it is
       in each case.

(i)

  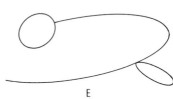

A   B   C   D   E

(ii)

   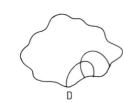 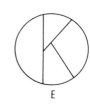

A   B   C   D   E

(iii)

 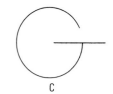 

A   B   C   D

(iv)

 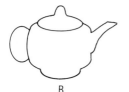 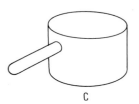

A   B   C   D

===== TAKE NOTE =====

Network X has been drawn on a rubber sheet.

It is transformed into network Y without cutting or joining the rubber sheet.

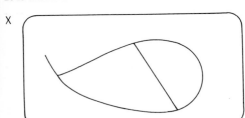

We say the networks are *topologically equivalent*.

2   Networks A and B are topologically equivalent. Write down the other equivalent pairs.

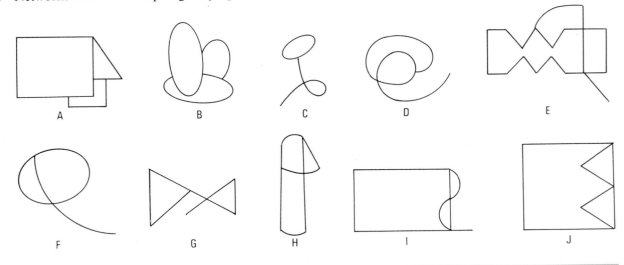

===== ACTIVITY =====

3   These sequences of drawings each show how network A might have been transformed into the topologically equivalent network B.

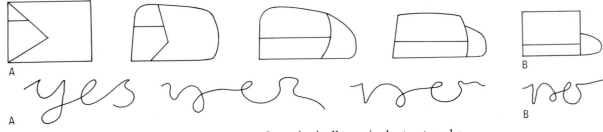

Draw an example of your own of a sequence of topologically equivalent networks.

Traversibility

━━━━━━━━ TAKE NOTE ━━━━━━━━

This network can be drawn

- without lifting the pencil from the paper
- without going along any already drawn line.

We say the network is *traversible*.

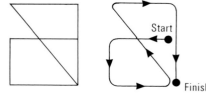

1   Find out which of these networks are traversible.

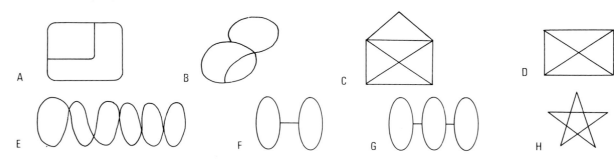

━━━━━━━━ EXPLORATION ━━━━━━━━

2   a) Draw a network that is traversible, for example:

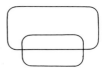

   b) Think of changing the network just *slightly*, for example:

   Draw slightly changed variations of the
   network that are:

   (i) still traversible
   (ii) no longer traversible.

or

   c) Try to find a rule that tells you whether or not
       a network is traversible. Use your rule to
       predict which one of these networks is traversible.

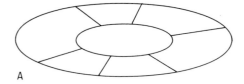

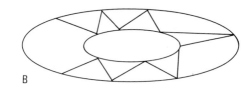

   d) Try to explain why your rule works (if it does!).

Nodes, arcs and regions

1 a) Check that networks A and B are topologically equivalent.

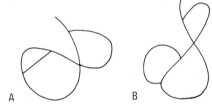

A   B

b) Network A has 5 nodes, 7 arcs and 4 regions:

How many nodes, arcs and regions does network B have?

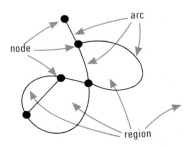

arc

node

region

2 a) Which of these two statements is *not* true?

A Networks that are topologically equivalent will have:

- the same number of nodes
- the same number of arcs
- the same number of regions

B Networks that have:

- the same number of nodes
- the same number of arcs
- the same number of regions

will be topologically equivalent.

b) Draw a pair of networks that *prove* that the statement you chose in a) is not true. Explain your answer.

CHALLENGE

3 If it is possible, draw networks with:

a) 7 nodes, 10 arcs and 5 regions (including an 'outside' region).

b) 3 nodes, 4 arcs and 4 regions.

EXPLORATION: EULER'S RULE

4 a) Try to draw networks with

lots of nodes and arcs but *few* regions

or   *few* nodes and arcs but *lots* of regions

or   *few* nodes and regions but *lots* of arcs, etc.

Which combinations seem to be possible?

b) For the networks that you have drawn, make a table of their number of nodes, arcs and regions. Find a rule that connects these numbers (Euler's rule).

B9

Odd and even nodes

1   Look at this network:

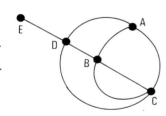

- We say node A is an odd node (there are 3 lines coming from A).

- We say node B is an even node (there are 4 lines coming from B).

a) Which other nodes are odd?

b) Which other nodes are even?

EXPLORATION

2   a) What restriction, if any, is there on the number of odd nodes and the number of even nodes that a network can have? (For example, is it possible to draw a network with 11 even nodes and 21 odd nodes?)

b) Think about traversible networks; what restriction, if any, is there on the number of odd nodes and even nodes that traversible networks can have? (Look back to question 2 on page 136.)

CHALLENGE

3   This map shows seven bridges linking two islands in the river Pregel in Königsberg (now Kaliningrad).

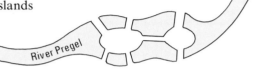

The Swiss mathematician Euler argued that it is impossible to walk across each bridge once and once only. Use the idea of odd and even nodes to show that Euler was right.

ENRICHMENT

1   Is a cube traversible (that is, by travelling only on the edges, is it possible to traverse each edge once and once only)?

2   It is easier to examine the traversibility of networks than of solids. Here is a way of transforming solids into networks:

| Imagine first that the faces of the solid are made of rubber | Imagine sticking one face to the page | Now cut open another face | Now pull open the solid, stretch it flat and stick it down onto the page |

   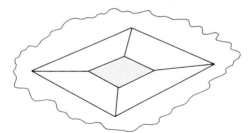

The resulting network is called a *Schlegel diagram*.

a) Is the Schlegel diagram of the cube traversible? Does your answer agree with your answer to question 1?

b) Which of the solids A to C goes with which Schlegel diagram X to Z?

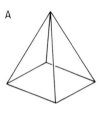
A

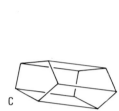
C

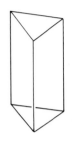
B

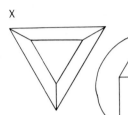
X

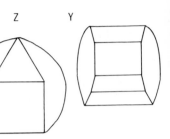
Z   Y

c) Draw a Schlegel diagram for these two solids.

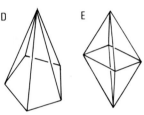
D   E

CHALLENGE

3   These Schlegel diagrams are both for the same solid.
Sketch the solid.

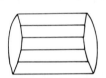

4   Here is a way of writing Euler's rule for networks:

$$N \quad - \quad A \quad + \quad R \quad = \quad 2$$

↑   ↑   ↑
number   number   number
of nodes   of arcs   of regions

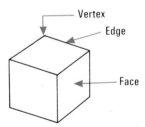

Vertex
Edge
Face

a) Write down Euler's rule for solids; use V for the number of vertices,
E for the number of edges, and
F for the number of faces.

b) Check the rule for: (i) a cube   (ii) a square-based pyramid   (iii) a closed cylinder.

CHALLENGE

c)   (i) How many vertices (V), edges (E) and
faces (F) does this solid have?
(ii) Does it fit Euler's rule?
(iii) Draw its Schlegel diagram.
(iv) How many nodes, arcs and regions does
the Schlegel diagram have?
(v) Does it (appear to) fit Euler's rule?
(vi) Compare your answers to (i) and (v). Can you explain the anomaly?

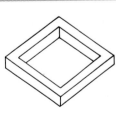

REVIEW

- Vectors which describe the position of a point on a grid relative to (0, 0) are called *position vectors*.

  For example, the position vector of A is $\begin{pmatrix} 4 \\ 1 \end{pmatrix}$.

- Vectors which represent displacements on a grid are called *displacement vectors*.
  For example, $\overrightarrow{PQ}$ has the displacement vector $\begin{pmatrix} 1 \\ -3 \end{pmatrix}$.

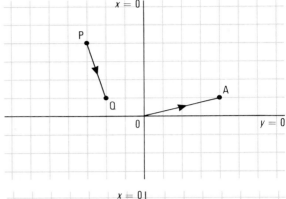

We can use position vectors to represent transformations of the (x, y) plane. For example, we can represent a reflection in the y axis ($x = 0$)

by the rule: $\begin{pmatrix} x \\ y \end{pmatrix} \longrightarrow \begin{pmatrix} -x \\ y \end{pmatrix}$.

For example,

$$\begin{pmatrix} 1 \\ 0 \end{pmatrix} \longrightarrow \begin{pmatrix} -1 \\ 0 \end{pmatrix}, \begin{pmatrix} 10 \\ -7 \end{pmatrix} \longrightarrow \begin{pmatrix} -10 \\ -7 \end{pmatrix}, \begin{pmatrix} 3 \\ 4 \end{pmatrix} \longrightarrow \begin{pmatrix} -3 \\ 4 \end{pmatrix},$$

etc.

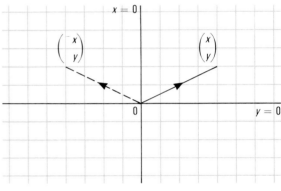

■ Write down a rule involving position vectors to represent a rotation of the plane through 90° clockwise about the origin, that is, $\begin{pmatrix} x \\ y \end{pmatrix} \longrightarrow \begin{pmatrix} ? \\ ? \end{pmatrix}$.

- If a transformation can be represented by a rule of the form $\begin{pmatrix} x \\ y \end{pmatrix} \longrightarrow \begin{pmatrix} ax+by \\ cx+dy \end{pmatrix}$ then the transformation can also be represented by a matrix.

  $\begin{pmatrix} ax+by \\ cx+dy \end{pmatrix}$ can be written as $\begin{pmatrix} a & b \\ c & d \end{pmatrix} \begin{pmatrix} x \\ y \end{pmatrix}$ and so we say that $\begin{pmatrix} a & b \\ c & d \end{pmatrix}$ is the *matrix of the transformation*.

- The rule $\begin{pmatrix} x \\ y \end{pmatrix} \longrightarrow \begin{pmatrix} -x \\ y \end{pmatrix}$ represents a reflection in $x = 0$.

  We can think of the rule as $\begin{pmatrix} x \\ y \end{pmatrix} \longrightarrow \begin{pmatrix} -1x+0y \\ 0x+1y \end{pmatrix}$.

  So, a reflection in $x = 0$ can be represented by the matrix $\begin{pmatrix} -1 & 0 \\ 0 & 1 \end{pmatrix}$.

■ Write down the matrix that represents a rotation through 90° clockwise about the origin.

CORE

B10

1 Here are four ways of representing a particular transformation:

• by a verbal statement   • by a diagram   • by a rule   • by a matrix

'A reflection in the
x-axis'

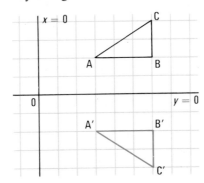

$$\begin{pmatrix} x \\ y \end{pmatrix} \longrightarrow \begin{pmatrix} x \\ -y \end{pmatrix}$$

$$\begin{pmatrix} 1 & 0 \\ 0 & -1 \end{pmatrix}$$

Each of the transformations below is described in just one of the ways shown above. Describe each transformation in the other three ways.

a) A reflection in the line $y = x$.   b) $\begin{pmatrix} x \\ y \end{pmatrix} \longrightarrow \begin{pmatrix} 3x \\ 3y \end{pmatrix}$ c) A rotation of $180°$ about the origin

d)   e) $\begin{pmatrix} 1 & 2 \\ 0 & 1 \end{pmatrix}$.

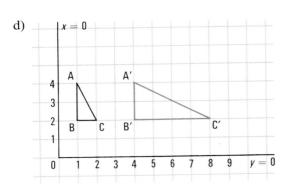

2 Write down the position vector of the image of the point $(2, 0)$ under each of these transformations:

a) A reflection in the line $x = 0$.

b) $\begin{pmatrix} x \\ y \end{pmatrix} \longrightarrow \begin{pmatrix} x+3y \\ y \end{pmatrix}$ c) $\begin{pmatrix} 2 & 5 \\ 1 & 0 \end{pmatrix}$ d) $\begin{pmatrix} 4 & 0 \\ 0 & 4 \end{pmatrix}$ e) $\begin{pmatrix} x \\ y \end{pmatrix} \longrightarrow \begin{pmatrix} x \\ x+y \end{pmatrix}$.

3 Write down the matrix for each of these transformations:

a) $\begin{pmatrix} x \\ y \end{pmatrix} \longrightarrow \begin{pmatrix} -x \\ 2x+y \end{pmatrix}$ b) $\begin{pmatrix} x \\ y \end{pmatrix} \longrightarrow \begin{pmatrix} 2x+3y \\ 3x-y \end{pmatrix}$ c) $\begin{pmatrix} x \\ y \end{pmatrix} \longrightarrow \begin{pmatrix} -y \\ x \end{pmatrix}$.

4 Write the transformations which have these matrices in the form $\begin{pmatrix} x \\ y \end{pmatrix} \longrightarrow \begin{pmatrix} \cdots \\ \cdots \end{pmatrix}$

a) $\begin{pmatrix} 2 & 3 \\ 1 & 5 \end{pmatrix}$ b) $\begin{pmatrix} 0 & 2 \\ 1 & -2 \end{pmatrix}$ c) $\begin{pmatrix} 1 & 0 \\ 0 & -1 \end{pmatrix}$.

B10

5   You need 5 mm squared paper.

a) The position vector of A is $\begin{pmatrix} 2 \\ 1 \end{pmatrix}$.

Check that $\begin{pmatrix} 2 \\ 11 \end{pmatrix}$ is the position vector of the image

of A under the transformation matrix $\begin{pmatrix} 3 & ^-4 \\ 4 & 3 \end{pmatrix}$.

[Work out $\begin{pmatrix} 3 & ^-4 \\ 4 & 3 \end{pmatrix} \begin{pmatrix} 2 \\ 1 \end{pmatrix}$.]

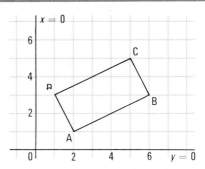

b) Find the position vectors of the images of B, C and D under the transformation $\begin{pmatrix} 3 & ^-4 \\ 4 & 3 \end{pmatrix}$.

c) Draw the image of the rectangle ABCD under the transformation $\begin{pmatrix} 3 & ^-4 \\ 4 & 3 \end{pmatrix}$. (Use 5 mm squared paper.)

d) Describe as fully as you can, the transformation represented by the matrix $\begin{pmatrix} 3 & ^-4 \\ 4 & 3 \end{pmatrix}$.
Use your drawing to help you.

(Hint: the transformation can be thought of as a combination of two simpler transformations, that is, one transformation of the plane followed by another one.)

EXPLORATION

6   Explore the kinds of transformations
which are represented by matrices of the form $\begin{pmatrix} a & ^-b \\ b & a \end{pmatrix}$. [For example, $\begin{pmatrix} 1 & ^-1 \\ 1 & 1 \end{pmatrix}$, $\begin{pmatrix} 3 & ^-8 \\ 8 & 3 \end{pmatrix}$, $\begin{pmatrix} 2 & 1 \\ ^-1 & 2 \end{pmatrix}$.]

What happens when $a = b$ and when a or b equals 0. Also try $a = \sqrt{3}$, $b = 1$, and describe the transformation.
(Hint: use the method of question 5, that is: draw a simple shape (*e.g.*, a rectangle) in the (x, y) plane; find the position vector of the image of each vertex under your chosen matrix; draw the image of the shape.)

EXPLORATION

7   a) The transformation represented in the
diagram can be thought of as a combination of
two transformations:
a reflection in $y = 0$, followed by
an enlargement, scale factor $\times 3$, centre the origin.

Copy and complete the rule and the matrix for
the combined transformation:

(i) $\begin{pmatrix} x \\ y \end{pmatrix} \longrightarrow \begin{pmatrix} 3x \\ \square \end{pmatrix}$ (ii) $\begin{pmatrix} 3 & \square \\ \square & \square \end{pmatrix}$

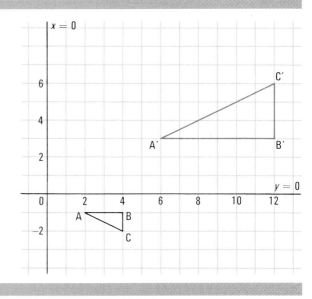

b) Explore some other combinations of
reflections and enlargements. Find the rule
and matrix for each combination.
Compare the matrix with the matrices for the
individual transformations.
Describe any connections that you see.

8   Sometimes it is possible to give a rule in the form $\begin{pmatrix} x \\ y \end{pmatrix} \longrightarrow \begin{pmatrix} \Box \\ \Box \end{pmatrix}$ for a transformation but not as a matrix.

   a) Copy and complete the rule for the transformations represented in each diagram.

   b) *Where possible*, write down the matrix for the transformation.

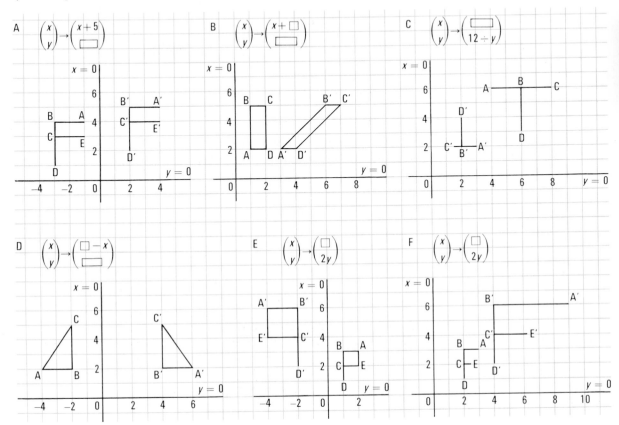

A $\begin{pmatrix} x \\ y \end{pmatrix} \longrightarrow \begin{pmatrix} x+5 \\ \Box \end{pmatrix}$

B $\begin{pmatrix} x \\ y \end{pmatrix} \longrightarrow \begin{pmatrix} x+\Box \\ \Box \end{pmatrix}$

C $\begin{pmatrix} x \\ y \end{pmatrix} \longrightarrow \begin{pmatrix} \Box \\ 12 \div y \end{pmatrix}$

D $\begin{pmatrix} x \\ y \end{pmatrix} \longrightarrow \begin{pmatrix} \Box - x \\ \Box \end{pmatrix}$

E $\begin{pmatrix} x \\ y \end{pmatrix} \longrightarrow \begin{pmatrix} \Box \\ 2y \end{pmatrix}$

F $\begin{pmatrix} x \\ y \end{pmatrix} \longrightarrow \begin{pmatrix} \Box \\ 2y \end{pmatrix}$

━━━━━━━━━━━ TAKE NOTE ━━━━━━━━━━━

We can represent a transformation of the plane by a 2×2 matrix only if the origin is invariant *and* the plane is transformed 'uniformly'; such a transformation is called a *linear transformation*.

In question 8, transformation F can be represented by the rule $\begin{pmatrix} x \\ y \end{pmatrix} \longrightarrow \begin{pmatrix} x^2 \\ 2y \end{pmatrix}$.

However,
it cannot be represented in the form $\begin{pmatrix} x \\ y \end{pmatrix} \longrightarrow \begin{pmatrix} ax+by \\ cx+dy \end{pmatrix}$ and therefore not by a matrix $\begin{pmatrix} a & b \\ c & d \end{pmatrix}$.

━━━━━━━━━━━ CHALLENGE ━━━━━━━━━━━

9   Explain what you think is meant by 'uniformly' in the *Take note*. Illustrate your explanation with some examples. You might like to start with a comparison of $\begin{pmatrix} x \\ y \end{pmatrix} \longrightarrow \begin{pmatrix} 2x \\ 2y \end{pmatrix}$ and $\begin{pmatrix} x \\ y \end{pmatrix} \longrightarrow \begin{pmatrix} x^2 \\ 2y \end{pmatrix}$.

Base vectors and matrices

1   When a transformation is applied, the whole (x, y) plane changes in some way. For example, this diagram shows what happens to the plane under a one-way stretch of scale factor $\times 3$ parallel to $y = 0$, with $x = 0$ invariant:

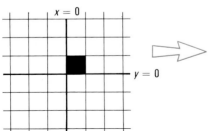 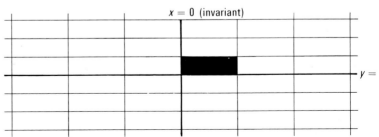

Looking at what happens to the shaded square gives us a good idea of the transformation. What is the image of each of these points under the transformation:

(i) $(1, 0)$ (ii) $(0, 1)$ (iii) $(0, 0)$ (iv) $(1, 1)$ (v) $(3, 1)$ (vi) $(^-2, ^-1)$ (vii) $(^-9, 14)$?

2   a)   The diagram represents a transformation of the plane in which $(0, 0) \rightarrow (0, 0)$, $(1, 0) \rightarrow (1, 0)$, $(0, 1) \rightarrow (1, 1)$ and $(1, 1) \rightarrow (2, 1)$.

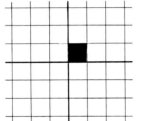 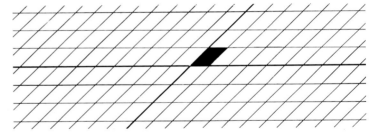

What is the image of each of these points under the same transformation:

(i) $(2, 0)$ (ii) $(0, 2)$ (iii) $(2, 2)$ (iv) $(7, 1)$ (v) $(1, 7)$ (vi) $(^-1, ^-1)$ (vii) $(^-7, 14)$?

b)   This diagram shows an original plane and its transformed plane together:

The image of $(1, 0)$ is $(2, 1)$.
The image of $(0, 1)$ is $(1, 2)$.
What is the image of
(i) $(1, 1)$ (ii) $(^-1, ^-1,)$
(iii) $(7, 3)$ (iv) $(3, ^-7)$?

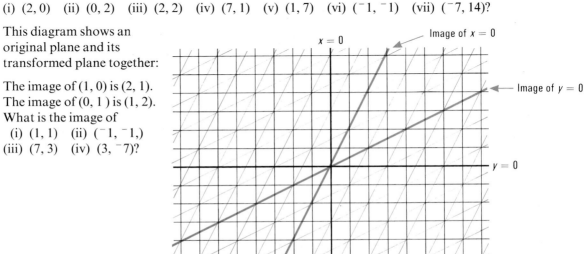

3 a) The diagram shows a one-way stretch with scale factor × 3. The origin remains invariant but the stretch is not in a horizontal or vertical direction. Only one quadrant of the plane is shown.

Try to find the matrix of the transformation. If you have not succeeded after five minutes, go on to part b).

b) The diagram shows the same transformation, and also how a section of the grid has been transformed. (You can see easily from this drawing what has happened to the square $(0, 0)$ $(1, 0)$ $(0, 1)$ $(1, 1)$, that is, $(0, 0) \rightarrow (0, 0)$, $(1, 0) \rightarrow (2, 1)$, $(0, 1) \rightarrow (1, 2)$, $(1, 1) \rightarrow (3, 3)$.)

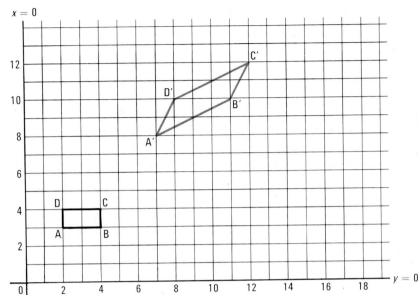

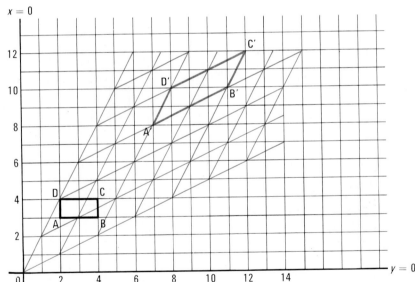

(i) Check that $\overrightarrow{OA'}$, the position vector of A', is $\begin{pmatrix} 7 \\ 8 \end{pmatrix}$.

(ii) Notice that we can also write

$$\overrightarrow{OA'} = 2\begin{pmatrix} 2 \\ 1 \end{pmatrix} + \square\begin{pmatrix} 1 \\ 2 \end{pmatrix}.$$

What is $\square$?

(iii) Copy and complete these vector sentences for the position vectors of B′, C′ and D′:

(i) $\overrightarrow{OB'} = \square\begin{pmatrix} 2 \\ 1 \end{pmatrix} + \square\begin{pmatrix} 1 \\ 2 \end{pmatrix} = \begin{pmatrix} 11 \\ 10 \end{pmatrix}$ (ii) $\overrightarrow{OC'} = \square\begin{pmatrix} 2 \\ 1 \end{pmatrix} + \square\begin{pmatrix} 1 \\ 2 \end{pmatrix} = \begin{pmatrix} 12 \\ 12 \end{pmatrix}$

(iii) $\overrightarrow{OD'} = \square\begin{pmatrix} 2 \\ 1 \end{pmatrix} + \square\begin{pmatrix} 1 \\ 2 \end{pmatrix} = \begin{pmatrix} 8 \\ 10 \end{pmatrix}$

c) E is a point with original position vector $\begin{pmatrix} 15 \\ 50 \end{pmatrix}$. E′ is the image of E under the transformation.

Copy and complete this vector sentence for the position vector of E′:

$$\overrightarrow{OE'} = \square\begin{pmatrix} 2 \\ 1 \end{pmatrix} + \square\begin{pmatrix} 1 \\ 2 \end{pmatrix} = \begin{pmatrix} \square \\ \square \end{pmatrix}$$

d) M is a point with position vector $\begin{pmatrix} e \\ f \end{pmatrix}$ and M′ is its image under the transformation.

  Copy and complete this vector sentence for the position vector of M′: $\overrightarrow{OM'} = \square \begin{pmatrix} 2 \\ 1 \end{pmatrix} + \square \begin{pmatrix} 1 \\ 2 \end{pmatrix} = \begin{pmatrix} \square \\ \square \end{pmatrix}$

e) Write down:

  (i) the rule for the transformation, in the form $\begin{pmatrix} x \\ y \end{pmatrix} \longrightarrow \begin{pmatrix} \square \\ \square \end{pmatrix}$

  (ii) the matrix for the transformation.

f) This is the matrix that you should have found in e): $\begin{pmatrix} 2 & 1 \\ 1 & 2 \end{pmatrix}$.

  Check that this matrix multiplication gives the correct position vector for $\overrightarrow{OA}'$: $\begin{pmatrix} 2 & 1 \\ 1 & 2 \end{pmatrix} \begin{pmatrix} 2 \\ 3 \end{pmatrix} = \begin{pmatrix} \square \\ \square \end{pmatrix}$

B10

4 You need 5 mm squared paper.
   The diagram shows the effect of a
   transformation on the rectangle
   ABCD and on a portion of the grid.

   a) Draw the image of the rectangle
      EFGH.

   b) Write down the image of these
      position vectors:

      (i) $\begin{pmatrix} 8 \\ 5 \end{pmatrix}$ (ii) $\begin{pmatrix} m \\ n \end{pmatrix}$

   c) Write down the matrix of the
      transformation (check that the
      matrix maps $\begin{pmatrix} 2 \\ 3 \end{pmatrix}$ onto $\begin{pmatrix} 7 \\ 11 \end{pmatrix}$,
      that is, C onto C′).

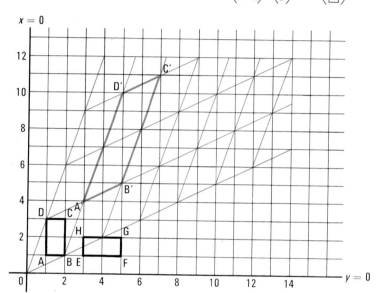

5 You need 5 mm squared paper
   The diagram shows the effect of a
   transformation on the rectangle
   ABCD and on a portion of the grid.

   a) Draw the image of the square
      EFGH.

   b) Write down the matrix of the
      transformation (check that the
      matrix maps $\begin{pmatrix} 2 \\ 3 \end{pmatrix}$ onto $\begin{pmatrix} 1 \\ 5 \end{pmatrix}$,
      that is, A onto A′).

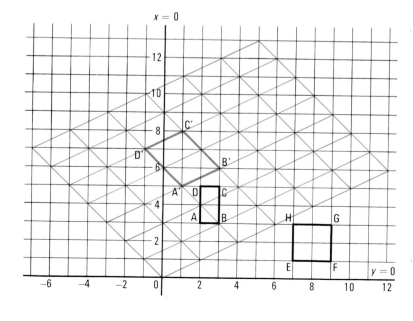

6   The position vectors $\begin{pmatrix} 1 \\ 0 \end{pmatrix}$ and $\begin{pmatrix} 0 \\ 1 \end{pmatrix}$ are called *base vectors*.

The diagram shows the effect of a transformation on a portion of the grid and on the base vectors, that is,

$$\begin{pmatrix} 1 \\ 0 \end{pmatrix} \rightarrow \begin{pmatrix} 2 \\ -1 \end{pmatrix} \text{ and } \begin{pmatrix} 0 \\ 1 \end{pmatrix} \rightarrow \begin{pmatrix} 1 \\ 3 \end{pmatrix}$$

Find the image of A.

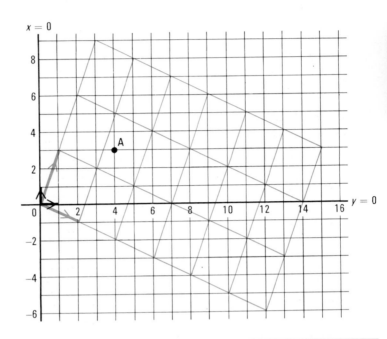

B10

■■■■■■■■■ THINK IT THROUGH ■■■■■■■■■

7   A transformation maps $\begin{pmatrix} 1 \\ 0 \end{pmatrix} \rightarrow \begin{pmatrix} 1 \\ 3 \end{pmatrix}$ and $\begin{pmatrix} 0 \\ 1 \end{pmatrix} \rightarrow \begin{pmatrix} 2 \\ 7 \end{pmatrix}$.

a) Copy and complete   (i) $\begin{pmatrix} 7 \\ 4 \end{pmatrix} \rightarrow \begin{pmatrix} \square \\ \square \end{pmatrix}$ (ii) $\begin{pmatrix} x \\ y \end{pmatrix} \rightarrow \begin{pmatrix} \square \\ \square \end{pmatrix}$

b) Write down the matrix of the transformation.

c) Write down some examples of images of $\begin{pmatrix} 1 \\ 0 \end{pmatrix}$ and $\begin{pmatrix} 0 \\ 1 \end{pmatrix}$ of your own for transformations which leave the origin invariant.
For each of your examples, find the matrix of the transformation.
You should discover a connection between the images of the base vectors, and the matrix itself. Describe what you discover.

d) What effect does the transformation matrix $\begin{pmatrix} 2 & 1 \\ 3 & -4 \end{pmatrix}$ have on the base vectors $\begin{pmatrix} 1 \\ 0 \end{pmatrix}$ and $\begin{pmatrix} 0 \\ 1 \end{pmatrix}$?

e) A transformation maps $\begin{pmatrix} 1 \\ 0 \end{pmatrix} \rightarrow \begin{pmatrix} 2 \\ 4 \end{pmatrix}$ and $\begin{pmatrix} 0 \\ 1 \end{pmatrix} \rightarrow \begin{pmatrix} 3 \\ -1 \end{pmatrix}$.

(i) What is the matrix of the transformation?

(ii) What is the image of $\begin{pmatrix} 1 \\ 1 \end{pmatrix}$?

▨▨▨▨▨▨▨▨▨▨▨▨ TAKE NOTE ▨▨▨▨▨▨▨▨▨▨▨▨▨▨▨▨▨▨▨▨▨▨▨▨▨▨▨▨▨

If a transformation is *linear* (that is, the origin does not move and the plane is transformed uniformly), we can find the matrix of the transformation by first finding the images of the base vectors.

For example, if $\begin{pmatrix} 1 \\ 0 \end{pmatrix} \rightarrow \begin{pmatrix} 2 \\ 5 \end{pmatrix}$ and $\begin{pmatrix} 0 \\ 1 \end{pmatrix} \rightarrow \begin{pmatrix} ^-1 \\ 3 \end{pmatrix}$, then the matrix is $\begin{pmatrix} 2 & ^-1 \\ 5 & 3 \end{pmatrix}$

The image of $\begin{pmatrix} 1 \\ 0 \end{pmatrix}$ becomes the first column of the matrix.

The image of $\begin{pmatrix} 0 \\ 1 \end{pmatrix}$ becomes the 2nd column of the matrix.

$\begin{pmatrix} 2 & ^-1 \\ 5 & 3 \end{pmatrix}$

Also, $\begin{pmatrix} 1 \\ 1 \end{pmatrix} \rightarrow \begin{pmatrix} 2+ {}^-1 \\ 5+ \ 3 \end{pmatrix} = \begin{pmatrix} 1 \\ 8 \end{pmatrix}$

Conversely, if the matrix is $\begin{pmatrix} 2 & 3 \\ 1 & 5 \end{pmatrix}$, then we know that

First column of matrix ↓

$\begin{pmatrix} 1 \\ 0 \end{pmatrix} \rightarrow \begin{pmatrix} 2 \\ 1 \end{pmatrix}$

2nd column of matrix

$\begin{pmatrix} 0 \\ 1 \end{pmatrix} \rightarrow \begin{pmatrix} 3 \\ 5 \end{pmatrix}$

and $\begin{pmatrix} 1 \\ 1 \end{pmatrix} \rightarrow \begin{pmatrix} 5 \\ 6 \end{pmatrix}$ ⟵ Sums of the numbers in the columns of the matrix

▨▨▨▨▨▨▨▨▨▨▨▨ IN YOUR HEAD ▨▨▨▨▨▨▨▨▨▨▨▨▨▨▨▨▨▨▨▨▨▨▨▨▨

8 a) Think about the images of $\begin{pmatrix} 1 \\ 0 \end{pmatrix}$ and $\begin{pmatrix} 0 \\ 1 \end{pmatrix}$, and write down the matrix for each of these transformations:

   (i) a reflection in $x = 0$
   (ii) a half turn about the origin
   (iii) an enlargement, scale factor $\times 5$, with centre the origin
   (iv) a reflection in $y = x$.

   b) Write down the images of the vertices of the unit square [that is, the square $(0, 0)$ $(1, 0)$ $(0, 1)$ $(1, 1)$] under the transformations which have the matrices:

   (i) $\begin{pmatrix} 1 & 2 \\ 2 & 1 \end{pmatrix}$ (ii) $\begin{pmatrix} ^-1 & 0 \\ 3 & 0 \end{pmatrix}$ (iii) $\begin{pmatrix} 5 & 5 \\ 5 & 5 \end{pmatrix}$ (iv) $\begin{pmatrix} a & c \\ b & d \end{pmatrix}$.

   c) Think about the images of $\begin{pmatrix} 1 \\ 0 \end{pmatrix}$ and $\begin{pmatrix} 0 \\ 1 \end{pmatrix}$ after each combined transformation, and write down the matrix for the combined transformation. [For example, for a reflection in $y = 0$ followed by a reflection in $x = 0$, $\begin{pmatrix} 1 \\ 0 \end{pmatrix} \rightarrow \begin{pmatrix} ^-1 \\ 0 \end{pmatrix}$ and $\begin{pmatrix} 0 \\ 1 \end{pmatrix} \rightarrow \begin{pmatrix} 0 \\ ^-1 \end{pmatrix}$

   So the matrix for the combined transformation is $\begin{pmatrix} ^-1 & 0 \\ 0 & ^-1 \end{pmatrix}$.]

   (i) A reflection in $x = 0$ followed by a half turn, centre $(0, 0)$.
   (ii) A quarter clockwise turn, centre $(0, 0)$, followed by a reflection in the y axis.
   (iii) A reflection in $x = y$ followed by an enlargement, scale factor $\times 2$, centre $(0, 0)$.

ENRICHMENT

EXPLORATION

1 a) Think of two linear transformations (for example, a reflection in $x = 0$ and a rotation of $90°$ anticlockwise about the origin).

Think of their combined effect on the base vectors $\begin{pmatrix} 1 \\ 0 \end{pmatrix}$ and $\begin{pmatrix} 0 \\ 1 \end{pmatrix}$. That is, what is the image

of $\begin{pmatrix} 1 \\ 0 \end{pmatrix}$ and $\begin{pmatrix} 1 \\ 0 \end{pmatrix}$ after a reflection in $x = 0$ followed by a rotation of $90°$ anticlockwise about $(0, 0)$?

Write down the matrices for the individual and combined transformations.

b) Multiply the two matrices for the individual transformations together. Do they give you the combined transformations matrix? If not, try multiplying them the other way round. Does this give you the combined transformations matrix?

c) Explore other pairs of linear transformations. Find out how the order in which the matrices are multiplied relates to the order in which the transformations are carried out.
Are there any transformations for which the order in which they are combined is unimportant in so far as multiplying the matrices together is concerned?

B10

REVIEW

We already know what trigonometrical ratios mean for angles less than 90°.

For example, $\sin 39° = \dfrac{AB}{AC}$

$\cos 39° = \dfrac{BC}{AC}$

$\tan 39° = \dfrac{AB}{BC}$

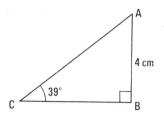

■ For triangle ABC find the lengths of
(i) BC (ii) AC.

CORE

B11

Angles between 0° and 180°

In this section we are going to consider the meaning of trigonometrical ratio for angles greater than 90° (for example, what is sin 123°? What is cos 210°?). When we deal with angles between 0° and 180° you will see that we are interested in positions relative to a point O rather than lengths of sides of right-angled triangles.

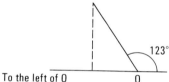

To the left of O

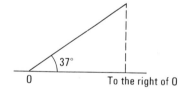

To the right of O

1   Study this diagram in which OP is a rotating line of length 1 unit.

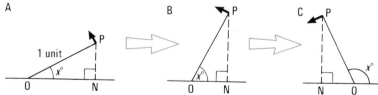

As the line rotates, x increases from 0 to 180.

a) In diagrams A and B check that

$$\cos x° = \dfrac{ON}{OP} = ON \quad \text{(because OP is 1)}$$

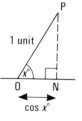

$\cos x°$ is therefore the distance of N from O. How far is N from O when x is 37?

b) In diagram C, x is greater than 90. However, we continue to refer to the distance ON as $\cos x°$. If x is 143, where is N relative to O?

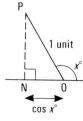

c) Do you think it is sensible to write

$\cos 143° = \cos 37°$?   Why?

2   Check that cos 37° = 0.80
The *position* of N relative to O is different for an angle of 143° to its *position* for an angle of 37°, even though its *distance* from O is the same in both cases.

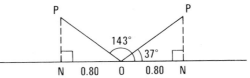

To show this we write

        cos 37° = 0.80 (so N is to the right of O)
and cos 143° = ⁻0.80 (meaning that N is to the left of O)

THINK IT THROUGH

3   Do not use your calculator. Study the diagram of the rotating pole, OP, in question 2. Which of these graphs best describes the way in which cos $x°$ varies as $x°$ changes from 0° to 180°?

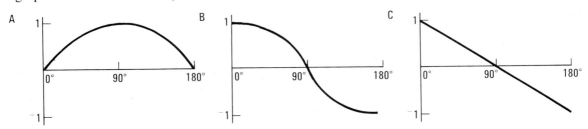

4   Do not use your calculator.
You are given these values of cosines (correct to 2 DP).

    cos 12° = 0.98   cos 88° = 0.03
    cos 120° = ⁻0.5   cos 172° = ⁻0.99

Find   a) cos 168°   b) cos 92°   c) cos 8°   d) cos 60°.

Check your results with your calculator.

5   Which of these is correct:

    cos (180 − x)° = cos $x°$;   cos (180 − x)° = ⁻cos $x°$?

Give an example to explain your answer.

6   Sketch diagrams of the line OP in question 1, when it has turned through 63° and 117°.
Copy and complete: cos 117° = ⁻cos □° = □

TAKE NOTE

cos 120° = ⁻cos 60°   Generally, cos (180 − x)° = ⁻cos $x°$.
cos 179° = ⁻cos 1°
cos 101° = ⁻cos 79°

B11

7   Do not use a calculator.

a) Check from the diagram that $PN = \sin x°$ and decide between
   you which of these you think we should accept as true: $\sin (180-x)° = ^-\sin x°$
   or $\sin (180-x)° = \sin x°$

   Explain why you made the choice you did.

b) Decide which of these graphs best describes the way in which $\sin x°$ varies as x changes from 0 to 180.

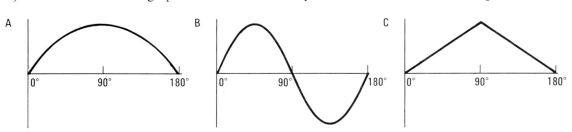

c) Use your calculator to check your decisions in a) and b).

d) Decide between you which of these you think we should accept as true:

   $\tan (180° -x°) = \tan x°$ or $\tan (180° -x°) = ^-\tan x°$ Explain why you made the choice you did.

e) Decide which of the graphs best describes how $\tan x°$ varies.

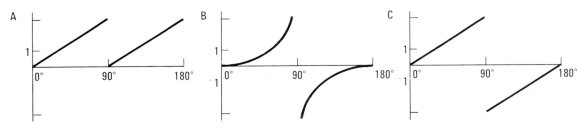

f) Use your calculator to check your decisions in d) and e).

8   Do not use a calculator. You are given these values of sin, cos and tan (correct to 2 DP). Use them to find
    the other trigonometrical ratios.

$\cos 60° = 0.5$	$\sin 110° = 0.94$	$\tan 70° = 2.7$
$\cos 110° = ^-0.34$	$\tan 150° = ^-0.58$	$\sin 40° = 0.64$

a) $\cos 120°$ b) $\tan 30°$ c) $\tan 110°$ d) $\cos 50°$
e) $\sin 140°$ f) $\cos 70°$ g) $\sin 20°$ (use your result in f))

Check your results with your calculator.

▨▨▨▨▨▨▨▨▨▨ TAKE NOTE ▨▨▨▨▨▨▨▨▨▨▨▨▨▨▨▨▨▨▨▨▨▨▨▨▨▨▨

Generally,

$\sin 120° = \sin 60°$	$\tan 120° = ^-\tan 60°$	$\sin (180-y)° = \sin y°$
$\sin 179° = \sin 1°$	$\tan 179° = ^-\tan 1°$	$\tan (180-y)° = ^-\tan y°$
$\sin 101° = \sin 79°$	$\tan 101° = ^-\tan 79°$	

WITH A FRIEND: TRIG. RATIO GUESSING GAMES

9   There are three games: one for sin, one for cos and one for tan. Play each game four times (so that each of you has two turns guessing and two turns choosing).

Sin game   Player 1 – chooses an angle between 0° and 180°.
              Player 2 – has three guesses to get within 0.1 of the correct value for sin.
                         After each guess Player 1 must say 'too low' or 'too high'.
              Scoring: 3 points for a correct guess on the first attempt
                        2 points for a correct guess on the second attempt
                        1 point for a correct guess on the third attempt
                        (Don't forget that in each game the sign of the ratio must be correct, for example, cos 120° = ⁻0.5.)

Cos game   Identical to the sin game except Player 1 asks for the cos of an angle between 0° and 180°.

Tan game   Player 1 – chooses the tan of an angle between 0° and 180°.
              Player 2 – has three guesses to get within 5° of the angle.
                         The scoring is as for the sin game.

10   a) Calculate   (i) DC   (ii) AD.

     b) If you used your calculator for cos 123° in a)
        you would have got the result DC = ⁻2.2 cm
        (1 DP). What does the negative sign tell us?

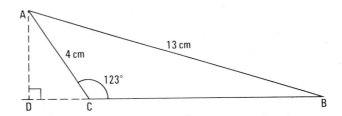

CHALLENGE

11   Do not use a calculator.

     a) Consider what happens to ON and PN as P makes a full turn
        about O. Decide whether these are positive or negative:

        sin 80°   cos 80°   tan 80°
        sin 130°   cos 130°   tan 130°
        sin 220°   cos 220°   tan 220°
        sin 310°   cos 310°   tan 310°

     b) Copy and complete the diagram to show whether sin, cos and
        tan are positive or negative for each range of values.

     c) Use your calculator to check your decisions in a) and b).

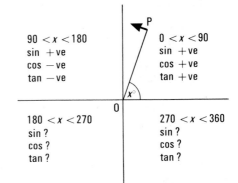

━━━━━━ ACTIVITY ━━━━━━

12   You need 1 mm graph paper.
Use your calculator to help you to draw accurate graphs of sin $x°$, cos $x°$, and tan $x°$ for $0 < x < 360$.

━━━━━━ TAKE NOTE ━━━━━━

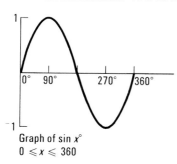

Graph of sin $x°$
$0 \leqslant x \leqslant 360$

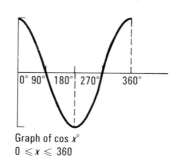

Graph of cos $x°$
$0 \leqslant x \leqslant 360$

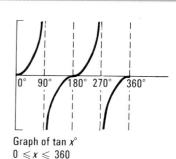

Graph of tan $x°$
$0 \leqslant x \leqslant 360$

$\sin(180-x)° = \sin x°$
$\cos(180-x)° = {}^{-}\cos x°$
$\tan(180-x)° = {}^{-}\tan x°$

$\sin(180+x)° = {}^{-}\sin x°$
$\cos(180+x)° = {}^{-}\cos x°$
$\tan(180+x)° = \tan x°$

	$\left.\begin{array}{l}\sin \\ \cos \\ \tan\end{array}\right\}$ +ve
sin +ve	
tan +ve	cos +ve

$\sin x°$
$\cos x°$
$\tan x°$

$\sin(360-x)° = {}^{-}\sin x°$
$\cos(360-x)° = \cos x°$
$\tan(360-x)° = {}^{-}\tan x°$

13   a) $\sin x° = 0.5$
x can have two possible values between 0 and 360. What are they (to 1 DP)?

b) Find the two possible values of x (to 1 DP) between 0 and 360 for which $\cos x° = 0.5$.

c) $\tan x° = {}^{-}2$.
Find all the possible values of x (to 1 DP) between 0 and 360.

━━━━━━ CHALLENGE ━━━━━━

14   a) Do not use a calculator.
Imagine that P continues rotating around and around O. You are given that $\sin 30° = 0.5$.

What is   (i) sin 690°,   (ii) cos 570°,   (iii) tan 1290°?

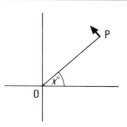

b) Use your calculator to check your results in a).

c) *Sketch* graphs for sin $x°$, cos $x°$ and tan $x°$ for $0 \leqslant x \leqslant 1440$.

ENRICHMENT

The sine rule

1   The triangle has a right angle at A, so

   $\tan \theta° = \frac{7}{4}$.

   a) Find $\theta°$ to the nearest 0.1°.

   b) Find the size of angle ABC to the nearest 0.1°.

   c) Find BC to the nearest 0.1 cm.

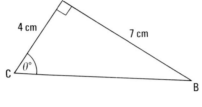

2   In the diagram, find:

   a) $\alpha°$ to the nearest 0.1°

   b) x to the nearest 0.1 cm

   c) $\theta°$ to the nearest 0.1°.

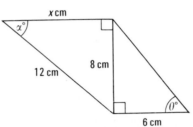

CHALLENGE

3   a) $\sin x° = \cos x°$.
      Find x.

   b) What is the maximum value of $2 \sin x°$?
      Explain your answer.

   c) $\sin 2x° = 0.5$.
      Find x.

   d) $\sin x° = 0.866$.
      Find   (i) $\tan x°$ (ii) $\cos x°$.

Non-right-angled triangles

1   Suppose we wish to find $\angle ABC$ in this triangle.

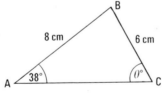

   There are no right angles to help us but we can draw a perpendicular BX.

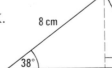

   a) Find BX to the nearest 0.01 cm.

   b) Now find $\theta°$ to the nearest 0.01°.

   c) Use your result in b) to help you to find
      $\angle ABC$ to the nearest degree.

2   In triangle XYZ, drop a perpendicular from Z to
   XY. Hence find:

   a) $\theta°$, to the nearest 0.01°

   b) XY to the nearest 0.1 cm

   c) $\angle XZY$ to the nearest 0.1°.

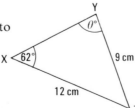

▓▓▓▓▓▓▓▓▓▓▓▓ TAKE NOTE ▓▓▓▓▓▓▓▓▓▓▓▓

When we know the size of an angle and the length of two sides (one of them opposite the angle), we can find the other angles and side by dropping a perpendicular.

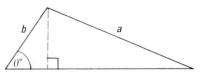

---

3   In triangle XYZ, ∠XZY is 120°. YP is the perpendicular from Y to XZ extended.

   Find: a) YP

            b) ZP

            c) XZ

            d) ∠ZXY.

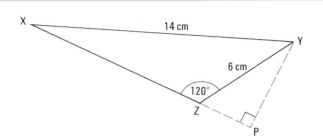

▓▓▓▓▓▓▓▓▓▓▓▓ THINK IT THROUGH ▓▓▓▓▓▓▓▓▓▓▓▓

4   In a triangle ABC, ∠ABC is 150°, AC is 26 cm and BC is 15 cm. Find ∠BAC.

---

5   a) In triangle ABC, check that AP is $b \sin C°$.

   b) Write a similar expression for AP using $B°$ and c.

   c) Use your results in a) and b) to complete this rule:

   $$\frac{b}{\sin \square°} = \frac{c}{\sin \square°}$$

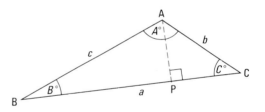

▓▓▓▓▓▓▓▓▓▓▓▓ CHALLENGE ▓▓▓▓▓▓▓▓▓▓▓▓

   d) The diagram shows triangle ABC again. CT is the perpendicular to BA extended.

   Copy and complete:

   (i) $CT = a \sin \square°$
   (ii) $CT = \square \sin \angle TAC = \square \sin A°$.

   e) Use your results in c) and d) to complete:

   $$\frac{a}{\sin \square°} = \frac{b}{\sin \square°} = \frac{c}{\sin \square°}$$

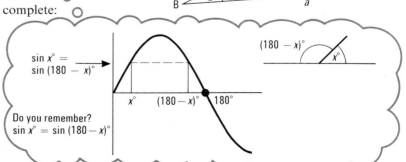

$\sin x° = \sin (180 - x)°$

Do you remember?
$\sin x° = \sin (180 - x)°$

6   Find

a) ∠QRP

b) QR.

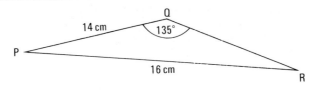

In any triangle ABC,

$$\frac{a}{\sin A^\circ} = \frac{b}{\sin B^\circ} = \frac{c}{\sin C^\circ}$$

This is called the *sine rule*.

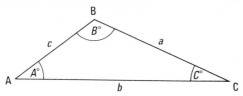

The cosine rule

1   a) In triangle ABC,
       find (i) ∠BAC   (ii) ∠BCA.

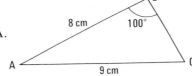

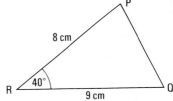

b) In triangle PQR two sides and an angle are known. Explain
    why we cannot use the sine rule to obtain any more information about the triangle.

c) What is the least which must be known about a triangle in order that the sine rule can be
    used to obtain more information?

2   a) PQR is the triangle in question 1 b).
       The perpendicular PT to RQ has been drawn.

   (i) Find the length of PT.
   (ii) Find the length of RT.
   (iii) Find the length of TQ.
   (iv) Find ∠PQR.
   (v) Find PQ.

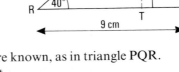

b) In triangle ABC, two sides and an angle are known, as in triangle PQR.
    Follow the same steps as in a) to show that

$$\tan B = \frac{b \sin \theta}{a - b \cos \theta}$$

c) In triangle LMN, explain why

   (i) $NL^2 = a^2 (\sin \theta)^2$
   (ii) $LM^2 = a^2 (\cos \theta)^2$
   (iii) $a^2 = a^2 (\sin \theta)^2 + a^2 (\cos \theta)^2$.

d) Use your result in c) (iii) to explain why

   $(\sin \theta)^2 + (\cos \theta)^2 = 1$.

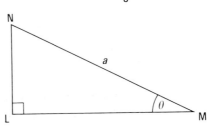

B11

3   This is the triangle from question 2 b).

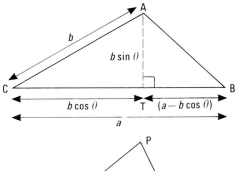

In question 2 you should have found that

CT $= b \cos \theta$
TB $= a - b \cos \theta$
AT $= b \sin \theta$

a) Find AB^2 in terms of a, b, $\sin \theta$ and $\cos \theta$.

b) Use your result in a) to explain why

AB$^2 = a^2 + b^2 - 2ab \cos \theta$.

c) Use the result in b) to calculate PQ. Check that your result is the same as that you obtained by a different method in question 2 a).

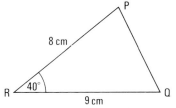

B11

When we know two sides of a triangle and an included angle, we can find the side opposite the angle by using the rule

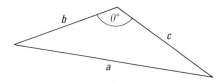

$a^2 = b^2 + c^2 - 2bc \cos \theta$.

This is called the *cosine rule*.

4   Use the cosine rule to find
     (i) PQ
     (ii) MN (remember, $\cos 110° = -\cos 70°$).

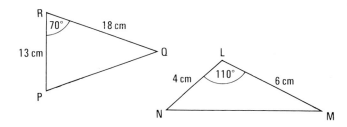

5   a) Use the cosine rule to find $\angle$ PRQ.

     b) Find $\angle$ QPR and $\angle$ RQP.

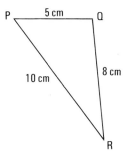

REVIEW

- *Vulgar* fractions (often called just 'fractions') are numbers such as $\frac{5}{7}, \frac{2}{3}, \frac{1}{2}, \ldots$

- *Decimal* fractions are numbers such as $0.12, 1.769, 17.04, \ldots$
  Each decimal fraction goes with a whole family of (vulgar) fractions, for example,

  0.5 is equal to every member of $\{\frac{1}{2}, \frac{2}{4}, \frac{3}{6}, \frac{4}{8}, \ldots\}$
  0.32 is equal to every member of $\{\frac{8}{25}, \frac{16}{50}, \frac{24}{75}, \frac{32}{100}, \ldots\}$

■ Write down four members of the family whose members are equal to the decimal fraction 0.418.

- $1\frac{3}{7}$ is a *mixed number*. $1\frac{3}{7} = \frac{10}{7}$; $\frac{10}{7}$ is a 'top-heavy' (vulgar) fraction.

- $0.123\,123\,123\ldots$ and $0.587\,474\,74\ldots$ are *recurring decimals*.

- $0.010\,010\,001\,000\,01\ldots$ is a *non-recurring decimal*.

  π is another example of a non-recurring decimal number.

- $0.274\,(0000)$ is a *terminating decimal*.

■ Continue 4.7181... so that it becomes:

  a) a recurring decimal

  b) a non-recurring decimal.

CONSOLIDATION

1 a) Write each of these as decimal fractions:

   (i) $\frac{1}{4}$ (ii) $\frac{1}{5}$ (iii) $\frac{3}{5}$ (iv) $\frac{7}{10}$ (v) $\frac{1}{3}$.

   b) Write each of these as mixed numbers:

   (i) $\frac{7}{3}$ (ii) $\frac{15}{7}$ (iii) $\frac{27}{19}$ (iv) $\frac{36}{10}$.

   c) Write each of these as vulgar fractions (or mixed numbers):

   (i) 0.12   (ii) 0.666 66...   (iii) 1.75   (iv) 8.88.

   d) Which fraction is larger, $\frac{8}{13}$ or $\frac{15}{26}$? Explain how you know.

In mathematics we deal with different types of numbers.

For example, equations such as

$$x + 1 = 3, \quad 3 - x = 1, \quad 8 \div x = 2$$

all have whole number solutions.

We could imagine a world in which only the whole numbers 1, 2, 3, 4, 5,... were used. Indeed, very early in our history these *were* the only numbers used – for counting and recording. They are called *counting numbers* or *natural numbers*.

1 a) Write down three equations (different from those in the *Take note*) which involve only natural numbers, and whose solutions are natural numbers.

   b) Write down three equations which involve only natural numbers, but whose solutions are *not* natural numbers.

2 Solve each of these equations:

   a) $2x = 1$ b) $3x - 1 = 12$ c) $\dfrac{2}{x} = \dfrac{5}{3}$.

3 The solutions to the equations in question 2 are fractions.

   a) Write down three equations of your own whose solutions are fractions.

   b) Write down an example of an equation whose solution is *neither* a fraction *nor* a counting number.

4   We can represent fractions on a *number line*, like this:

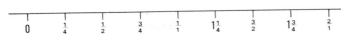

(Notice that $\frac{1}{1}, \frac{2}{1}, \ldots$ are fractions which we normally write as $1, 2, \ldots$)

a) Given any two fractions, for example, $\frac{101}{199}$ and $\frac{102}{199}$, is it always possible to find a fraction which lies between them? If you say 'yes', explain how you can do this.

b) Find two different fractions x which satisfy the relation
    $\frac{2888}{3000} < x < \frac{2889}{3000}$

====== TAKE NOTE ======

In question 3 b), you were asked to find an equation whose solution is not a fraction and not a natural number.

Here are two examples: (i) $x + 4 = 0$ (ii) $x^2 = 2$.

The solution to (i) is $x = {}^-4$. ${}^-4$ is an example of a *negative number*.
Positive and negative numbers such as ${}^+\frac{1}{2}, {}^-1.1, {}^+10, {}^-12, \ldots$ are called *directed numbers*. Directed numbers which are also whole numbers, such as ${}^-5, {}^-4, {}^-3, {}^-2, \quad 0, {}^+1, {}^+2, {}^+3, {}^+4, \ldots$ are called *integers*.

B12

5   a) Write down your own example of an equation which has a negative number solution.

b) The solution to equation (ii) above is $x = \sqrt{2}$.
    $\sqrt{2}$ cannot be represented as a (vulgar) fraction. It is, in fact, a non-recurring decimal which begins $1.4142136\ldots$ and which continues forever without ending or recurring.
    $\sqrt{3}$ is another non-recurring decimal. Write an equation whose solution is $\sqrt{3}$.

c) $0.121\,121\,112\,111\,12\ldots$ is a non-recurring decimal. Write down your own example of a non-recurring decimal which is:

   (i) larger than 0.152 but smaller than 0.153
   (ii) larger than $0.787\,878\,7878\ldots$ but smaller than $0.797\,979\,7979\ldots$

====== TAKE NOTE ======

We can represent the positive and negative numbers (including the recurring and non-recurring decimals) on a number line, like this:

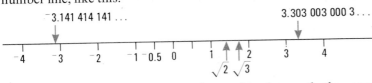

It is not possible of course to place the numbers in exactly the correct position.
The numbers which are represented on this number line are, together, all called *real* numbers.

====== FIND OUT FOR YOURSELF ======

6   What is an '*unreal*' or '*imaginary*' number? Write down an equation whose solution is an imaginary number.

████████████████ TAKE NOTE ████████████████

REAL NUMBERS

	Rational numbers	Irrational numbers
The *real* numbers are made up of two different sets:	Numbers which can be represented by vulgar fractions and mixed numbers: $0.121212\ldots$ ($\frac{12}{99}$) 3.4 ($3\frac{2}{5}$) $\ldots$	Numbers which cannot be represented by vulgar fractions and mixed numbers: $0.121\,121\,112\,111\,12$ π $\sqrt{2}$ $\ldots$

7 a) Write down a rational number which lies between the two irrational numbers

   $0.434\,334\,333\,433\,334\ldots$ and $0.433\,433\,343\,333\ldots$

   b) Write down an irrational number which lies between the two rational numbers

   0.8444 and $0.844\,4444\ldots$

████████████████ CHALLENGE ████████████████

8 a) Explain how we know that there must be an infinite number of rational numbers which lie between 0.1 and 0.2.

   b) Explain how we know that there must be an infinite number of irrational numbers which lie between 0.1 and 0.2.

ENRICHMENT

1   In the Core section, you have had to take our word for it that $\sqrt{2}$ is an irrational number. That is, it *cannot* be written as a fraction a/b.

   a) Study this argument, which *proves* that $\sqrt{2}$ cannot be written in the form a/b.

Step 1   Assume that $\sqrt{2}$ *can* be written in the form a/b.

Step 2   Assume that a/b written in its simplest ('cancelled down') form is n/m
   (For example, $\frac{14}{22}$ is $\frac{1}{2}$, $\frac{16}{160}$ is $\frac{1}{10}$ ... In the same way, a/b is n/m.)

Step 3   Then $\sqrt{2} = n/m$, where n and m do not have any common factors.
   So $2 = n^2/m^2$ (squaring both sides).
   So $2m^2 = n^2$.
   Now $2m^2$ is an even number (any number, $2 \times \ldots$ is even).
   So n^2 must be an *even* number.
   If n^2 is an even number, then n must be even (convince yourself that this must be true).

Step 4   Since n is even, then n can be written as $2k$.
   So $n^2 = 4k^2$.

Step 5   In step 3 we had the equation $2m^2 = n^2$, and in step 4 the equation $n^2 = 4k^2$.
These two give $2m^2 = 4k^2$.
So $m^2 = 2k^2$.
So m must be even (convince yourself that *this* is true).

Step 6   We have now shown that, by assuming that $\sqrt{2}$ can be written as n/m where n and m have no common factors, we arrive at the contradictory conclusion that both n and m can be divided by 2. This means that our original assumption must have been incorrect.
$\sqrt{2}$ cannot therefore be written in the form n/m, and it is therefore not a rational number.

b) Use a similar argument to that in a) to prove that $\sqrt{3}$ is irrational.

2   We can change a vulgar fraction to a recurring or terminating decimal by 'dividing out', for example,

$$\frac{8}{14} \text{ is } 14 \overline{\smash)\,8.\,000\;\;000\;\;0} \;\;0.\,571\;\;428\;\;5\ldots$$

We write $0.571\,428\,571\,428\,5\ldots$ or $0.\dot{5}71\,42\dot{8}$, the two dots meaning that this string of digits repeats itself again and again.

a) By 'dividing out', write each of these as a recurring or terminating decimal: (i) $\frac{3}{7}$ (ii) $\frac{7}{8}$ (iii) $\frac{1}{11}$.

b) Which fractions do these recurring and terminating decimals represent:
(i) 0.84 (ii) $0.8888\ldots$ (iii) $0.\dot{3}$ (iv) $0.919\,191\ldots$?

(You might have to use trial and improvement with your calculator.)

3   Here is how we can change a recurring decimal to fraction form. (If you found question 2 b) difficult you can use this method.)
Put $x = 0.333\,333\ldots$
Multiply each side of the equation by 10:
$10x = 3.333\,333\ldots$
Subtract the two equations:
$9x = 3$
so $x = \frac{1}{3}$

a) Use the same method to change $0.6666\ldots$ to fraction form.

b) Copy and complete this for changing the decimal $0.848\,484\ldots$ to fraction form:

Put $x = 0.848\,484\ldots$
Multiply both sides of the equation by 100:
$100x = 84.848484\ldots$
Subtract the two equations:
$99x = \square$
So $x = \square$.

c) Change $0.737\,373\,73\ldots$ to fraction form.

d) Change $1.123\,123\,123\ldots$ to fraction form.

e) Change $0.223\,333\,3\ldots$ to fraction form.

f) Explain why the method you use in parts a) to e) enables you to write recurring decimals as fractions, but not to write non-recurring decimals as fractions.

REVIEW

- Quadratic functions are functions of the form $x \rightarrow ax^2 + bx + c$,
  which we can also write as $f(x) = ax^2 + bx + c$.

For example, $y = 2x^2 + 1$
$$f(x) = 2x^2 - 4$$
$$f(x) = \tfrac{1}{2}x^2$$
are all quadratic functions.

 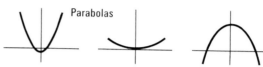

Parabolas

- The graphs of quadratic functions are *parabolas*.

- $2x^2 + 3x + 1$ is a quadratic expression.

  Quadratic expressions can be expressed as
  the product of two factors (factorized):

  $$2x^2 + 3x + 1 \equiv (2x + 1)(x + 1)$$

  $$3x^2 + x \equiv x(3x + 1)$$

  Not all factors, however, are as easy to find
  as these.

■ Factorize:
   a) $x^2 + 5x - 6$ b) $x^2 - 4$ c) $5x^2 - 90x$.

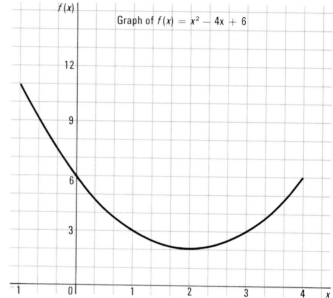

$f(x)$

Graph of $f(x) = x^2 - 4x + 6$

B13

CORE

Solving quadratic equations

▬▬▬▬▬▬▬▬ TAKE NOTE ▬▬▬▬▬▬

Equations which have an x^2 term in them (but not an x^3, x^4, ... term) are called *quadratic equations*:

For example, $2x^2 - x = 0$ $3x = x^2$
$$x^2 + 3x + 4 = 0 \qquad x^2 = 12$$
$$x^2 = 2x - 7$$
are quadratic equations.

1   Use trial and improvement or any other method to find the *two* solutions of each of these equations:

   a) $x^2 + x = 3$ b) $x^2 - 4 = 0$ c) $3 - x^2 = 2x$.

2 a) Decide together how the graph helps you to
      solve the equations:

    (i) $x^2 - x - 6 = {}^-4$
    (ii) $x^2 - x - 6 = 0$
    (iii) $x^2 - x = 6$.

  b) Roughly, what are the solutions of:

    (i) $x^2 - x - 6 = 4$
    (ii) $x^2 - x = 10$?

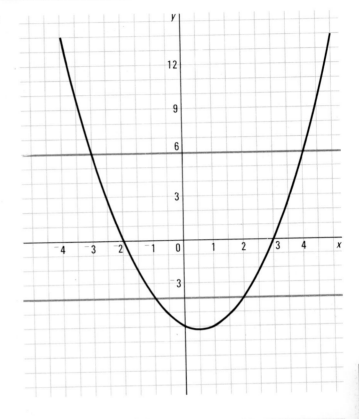

3 a) The equation $x^2 - 8x + 16 = 0$ has only one
      solution. What is it?

  b) Find another quadratic equation which
      has only one solution.

B13

Some quadratic equations have *two* (real number) solutions.

For example, the solutions of $2x^2 - 4x = 0$ are $x = 0$ and $x = 2$.

Some have only *one* (real number) solution.

For example, $x^2 - 6x + 9 = 0$ has only the one solution, $x = 3$.

And some have *no* (real number) solutions.

For example, $x^2 + 2x + 4 = 0$.

4 a) On separate axes, draw the graphs of the functions:

    (i) $y = 2x^2 - 4x$ (ii) $y = x^2 - 6x + 9$ (iii) $y = x^2 + 2x + 4$.

  b) On each of your graphs, draw in red (or another colour) the line $y = 0$. Explain the connection between
      what you have drawn and the information in the *Take note*.

5 a) Match each graph with one of these functions:

   (i) $y = x^2 - 4x + 4$
   (ii) $y = 6 + x - x^2$
   (iii) $y = x^2 - 3x - 4$
   (iv) $y = x^2 - 2x + 3$.

   b) For each graph, find the value(s) of x for which y is 0 (if they exist).

   c) Use your results in a) and b) to decide which of the equations

   $x^2 - 4x + 4 = 0$
   $6 + x - x^2 = 0$
   $x^2 - 3x - 4 = 0$
   $x^2 - 2x + 3 = 0$

   has   (i) two solutions   (ii) one solution   (iii) no solutions.

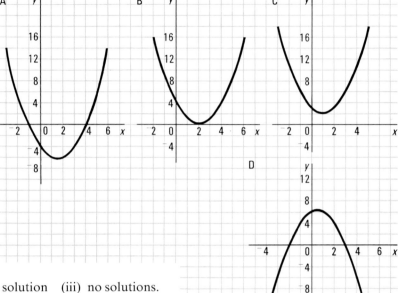

6 You need 1 mm graph paper.

   a) On separate axes draw the graph of each quadratic function:

   (i) $x \rightarrow x^2 - x - 2$ (ii) $x \rightarrow x^2 - x + 6$ (iii) $x \rightarrow x^2 - 6x + 9$.

   b) *From your graphs*:   (i) explain how you know that the solutions of $x^2 - x - 2 = 0$ are $x = 2$ and $x = {}^-1$
                            (ii) explain how you know that $x^2 - x + 6 = 0$ does not have a solution
                            (iii) explain how you know that $x^2 - 6x + 9 = 0$ has only one solution.

B13

▓▓▓▓▓▓ TAKE NOTE ▓▓▓▓▓▓

Quadratic equations, $ax^2 + bx + c = 0$, have either 2, 1 or 0 solutions.

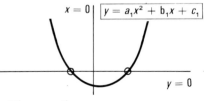

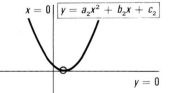

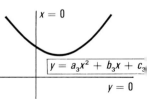

- The equation

  $a_1x^2 + b_1x + c_1 = 0$

  has *two solutions*. These are the two values of x for which y is zero (that is, for which $y = a_1x^2 + b_1x + c_1 = 0$). The values of x are those ringed – where the graph cuts the $y = 0$ line.

- The equation

  $a_2x^2 + b_2x + c_2 = 0$

  has only *one solution*. (Or, we might say that its two solutions are equal.) The solution is ringed. The curve touches the line $y = 0$ at one point, so there is only one value for which
  $y = a_2x^2 + b_2x + c_2 = 0$.

- The equation

  $a_3x^2 + b_3x + c_3 = 0$

  has *no solutions*. the curve does not cut the $y = 0$ line, and there are therefore no values of x for which $y = a_3x^2 + b_3x + c_3 = 0$.

THINK IT THROUGH

7   a) Write down your own examples of equations (different to those in question 1) which have
       (i) 2 solutions   (ii) 1 solution   (iii) no solutions.

    b) Find the number of solutions of each of these equations:
       (i) $2x^2 + 3x + 4 = 0$ (ii) $6 - x^2 - 3x = 0$ (iii) $x^2 - 2x + 1 = 0$.

Quadratic equations: factorizing and solving

1   a) Explain why one solution of the equation

       $(x+2)(x-1) = 0$

       is $x = {}^-2$.

    b) What is the other solution?

    c) Write the equation in a) in the form $ax^2 + bx + c = 0$.

    d) What are the solutions to the equation $x^2 + x - 2 = 0$?

2   a) Solve the equation $(x+3)(x-5) = 0$.

    b) Write the equation $(x+2)(x-7) = 0$ in the form $ax^2 + bx + c = 0$.

    c) Solve the equation $(x+2)(x-7) = 0$.

    d) Solve the equation $x^2 - 5x - 14 = 0$.

3   a) Write down an equation of the form $(x\ .....)(x\ .....) = 0$
       whose solutions are $x = 4$ and $x = {}^-1$.

    b) Write your equation in the form $ax^2 + bx + c = 0$.

    c) Solve the equation $x^2 - 3x - 4 = 0$.

THINK IT THROUGH

4   Write down an equation in the form: (i) $(x......)(x......) = 0$ ii) $ax^2 + bx + c = 0$

    a) whose solutions are $x = 5$, $x = 1$

    b) whose only solution is $x = 2$

    c) whose solutions are $x = \frac{1}{2}$, $x = 1$.

B13

TAKE NOTE

$x^2 + x - 12 = 0$ can be written as $(x - 3)(x + 4) = 0$.

$(x - 3)(x + 4)$ is zero when   (i) x is 3   (because then we get $0 \times 7 = 0$)
                                 (ii) x is $^-4$ (because then we get $^-7 \times 0 = 0$)

So the solutions of $x^2 + x - 12 = 0$ are $x = 3$ and $x = {}^-4$.

$x^2 - 6x + 9 = 0$ can be written as $(x - 3)(x - 3) = 0$ or $(x - 3)^2 = 0$.

The only solution is $x = 3$ because then we get $0 \times 0 = 0$.
To solve quadratic equations we can first factorize, and then find the value(s) of the variable which make each bracket zero.

---

5   By first factorizing the quadratic expression, find the solutions to each equation. Check each time that your results fit the original equation.

a) $x^2 - 3x + 2 = 0$ b) $x^2 + x - 2 = 0$ c) $x^2 - x - 2 = 0$
d) $x^2 - 5x + 6 = 0$ e) $x^2 + x - 6 = 0$ f) $x^2 - x - 6 = 0$
g) $x^2 - 8x + 15 = 0$ h) $x^2 - 2x - 15 = 0$ i) $x^2 + 2x - 15 = 0$
j) $2x^2 - 2x - 4 = 0$ k) $2x^2 + 6x + 4 = 0$ l) $2x^2 - 6x + 4 = 0$
m) $2x^2 + x - 1 = 0$ n) $2x^2 + 3x + 1 = 0$ o) $x^2 - 9 = 0$
p) $x^2 - x = 0$ q) $x^2 + 2x + 1 = 0$ r) $x^2 + 8x + 16 = 0$
s) $2x^2 - 3x = 0$ t) $21 - x^2 - 4x = 0$ u) $3 - 2x^2 - 5x = 0$

EXPLORATION

6   All quadratic equations are of the form $ax^2 + bx + c = 0$ (sometimes b is 0, or c is 0).
For example, in $5x^2 + 4x - 7 = 0$, a is 5, b is 4 and c is $^-7$.
Some quadratic equations have only one solution, for example

$x^2 - 4x + 4 = 0$ has $x = 2$ as its only solution.
$[x^2 - 4x + 4 \equiv (x - 2)(x - 2)]$

In this case, a is 1, b is $^-4$ and c is 4.
Investigate quadratic equations which have only one solution.
(First investigate equations for which a is 1, for example, $x^2 + 2x + 1 = 0$, and then equations for which a is some other number.)
What can you say about a, b and c for equations which have only one solution?
Write a short report to explain what you discover.

---

7   $f(x) = x^2 - 5x + 6$
Find the values of x for which   (i) $f(x) = 0$ (ii) $f(x) = 6$.
(There are two values in each case.)

CHALLENGE

8   For a quadratic function $f(x) = x^2 + bx + c$,

$f(^-1) = 0$ and $f(2) = 0$.

Find b and c.

Finding solutions by calculator methods

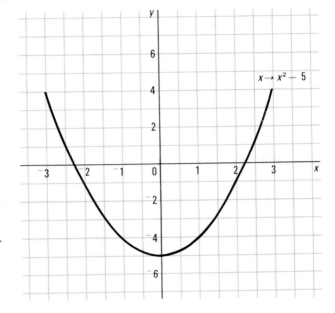

1   This is the graph of the function

$x \rightarrow x^2 - 5$

(or, $y = x^2 - 5$)

a) Explain how we know from the graph that a solution of the equation $x^2 - 5 = 0$ lies between $x = 2$ and $x = 3$.

b) Roughly, what are the two solutions of the equation?

c) Since $x^2 - 5 = 0$
   then $x^2 = 5$.

   Use your calculator to find the two values of x which satisfy this equation correct to 2 DP.

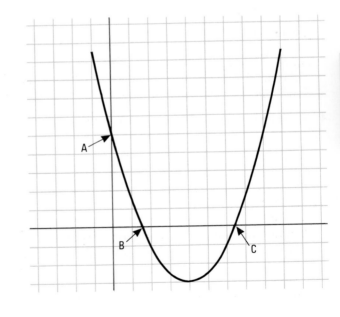

2   This is a sketch graph of $x \rightarrow x^2 - 8x + 10$ (that is, $y = x^2 - 8x + 10$).

a) What is the value of y at the point A?

b) The point B represents one solution of

$x^2 - 8x + 10 = 0$.

If we put $x = 2$ in $x^2 - 8x + 10 = 0$, we get

$2^2 - (8 \times 2) + 10 = {}^-2$

so $x = 2$ is too large for the solution at B.
Try $x = 1$.
Is $x = 1$ too large or too small for the solution at B?

c) You should have found in b) that the solution at B lies between 1 and 2. Use your calculator to try $x = 1.5$ as a solution of

$x^2 - 8x + 10 = 0$.

Is this too large or too small?
Test and check again until you find the solution at B correct to 1 DP.

d) Find the solution at C correct to 1 DP.

3   Each of the following equations has two solutions. Use your calculator to find each one correct to 1 DP.

a) $x \rightarrow x^2 - 11 = 0$ b) $x \rightarrow x^2 - 3x - 6 = 0$.

ENRICHMENT

CHALLENGE

1 $f(x) = ax^2 + bx + c$, is a quadratic function.

a) For all values of p, $f(p) = f(^-p)$.
What can you say about the graph of the function?

b) $f(0) = 32$. What can you say about c?

c) One solution of the equation $ax^2 + bx + c = 0$ is $x = {}^-4$. Write down the other solution.

d) Make a rough sketch of the graph of $f(x)$.

e) Find the values of a and b.

2 For a quadratic function $f(x) = ax^2 + bx + c$, $f(^-1) = 0$, $f(2) = 0$ and $f(0) = {}^-8$. Find a, b and c.

WITH A FRIEND: THE QUADRATIC EQUATION GAME

3 Each of you choose a quadratic function of the form $f(x) = x^2 + bx + c$ (for example $f(x) = x^2 - 4x + 3$; $f(x) = x^2 + 2x - 1$). Restrict the values of b and c to whole numbers between 4 and $^-4$.
By asking questions, in turn, of the form

'What is $f(a)$', for example, 'What is $f(0)$', 'What is $f(2)$'

try to discover the function which your partner has chosen.
The first to find the function wins the game.

4 a) Spend not more than 5 minutes trying to solve the equation:

$x^2 - 6x - 2 = 0.$

Try any method you wish: trial and improvement, factorizing, ...

b) Check that the equation in a) can be written as:

$(x-3)^2 = 11$

c) Copy and complete this solution to find x:

$$(x-3)^2 = 11$$

$\sqrt{\ }$: $\quad x - 3 = \pm\sqrt{\square}$

$+3$: $\quad x = \square \pm \sqrt{\square}$

$x = 6.3$ (to 1 DP) or $\square$ (to 1 DP).

CHALLENGE

5 Rearrange the equation $x^2 - 8x + 4 = 0$ into the form $(x \ldots)^2 = \ldots$
Hence find the two solutions for x correct to 1 DP.

6   a) Copy and complete this solution of the equation $2x^2 + 8x - 1 = 0$:

$$2x^2 + 8x - 1 = 0$$

$\div 2$: $x^2 + \Box x - \tfrac{1}{2} = 0$

insert brackets:

$$x^2 + 4x - \tfrac{1}{2} = 0$$
$$(x + 2)^2 - 4\tfrac{1}{2} = 0$$

$+4\tfrac{1}{2}$: $(x + 2)^2 = 4\tfrac{1}{2}$

$\sqrt{\ }$: $x + 2 = \pm\sqrt{4\tfrac{1}{2}} = \pm 2.1 \ (1 \ DP)$

-2: $x = -2 \pm 2.1 = -4.1 \ or \ 0.1 \ (1 \ DP)$

   b) Use the method in part a) to solve:

   (i) $2x^2 + 6x - 3 = 0$ (ii) $4x^2 - 12x - 3 = 0$.

━━━━━━━━━━━━ TAKE NOTE ━━━━━━━━━━━━

We can solve quadratic equations by first expressing them in the form: $(x \dots \Box)^2 = \Box$
This method is called 'completing the square'.

━━━━━━━━━━━━━━━━━━━━━━━━━━━━━━━

7   When we 'complete the square' for $x^2 + bx + c = 0$, the number we choose to go with x inside the
    bracket is $\dfrac{b}{2}$: $\left(x + \dfrac{b}{2}\right)^2 + \dots = 0$. Why?

8   $ax^2 + bx + c = 0$, $a \neq 0$, is any quadratic equation. (We can choose a, b and c to be any number we wish.)

   a) We can solve the equation by completing the square.
      Copy and complete each step:

   Divide by a: $x^2 + \Box x + \dfrac{c}{a} = 0$

   Insert a bracket:

   $$\left(x + \dfrac{b}{2a}\right)^2 + \dfrac{c}{a} - \Box = 0$$

   So $\left(x + \dfrac{b}{2a}\right)^2 \qquad = \dfrac{b^2}{4a^2} - \Box$

   $$\qquad\qquad = \dfrac{b^2 - \Box}{4a^2}$$

   Take the square root of both sides:

   $$\Box = \pm\sqrt{\dfrac{b^2 - 4ac}{4a^2}}$$

   Subtract $\dfrac{b}{2a}$ from both sides:

   $$x = \dfrac{-b}{2a} \pm \sqrt{\dfrac{b^2 - 4ac}{\Box}}$$

   $$= \dfrac{-b \pm \sqrt{b^2 - 4ac}}{2a}$$

B13

b) Given any quadratic equation, we can now find x using the result $x = \dfrac{-b \pm \sqrt{b^2 - 4ac}}{2a}$.

For example, the solution to the equation $3x^2 + 2x - 6 = 0$

$$\begin{array}{ccc} b & b^2 & \\ \downarrow & \downarrow & \end{array} \quad +72 \text{ is } -4ac \text{ which is } -4 \times 3 \times {}^-6$$

is $x = \dfrac{-2 \pm \sqrt{4 + 72}}{6}$ ← $2a$

$$x = \dfrac{-2 \pm \sqrt{76}}{6}$$

So x is $\dfrac{-2 + \sqrt{76}}{6}$ or $\dfrac{-2 - \sqrt{76}}{6}$

   (i) Find the two values of x correct to 1 DP.
   (ii) Check that your results approximately fit the original equation.

c) Use the formula in a) to solve the quadratic equations:

   (i) $x^2 - 3x + 1 = 0$ (ii) $2x^2 + 3x - 4 = 0$

TAKE NOTE

The solutions (roots) of the quadratic equation $ax^2 + bx + c = 0$ are given by the formula

$$x = \dfrac{-b \pm \sqrt{b^2 - 4ac}}{2a}$$

B13

EXPLORATION

9   Invent some equations of your own. Try to solve them using the formula in a). Which ones have real number solutions and which ones do not?

REVIEW

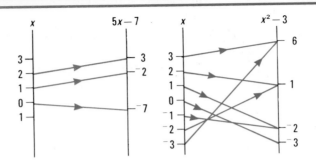

- Rules such as $x \rightarrow 5x - 7$
  $$x \rightarrow x^2 - 3$$

  are called *functions*.

  When we draw an arrow diagram,
  only one arrow leaves each value of x.

- The rule $x \rightarrow \pm\sqrt{x}$

  is *not* a function because more than one arrow leaves some values of x.

- $x \rightarrow 5x - 7$ is the function 'multiply by 5 then subtract 7'.

  $x \rightarrow x^2 - 3$ is the function 'square then subtract 3'.

■ Write the function $x \rightarrow \frac{1}{2}x + 4$ in words.

- The function which returns us to the number we began with, for each value of x, is called the *inverse* function.

  For example, the inverse of

  $$x \rightarrow 5x - 7 \qquad \text{is} \qquad x \rightarrow \tfrac{1}{5}(x + 7)$$
  Multiply by 5 then subtract 7   Add 7 then multiply by $\frac{1}{5}$

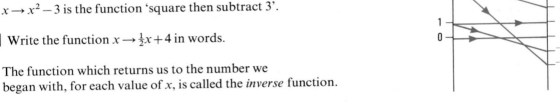

Original function $x \xrightarrow{\text{Multiply by 5}} 5x \xrightarrow{\text{Subtract 7}} 5x - 7$

$\xleftarrow[\text{(or divide by 5)}]{\text{Multiply by } \frac{1}{5}} 5x \xleftarrow{\text{Add 7}}$

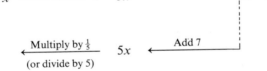

$\tfrac{1}{5}(x + 7) \longleftarrow x + 7 \longleftarrow x$ **Inverse function**

For example:

Original function $7 \xrightarrow{\text{Multiply by 5}} 35 \xrightarrow{\text{Subtract 7}} 28$

Inverse function $28 \xrightarrow{\text{Add 7}} 35 \xrightarrow[\text{(or multiply by } \frac{1}{5})]{\text{Divide by 5}} 7$

■ Write in words, the function $x \rightarrow 2x + 3$.
  Write the inverse function   a) in words   b) in the form $x \rightarrow \ldots$

CONSOLIDATION

1   For the function $n \rightarrow 2n^2 + 4$:

   a) find the image (that is, the number which n maps onto) of   (i) 5   (ii) $^-5$.

   b) The image of p is 22. What is p?

2 a) For each function in list A,
find the image of
(i) 7 (ii) $^-1$
(iii) 4.

List A	*List B*
$x \longrightarrow 4x - 2$	$x \longrightarrow \frac{1}{2}x$
$x \longrightarrow 2x$	$x \longrightarrow \frac{1}{4}(2-x)$
$x \longrightarrow 2 - 4x$	$x \longrightarrow \frac{1}{4}(x-2)$
$x \longrightarrow \frac{1}{2}x$	$x \longrightarrow 2x$
$x \longrightarrow 4x + 2$	$x \longrightarrow \frac{1}{4}(x+2)$
$x \longrightarrow 2x + 4$	$x \longrightarrow \frac{1}{2}(x-4)$

b) Match each function in List A with its inverse in List B.

CORE

Self-inverse functions

1 a) Find the image of (i) 2 (ii) 12 (iii) $^-4$ (iv) 5,   for the function $x \rightarrow 12 - x$.

b) Find the image of (i) 10 (ii) 0 (iii) 16 (iv) 7,   for the function $x \rightarrow 12 - x$.

c) Compare your results in a) and b).
What do they suggest about the inverse of the function $x \rightarrow 12 - x$ (that is, the *subtract from* 12 functio

2 a) Copy and complete:

Function A		*Function B*	
x	$\longrightarrow \dfrac{40}{x}$	x	$\longrightarrow \dfrac{40}{x}$
1	$\longrightarrow 40$	$40 \longrightarrow$	?
2	$\longrightarrow$?	? $\longrightarrow$	2
5	$\longrightarrow$?	? $\longrightarrow$	5
10	$\longrightarrow$?	? $\longrightarrow$	10
?	$\longrightarrow 1$	$1 \longrightarrow$	?

b) What do your results suggest about the inverse of the function $x \rightarrow \dfrac{40}{x}$?

▓▓▓▓▓▓▓▓▓▓ TAKE NOTE ▓▓▓▓▓▓▓▓▓▓

Some functions are their own inverses ('self inverse'), for example:

$x \rightarrow 20 - x$ (the 'subtract from 20' function)

$x \rightarrow \dfrac{20}{x}$ (the 'divide into 20' function).

You can check that they are self inverse by putting values of x into the function, and the results into the function again, for example:

$x \rightarrow 20 - x$: $14 \xrightarrow{\ x \rightarrow 20 - x\ } 6 \xrightarrow[\ x \rightarrow 20 - x\ ]{\qquad\qquad} 14$

For each replacement, we 'get back to the number we began with'.

EXPLORATION

3   a) Investigate which functions are their own inverses (that is, self inverse).

Begin with $x \rightarrow 12 - x$

and $x \rightarrow \dfrac{20}{x}$

and find others.

Write a report to explain what you find.

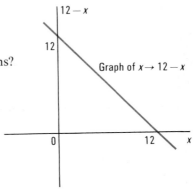

b) Draw a graph of some of the self-inverse functions you find.
Is there anything special about the graphs of self-inverse functions?

Using the notation $f(x) = ...,$ $f: x \longrightarrow$ and f^{-1}

TAKE NOTE

$x \rightarrow 2x + 1$ can also be written as
$$f(x) = 2x + 1$$
$$y = 2x + 1$$
and $f: x \rightarrow 2x + 1.$

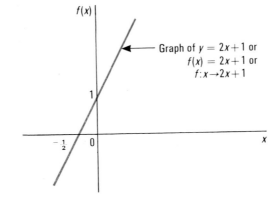

- We read $f(x)$ as 'f of x' or 'the function f of x'.

- '$y = ...$' is simply an alternative (and simpler) way of writing '$f(x) = ...$'.

- The third alternative, $f: x \rightarrow 2x + 1$, names the function $x \rightarrow 2x + 1$ as 'f'.

We say 'f takes x onto $2x + 1$'.

All three expressions mean exactly the same thing.
We can also write $g(x)$, the function g of x, etc.

1   Write each of these functions in two more ways, using either $f: x \rightarrow ...$, $y = ...$, or $f(x) = ...$

   a) $x \rightarrow 3x - 1$ b) $y - x^2 + 2 = 0$ c) $\dfrac{y}{x} = 4$ d) $f(x) = x$.

2   If $f(x) = x^2 + 2x - 4$

   then $f(7)$ is $7^2 + (2 \times 7) - 4 = 59$.

   What is   (i) $f(2)$ (ii) $f(^-2)$?

3   a) The function $x \rightarrow 2x - 1$ is the 'multiply by 2 and subtract 1' function.
       Check that its inverse is $x \rightarrow \frac{1}{2}(x + 1)$.

━━━━━━━━━━━━━━━━ TAKE NOTE ━━━━━━━━━━━━━━━━

To write the inverse function we use '$f^{-1}(x)$' like this:

   $f(x) = 2x - 1$ [Multiply by 2 then subtract 1]
So $f^{-1}(x) = \frac{1}{2}(x + 1)$ [Add 1 then divide by 2 (or, multiply by $\frac{1}{2}$)]

Notice that $f^{-1}(x)$ does *not* mean $1/f(x)$, but 'the inverse of the function $f(x)$'.

We can also write: $f^{-1}: x \rightarrow \frac{1}{2}(x + 1)$.

━━━

   b) $g(x) = \dfrac{x}{4} - 1$

      Which of these is correct?

      A $g^{-1}(x) = 4x + 4$ B $g^{-1}(x) = 4x + 1$ C $g^{-1}(x) = x + 4$.

   c) $f(x) = 3x + 4$

      Which of these is correct?

      A $f^{-1}: x \rightarrow 4x + 3$ B $f^{-1}: x \rightarrow \dfrac{1}{3x + 4}$ C $f^{-1}: x \rightarrow \frac{1}{3}(x - 4)$.

   d) $h^{-1}(x) = \dfrac{x}{2} - 1$

      Find   (i) $h^{-1}(2)$ (ii) $h(2)$.

   e) $k(x) = 4 - x$ and $h(x) = \dfrac{3}{x}$.

      Find   (i) $k^{-1}(x)$ (ii) $h^{-1}(x)$.

4   a) $f(x) = 2(x - 4)$

      On the same axes, sketch the graph of $f(x)$ and of $f^{-1}(x)$.

   b) $f(x) = \dfrac{24}{x + 10}$

      On the same axes, sketch the graph of $f(x)$ and of $f^{-1}(x)$.

   c) Explain how the graph of a function and its inverse are related (look for symmetry).

B14

5   Here are graphs of eight functions:

A

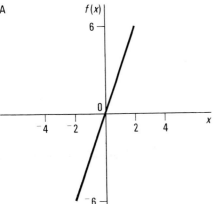

B

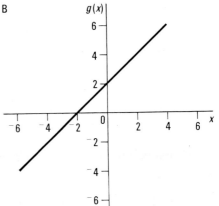

C

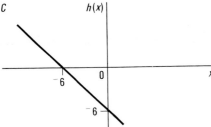

D

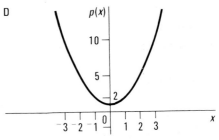

E

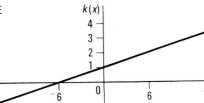

F

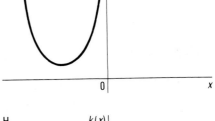

G

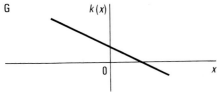

H

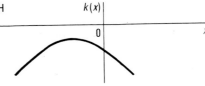

a) *Sketch* the graph of the inverse of each function.

b) For graphs A to E write each function and its inverse in the form:

$$g : x \rightarrow \dots \qquad g^{-1} : x \rightarrow \dots$$

B14

The general equation $y = mx + c$

1 a) On the same axes draw the graphs of:

$y = 2x + 1$
$y = 2x - 4$
$y = 2x$ Write down what you notice about the collection of graphs.
$y = 2x + 5.$ Write down the equations of three more lines which belong to the same collection.

b) Now draw the graphs of:

$y = 2 - 3x$
$y = 4 - 3x$
$y = -6 - 3x$ Write down what you notice about this collection of graphs.
$y + 3x = 0.$ Write down the equations of three more lines which belong to the same collection.

━━━━━━━━━━ TAKE NOTE ━━━━━━━━━━

The graphs you drew in question 1 a) and b) are all straight-line graphs. They have equations of the form

$y = mx + c$

(For example, in $y = 2x + 1$, m is 2 and c is 1.)
Functions of the form $f : x \rightarrow mx + c$ (that is, $y = mx + c$) are called *linear functions*.

━━━━━━━━━━ EXPLORATION ━━━━━━━━━━

2 Investigate the graphs of linear functions. Choose different values for m and c.

From your investigation decide what information:

(i) the value of m tells us about the graph of a function
(ii) the value of c tells us about the graph of a function.

━━━━━━━━━━ THINK IT THROUGH ━━━━━━━━━━

3 Write down the function whose graph:

a) meets the y axis at $(0, 4)$ and has a gradient of 3

b) meets the y axis at $(0, {}^-2)$ and has a gradient of $-\frac{1}{4}$

c) meets the y axis at $(0, 0)$ and has a gradient of 7

d) meets the x axis at 7 and has a gradient of $^-1$.

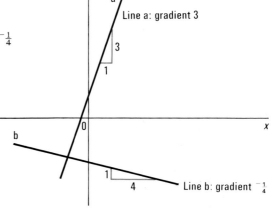

B14

In the equation $y = mx + c$, the value of m gives us the gradient of the line.

The value of c tells us the point at which the line meets the y axis. The gradient of each line is $\frac{1}{2}$.

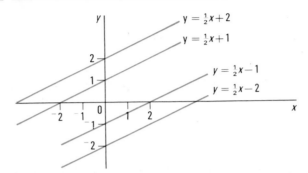

4   a) Write down the equation of the straight line which passes through $(0, \, ^-7)$ and $(7, 0)$.

   b) What is the equation of the straight line which passes through $(^-2, 3)$ and $(0, \, ^-1)$?

5   a) What is the gradient of the line $2y = 4x - 1$? (It is *not* 4.)

   b) Where does the line cut the y axis? (*Not* at $(0, \, ^-1)$.)

   c) Sketch the line.

6   Explain how you know, without drawing the graphs, that the graphs of:

   $y = 2x - 1$
   and $5y = 10x$ never meet.

7   What is the gradient of the graph of   a) $f : x \rightarrow 3x - 7$?   b) f^{-1}?

   c) The gradient of the graph of the function $g(x)$ is a.
      What is the gradient of the graph of $g^{-1}(x)$?

8   Find the equation of the line which is perpendicular to the line

   $y = 2x - 1$ and which passes through the point $(4, 0)$.

B14

ENRICHMENT

1   $f(x) = 2x - 3$.

   f is the 'multiply by 2 then subtract 3' function.

   a) Check that   (i) $f(2) = 1$ (ii) $f(^-1) = \, ^-5$ (iii) $f(a) = 2a - 3$ (iv) $f(2a) = 4a - 3$

   (multiply $2a$ by 2, then subtract 3)

   (v) $f(2x) = 4x - 3$ (vi) $f(x^2) = 2x^2 - 3$

   (multiply x^2 by 2, then subtract 3)

   (vii) $f(x - 1) = 2x - 5$.

   b) On the same axes, sketch the graphs of   (i) $f(x)$ (ii) $f(x - 1)$ (iii) $f(2x)$.

2    $f(x) = x^2 + 4$.

   f is the 'square then add 4' function.

   a) Check that   (i) $f(^-1) = 5$ (ii) $f(a) = a^2 + 4$ (iii) $f(2x) = 4x^2 + 4$ (iv) $f(^-x) = x^2 + 4$
       (v) $f(x+1) = x^2 + 2x + 5$.

   b) On the same axes, sketch the graphs of   (i) $f(x)$ (ii) $f(2x)$ (iii) $f(x+1)$.

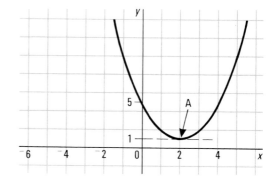
square 2x, then add 4

3    $y = f(x) = 3 - x^2$.

   a) Copy and complete:

       (i) $y_1 = f(x+1) =$ ...   (ii) $y_2 = f(3x) =$ ...
       (iii) $y_3 = f(x) + 4 =$ ...

   b) Sketch the graphs of y, y_1, y_2 and y_3.

4   a) Check that this is the graph of the function:

       $y = (x-2)^2 + 1$

       that is, $y = x^2 - 4x + 5$.

   b) Copy the graph. On the same axes, sketch the graphs of:

       (i) $y = x^2$ (ii) $y = (x-1)^2 + 2$ (iii) $y = (x+4)^2 - 3$ (iv) $y = (x-3)^2 - 2$.

   c) Can you see a connection between the forms in which the equations in part b) are written, and the
       position of the point A on each graph? (Point A is the 'bottom of the curve'.) If so, explain what the
       connection is.

EXPLORATION

5   Choose each of the functions in turn: $y = f(x) = 2x$ $y = g(x) = 3x^2$ $y = h(x) = \dfrac{36}{x}$.

   Sketch its graph.
   Investigate how the graph is related to the graphs of functions obtained from the original function by:

   A   Replacing x by ax, where a is any number. For example:

       $f(2x)$, $g(4x)$, $h(^-x)$.

       ↑   ↑   ↑
       a is 2 a is 4 a is $^-1$

   B   Replacing x by $x+a$, where a is any number. For example:

       $f(x-2)$, $g(x+2)$, $h(x-1)$.

   C   Replacing $f(x)$, $g(x)$ and $h(x)$ by $f(x) + a$, $g(x) + a$, $h(x) + a$, where a is any number. For example:

       $f(x) + 2$, $g(x) - 4$, $h(x) + 10$.

   D   Replacing x by $ax + b$, where a and b are any numbers. For example:

       $f(3x - 4)$, $g(2x + 1)$, $h(^-x - 1)$.

   Write a report to explain what you discover.

B14

6   This is the graph of the function:

$y = f(x) = x^3$.

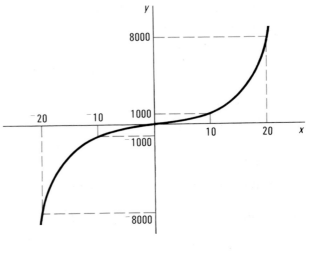

a) Copy the graph (a sketch will do).

b) Sketch these curves on the same axes. (You should be able to do this without doing any calculations.)

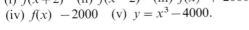

(i) $f(x+2)$ (ii) $f(x-2)$ (iii) $f(x) + 2000$
(iv) $f(x) - 2000$ (v) $y = x^3 - 4000$.

c) Make another copy of the original graph.

On the same axes, *sketch* the graphs of:

(i) $f(2x^3)$ (ii) $f(^-x^3)$ (iii) $f(^-x^3+2)$ (iv) $f(^-x^3)+2000$
(v) $f(2x^3)-1000$

B14

B15 ALGEBRAIC FRACTIONS

REVIEW

- To add or subtract fractions we first express each fraction with the same denominator.

$\frac{2}{5}+\frac{1}{8}=\frac{16}{40}+\frac{5}{40}=\frac{21}{40}$

$3\frac{3}{4}-1\frac{1}{6}=3\frac{9}{12}-1\frac{2}{12}=2\frac{7}{12}$

■ Calculate   (i) $2\frac{1}{3}-1\frac{7}{8}$ (ii) $\frac{3}{4}+4\frac{1}{5}+7\frac{5}{9}$.

- To multiply fractions we multiply the numerators and the denominators:

$\frac{2}{3}\times\frac{5}{8}=\frac{10^5}{24_{12}}=\frac{5}{12}$ $1\frac{1}{3}\times1\frac{1}{2}=\frac{4}{3}\times\frac{3}{2}=\frac{12}{6}=2$

- To divide fractions we find the reciprocal of the divisor, then multiply:

reciprocal of the divisor

$\frac{2}{3}\div\frac{5}{8}=\frac{2}{3}\times\frac{8}{5}=\frac{16}{15}=1\frac{1}{15}$ ○ ○ ○

$4\frac{1}{2}\div1\frac{1}{3}=\frac{9}{2}\div\frac{4}{3}=\frac{9}{2}\times\frac{3}{4}=\frac{27}{8}=3\frac{3}{8}$

because $\frac{2}{3}\div\frac{8}{5}=\left(\frac{2}{3}\times\frac{8}{5}\right)\div\left(\frac{5}{8}\times\frac{8}{5}\right)=\frac{2}{3}\times\frac{8}{5}$

■ Calculate   (i) $3\frac{1}{2}\times\frac{5}{7}$ (ii) $2\frac{1}{2}\div1\frac{5}{8}$.

- The common factors of 24 and 16 are 1, 2, 3, 4, 6, 8.
  The HCF (Highest Common Factor) of 24 and 16 is 8.

- The common multiples of 4 and 6 are 12, 24, 36, 48, ...
  The LCM (Lowest Common Multiple) of 4 and 6 is 12.

■ Find the HCF and LCM of:

a) 8 and 10   b) 4, 6 and 8.

CONSOLIDATION

1 You want to add $\frac{3}{8}$ and $\frac{1}{6}$: that is, $\frac{3}{8}+\frac{1}{6}=?$

First, you need to write each fraction with the same denominator $\frac{\square}{a}+\frac{\square}{a}=?$
where a is a whole number.

a) What is the smallest possible value of a that you can use?

b) Use this value of a to write $\frac{3}{8}+\frac{1}{6}$ as a single fraction.

c) What other values of a could you use to complete the same calculation?

d) (i) What is the smallest value of a you could use to complete this subtraction: $\frac{4}{16}-\frac{3}{48}=\frac{\square}{a}-\frac{\square}{a}$?

   (ii) Complete the subtraction in (i).

2 a) Find the LCM of 8, 12 and 16.

   Use your result to complete this calculation:

   $\frac{5}{8}+\frac{7}{12}-\frac{3}{16}=?$

   b) Find the LCM of 13 and 7.

   Use your result to complete each calculation:

   (i) $1\frac{1}{7}-\frac{12}{13}$ (ii) $2\frac{7}{13}+4\frac{6}{7}$

3   Calculate and write each result as a fraction in its simplest form:

a) $1\frac{3}{4} \times 1\frac{3}{4}$ b) $3\frac{1}{3} \div 4\frac{1}{4}$ c) $(\frac{2}{3} \div \frac{3}{4}) \times 1\frac{1}{2}$ d) $(\frac{1}{2} + 1\frac{1}{3}) \times \frac{3}{4}$ e) $(1\frac{5}{8} - \frac{2}{5}) \div \frac{1}{3}$

f) $\dfrac{\frac{1}{2}+\frac{1}{3}}{1-\frac{3}{7}}$ g) $\dfrac{3\frac{1}{4}-1\frac{9}{10}}{4-1\frac{1}{5}}$ h) $(1\frac{1}{2})^3$ i) $(1\frac{1}{3} - \frac{3}{5})^2$

4   The following argument explains why $\frac{a}{b} \div \frac{c}{d} \equiv \frac{a}{b} \times \frac{d}{c}$.

Copy and complete it:

$$\frac{a}{b} \div \frac{c}{d} \equiv \frac{a \times \square}{b} \div \frac{c \times d}{d}$$

$$\equiv \frac{a \times \square}{b} \div \square$$

$$\equiv \frac{a \times d}{b \times \square} \div \frac{c}{c} \equiv \frac{a \times d}{b \times \square} \div 1 \equiv \frac{a}{b} \times \frac{\square}{\square}.$$

CORE

Algebraic LCMs

1   a) Check that $\frac{3+4}{10} = \frac{3}{10} + \frac{4}{10} = \frac{3}{10} + \frac{2}{5}$.

b) Write each of these as a sum or difference of two fractions as in a).
   Simplify each fraction as much as possible:

(i) $\dfrac{8+4}{14}$ (ii) $\dfrac{3-2}{18}$ (iii) $\dfrac{a+b}{c}$ (iv) $\dfrac{p-q}{r}$ (v) $\dfrac{c+b}{cb}$

(vi) $\dfrac{a+2b}{4r}$ (vii) $\dfrac{ac+bd}{cd}$ (viii) $\dfrac{s-q}{rs}$ (ix) $\dfrac{ps-qr}{rs}$.

c) Use your result in b) (vii) to write as single fractions: (i) $\frac{a}{d} + \frac{b}{c}$ (ii) $\frac{3}{7} + \frac{4}{9}$.

d) Use your result in b) (ix) to write as single fractions: (i) $\frac{p}{r} - \frac{q}{s}$ (ii) $\frac{3}{7} - \frac{2}{9}$.

═════════ WITH A FRIEND ═════════

B15

2   a and b are any two whole numbers.

a) Decide between you which of these are common multiples of a and b.

(i) a (ii) ab (iii) $2ab$ (iv) $a+b$ (v) a^2 (vi) a^2b (vii) $\frac{1}{2}ab$.

b) Discuss together what we can say about the LCM of a and b. Each of you write down what you decide.

3    $2b$ and k^2 are whole numbers.

   a) Which of these are certain to be common multiples of $2b$ and k^2?

      (i) k (ii) k^2 (iii) b^2 (iv) $2bk^2$ (v) b^2k^2 (vi) $4bk$ (vii) $8b^3k^4$ (viii) $(2b+k^2)$.

   b) What can you say about the LCM of $2b$ and k^2?

TAKE NOTE

If p and q are whole numbers, then each of these is divisible by p and q.

$pq, 2pq, p^2q, (1+p)pq, \ldots$

We say that pq is the 'algebraic LCM' of p and q. It is the common multiple which is a factor of all other common multiples.

4   a) p and q are whole numbers. Their 'algebraic LCM' is pq. However, pq might not be the LCM of p and q for specific values of p and q.
       Find values of p and q for which pq (i) is *not* the LCM of p and q (ii) *is* the LCM of p and q.

   b) Explain in your own words the difference between the LCM for two numbers and the LCM for two variables.

THINK IT THROUGH

5   Find the algebraic LCM of:

   (i) a and b (ii) a and a^2 (iii) ab and b
   (iv) $2a$ and b (v) a^2b and b^2 (vi) ab^2 and a^2b
   (vii) $(a+b)$ and b (viii) $(a+b)$ and $(a-b)$ (ix) $(1+a)$ and a
   (x) $(1+a)$ and $(1+a)^2$ (xi) $(1+a)$ and $(a-1)$ (xii) $a(a+b)$ and $(a+b)$
   (xiii) $b(a-b)$ and $a(a-b)$ (xiv) b^2a and $b(a+b)$ (xv) $(a+b)^2$ and $b(a+b)(a-b)$
   (xvi) a, 2 and ab (xvii) a^2, $(a+b)$, and 3   (xviii) a^2b, $2ab$, $(a+b)$ and $2(a+b)$.

Adding, subtracting, multiplying and dividing with algebraic fractions

1    $\frac{a}{b}$ represents any fraction. $\frac{c}{d}$ represents any other fraction (which might or might not be equal to $\frac{a}{b}$).

   a) What is the algebraic LCM of b and d?

   b) Write each fraction with a denominator whose LCM is that which you found in a).

   c) Copy and complete:

   (i) $\dfrac{a}{b}+\dfrac{c}{d}=\dfrac{\square}{\text{LCM of }b\text{ and }d}+\dfrac{\square}{\text{LCM of }b\text{ and }d}=\dfrac{\square+\square}{\square}$

   (ii) $\dfrac{9}{12}+\dfrac{3}{8}=\dfrac{\square}{\text{LCM of 12 and 8}}+\dfrac{\square}{\text{LCM of 12 and 8}}=\dfrac{\square}{\square}$.

2   Copy and complete:

(i) $\dfrac{p}{q}-\dfrac{r}{s}=\dfrac{\Box}{\text{LCM of }q\text{ and }s}-\dfrac{\Box}{\text{LCM of }q\text{ and }s}=\dfrac{\Box-\Box}{\Box}$

(ii) $\dfrac{13}{14}-\dfrac{7}{21}=\dfrac{\Box}{\text{LCM of 14 and 21}}-\dfrac{\Box}{\text{LCM of 14 and 21}}=\dfrac{\Box}{\Box}.$

━━━━━━━━━ TAKE NOTE ━━━━━━━━━

• $\dfrac{a}{b},\dfrac{c}{d},\dfrac{a\times b}{bc},\dfrac{ad+bc}{bd},\dfrac{p-2}{k}$, etc., are called *algebraic fractions.*

• To add or subtract algebraic fractions, we first write each fraction with the same denominator (normally the 'algebraic LCM'), for example,

$\dfrac{a}{b}+\dfrac{c}{d}=\dfrac{\Box}{\text{LCM of }b\text{ and }d}+\dfrac{\Box}{\text{LCM of }b\text{ and }d}=\dfrac{ad}{bd}+\dfrac{cb}{bd}=\dfrac{ad+cb}{bd}$

$\dfrac{1}{v}-\dfrac{p}{2q}=\dfrac{\Box}{\text{LCM of }v\text{ and }2q}-\dfrac{\Box}{\text{LCM of }v\text{ and }2q}=\dfrac{2q}{2vq}-\dfrac{pv}{2vq}=\dfrac{2q-pv}{2vq}$

• To multiply and divide algebraic fractions we proceed as with numerical fractions:

$\dfrac{a}{b}\times\dfrac{c}{d}=\dfrac{ac}{bd}\qquad \dfrac{a}{b}\div\dfrac{c}{d}=\dfrac{a}{b}\times\dfrac{d}{c}=\dfrac{ad}{bc}$

3   Copy and complete these additions and subtractions:

(i) $\dfrac{3}{n}+\dfrac{k}{n^2}\equiv\dfrac{\Box}{n^2}+\dfrac{k}{n^2}$

  $\equiv\dfrac{\Box+k}{n^2}$

(ii) $\dfrac{b}{4}-\dfrac{4}{b}\equiv\dfrac{\Box}{\text{LCM of 4 and }b}-\dfrac{\Box}{\text{LCM of 4 and }b}$

  $\equiv\dfrac{\Box}{\Box}-\dfrac{\Box}{\Box}=\dfrac{\Box}{\Box}$

(iii) $\dfrac{1}{a}+\dfrac{1}{b}+\dfrac{1}{c}\equiv\dfrac{\Box}{abc}+\dfrac{\Box}{abc}+\dfrac{\Box}{abc}$

  $\equiv\dfrac{\Box+\Box+\Box}{abc}$

(iv) $\dfrac{a}{1+a}-\dfrac{a}{2}\equiv\dfrac{2a}{\Box}-\dfrac{a(1+a)}{\Box}$

  $\equiv\dfrac{2a-\Box-\Box}{\Box}$

  $\equiv\dfrac{a(\Box-\Box)}{\Box}.$

4   Write each of these as a single fraction, as in question 3. Simplify each result as much as possible.

a) $\dfrac{2}{k}+\dfrac{1}{n}$ b) $\dfrac{2}{3}-\dfrac{4}{n}$ c) $\dfrac{a}{b}-\dfrac{1}{2}$ d) $\dfrac{k}{4}+\dfrac{4}{k}$

e) $e-\dfrac{1}{e}$ f) $\dfrac{1}{u}-\dfrac{1}{v}$ g) $\dfrac{1}{u}-\dfrac{2}{u^2}$ h) $2-\dfrac{1}{h}$

i) $\dfrac{1}{pq}+\dfrac{1}{q}$ j) $\dfrac{p}{rs}-\dfrac{1}{2s}$ k) $\dfrac{a}{1+a}+\dfrac{a}{1-a}$ l) $\dfrac{1+a}{a}+\dfrac{1-a}{2}$

B15

5   Copy and complete each addition and subtraction:

a) $\dfrac{2}{1-a}-\dfrac{a}{1+a}\equiv\dfrac{2(1+a)}{\square}-\dfrac{a(1-a)}{(1-a)(1+a)}$

$\equiv\dfrac{2(1+a)-a(1-a)}{\square}\equiv\dfrac{2+2a-a+\square}{\square}$

$\equiv\dfrac{2+a+a^2}{1-\square}$

b) $\dfrac{n}{n-3}-\dfrac{1+n}{1-n}\equiv\dfrac{n(\square-\square)}{(n-3)(1-n)}-\dfrac{(1+n)(\square-\square)}{\square}$

$\equiv\dfrac{n(\square-\square)-(1+n)(\square-\square)}{(n-3)(1-n)}$

$\equiv\dfrac{n-n^2-(1+n)(n-3)}{(n-3)(1-n)}$

$\equiv\dfrac{3+\square n-\square n^2}{(n-3)(1-n)}.$

6   Show that:

(i) $\dfrac{n}{1-n}-\dfrac{n}{1+n}\equiv\dfrac{2n^2}{1-n^2}$

(ii) $\dfrac{a-b}{a+b}-\dfrac{a+b}{a-b}\equiv\dfrac{4ab}{b^2-a^2}$

(iii) $\dfrac{p}{1+p}-\dfrac{3p}{p-2}\equiv\dfrac{p(2p+5)}{(2-p)(1+p)}$

(iv) $\dfrac{2}{a(a+1)}-\dfrac{1-a}{a}\equiv\dfrac{a^2+1}{a^2+a}.$

ENRICHMENT

1   $\dfrac{3x}{(x+1)(x+2)}$ can be written in the form $\dfrac{A}{x+1}+\dfrac{B}{x+2}$. By trial and improvement or otherwise, find A and B.

2   By trial and improvement, or otherwise, write $\dfrac{4}{(a-1)(a+1)}$ in the form $\dfrac{A}{a-1}+\dfrac{B}{a+1}$.

3   Write as a single fraction:

a) $\dfrac{1}{2a}+\dfrac{1}{2b}-\dfrac{1}{2c}$ b) $\dfrac{a}{b}+\dfrac{b}{c}+\dfrac{c}{a}$ c) $\dfrac{1}{v^2}-\left(\dfrac{3}{m}+\dfrac{4}{v}\right).$

4   a) Assuming that x is not 0 or 1, show that $\dfrac{x^2-\dfrac{1}{x}}{x-\dfrac{1}{x^2}}=x.$

   Why must we assume that x is not 0 or 1?

   b) Assuming that x is not 0 or $^-1$, show that

   $\dfrac{1}{x}-\dfrac{1}{x+1}-\dfrac{x}{x+1}=\dfrac{1-x}{x}.$

   Why must we assume that x is not 0 or $^-1$?

REVIEW

- We can represent sequences by writing an expression for their nth term.

  For example, the sequence with nth term $2n+1$ $(n = 1, 2, 3, 4, 5, \ldots)$ is

  $3, 5, 7, 9, 11, 13, 15, \ldots$

- The formula $N = 3n+4$ $(n = 1, 2, 3, 4, 5, \ldots)$ gives the sequence

  $7, 10, 13, 16, 19, \ldots$

■ Find the first five members $(n = 1, 2, 3, \ldots)$ of the sequence with nth term   (i) $n^2 - 1$ (ii) $n(n+1)$.

We can often find an expression for the nth term of a sequence by studying the terms of the sequence and their position:

5,	6,	7,	8,	9, ...,	$n+4$
↑	↑	↑	↑	↑	↑
1st	2nd	3rd	4th	5th	nth
$(1+4)$	$(2+4)$	$(3+4)$	$(4+4)$	$(5+4)$	$(n+4)$

■ Find the nth term $(n = 1, 2, 3, 4, \ldots)$ of the sequences: (i) $2, 4, 6, 8, 10, \ldots$ (ii) $0, 1, 2, 3, 4, \ldots$

CONSOLIDATION

1   a) How many dots and how many crosses are there in the next pattern in the sequence?

b) How many dots are there in the nth pattern?

c) How many crosses are there in the nth pattern?

d) How many symbols (that is, dots and crosses together) are there in the nth pattern?

e) Suppose you know the number of dots in a particular pattern. Explain how you can find:

   (i) the number of dots in the next pattern
   (ii) the number of crosses in the next pattern.

f) Use d for the number of dots in any pattern, and c for the number of crosses. Which of these formulas gives the correct connection between d and c for any pattern?

   (i) $d^2 = 2c - 5$ (ii) $c^2 - d = 2$ (iii) $(c-1)^2 = 4d$.

g) The total number of symbols in a pattern is 729. How many dots and how many crosses are there?

2   Write down the first five terms of each of the sequences whose nth terms are

   (i) $n^2 - n$ (ii) $\dfrac{n}{4}$ (iii) $1 - \dfrac{n}{4}$.

Using a_n, and limits

1   We can represent the terms of any sequence like this:

$$a_1, a_2, a_3, a_4, a_5, \ldots, a_n, \ldots$$

For example, for the sequence

$$2, 4, 6, 8, 10, \ldots, 2n, \ldots$$

a_1 is 2, a_2 is 4, $\ldots$, a_n is $2n$, and so on.

a) In a sequence, $a_n = 3n + 10$.   (i) What is a_1?   (ii) What is a_{50}?   (iii) Calculate $a_{20} - a_5$.

b) We normally write the terms before a_n and the terms following a_n like this:

$$a_1, a_2, a_3, a_4, a_5, \ldots, a_{n-2}, a_{n-1}, a_n, a_{n+1}, a_{n+2}, \ldots$$

In the sequence $a_n = 2n$, calculate: (i) $a_n - a_{n-1}$ (ii) $2a_{n-3}$.

> notice that a_{n-2} is not the same as $a_n - 2$

c) In the sequence $a_n = n^2 + 2$, find an expression involving n, for

$$a_{n+1} - a_n$$

Simplify your expression as much as possible.
Check that your expression gives the correct result when n is chosen to be 10.

2   The terms of the sequence

$$2, 4, 6, 8, 10, \ldots, 2n, \ldots \quad \text{get larger and larger as } n \text{ increases.}$$

a) Write down another sequence whose terms get larger and larger.

b) Write down a sequence whose terms get smaller and smaller.

3   a) Write down the first 6 terms of each of the sequences: (i) $a_n = \dfrac{2}{n}$ (ii) $a_n = 2 - n$

b) As n increases, the terms of
   each sequence get smaller
   ... but there is a difference
   in the way that the
   sequences 'behave'.
   Explain what it is.

c) The graph shows the first
   10 terms of the sequence

   $$a_n = 1 + \frac{1}{n}$$

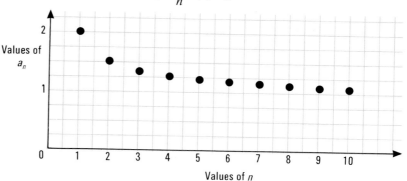

Values of a_n

Values of n

Although the terms of the sequence decrease as n increases, they never get smaller than a certain value.
What is that value?

d) Draw a graph like that in c) for each of these

   sequences: (i) $a_n = \dfrac{10}{n} + 1$ (ii) $a_n = \dfrac{1}{n} - 1$ (iii) $a_n = 1 + \dfrac{n}{n+1}$.

Choose n from 1 to 10 for each graph. What do you notice about the shapes of the graphs?

TAKE NOTE

We say that the terms of
sequences like

$$a_n = 1 + \frac{1}{n}$$

and $a_n = 1 + \dfrac{n}{n+1}$

tend towards a *limit*.
As n increases, the terms of
the sequence tend towards a
certain value.

The limit of $a_n = 1 + \dfrac{1}{n}$ is 1.

The limit of $a_n = 1 + \dfrac{n}{n+1}$ is 2.

The limit of sequence C is $^-2$.

The sequence $a_n = n^2$ does
not have a limit. As n
increases the terms of a_n
increase without bound.

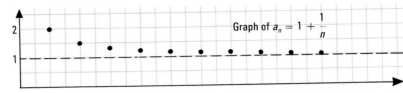

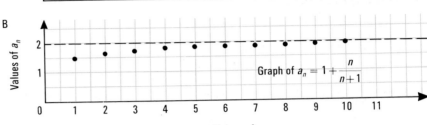

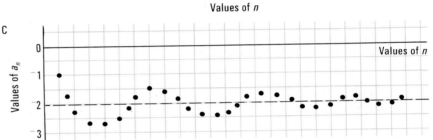

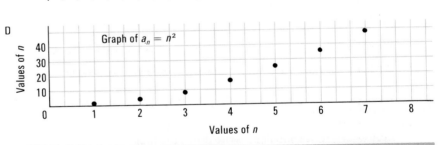

4   For the following sequences:

a) $a_n = \dfrac{1}{n^2}$ b) $a_n = 2n + 1$ c) $a_n = \dfrac{10}{n}$ d) $a_n = {}^-n$ e) $a_n = 10 + \dfrac{1}{n}$

   (i)   write down the first six terms of each sequence
   (ii) say whether or not each sequence has a limit
   (iii) if a sequence has a limit, say what it is.

CHALLENGE

5   Investigate how each of these sequences behaves. Draw a graph to show what happens to each one,
    as n increases.

a) $a_n = \sin n^\circ$ b) $a_n = \dfrac{(^-1)^n}{n}$ c) $a_n = \dfrac{\sin n^\circ}{n}$

B1

Finding the terms of a sequence

1 Find the next term in each of these sequences:
   A 1, 4, 7, 10, 13, ...
   B 2, 4, 8, 16, 32, ...
   C 4, 3, $2\frac{1}{2}$, $2\frac{1}{4}$, $2\frac{1}{8}$, ...
   D 1, 1, 2, 3, 5, 8, ...

2 These are the sequences in question 1.

   a) What does each row of smaller numbers represent?

A 1   4   7   10   13   ...
        3   3   3   3   ...

B 2   4   8   16   32   ...
        2   4   8   16   ...

   b) The smaller red numbers will help you to find the next term in each sequence. Explain how, and use them to check your results in question 1.

C 4   3 $2\frac{1}{2}$ $2\frac{1}{4}$ $2\frac{1}{8}$ ...
        1      $\frac{1}{2}$ $\frac{1}{4}$ $\frac{1}{8}$ ...

D 1   1   2   3   5   8   ...
        0   1   1   2   3   ...

   c) Find the next term in each of these sequences. (Writing the difference between successive terms below the sequence, as in a), will help.)
       (i)   2, 7, 17, 37, 77, ...
       (ii)   2, 5, 14, 41, ...
       (iii) 2, 3, 6, 11, 18, 27, ...
       (iv)   1, 2, 6, 15, 31, 56, ...

============ CHALLENGE ============

3 Find   a) the 20th term   b) the nth term in each sequence:

   a) 2, 5, 10, 17, 26, 37, 50, ...   b) 0, 2, 6, 12, 20, 30, ...

Iterative formulas

1 a) Follow this flow chart, and write down the first six numbers it produces.

   b) When I thought of a number, the 7th number I wrote down was 62. What was the number I first thought of?

   c) What number is produced when the first number is 7 and n is 20?

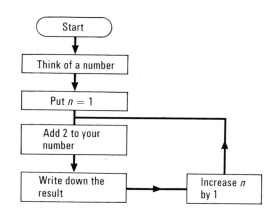

c) The flow chart produces a sequence. As you follow the chart you find the next term of the sequence from the previous term (by adding 2).
We can represent the process like this:

the new term   the previous term

$$a_n = a_{n-1} + 2 \qquad a_1 = \dots$$

Notice that we have to specify what a_1 is. Different values for a_1 will give different sequences.

What sequence do we get when a_1 is   (i) 4   (ii) 20?

2   This flow chart will produce a sequence.

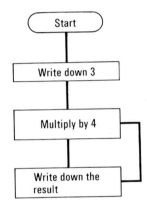

a) Write down the first six terms of the sequence.

b) In the sequence, a_1 is 3. Write down a formula for the sequence like that in question 1.

THINK IT THROUGH

3   Which of these formulas produces the sequence 5, 7, 12, 19, 31, …?

a) $a_n = a_{n-1} + 7, \quad a_1 = 5$ b) $a_n = a_{n-1} + a_{n-3}, \quad a_1 = 5$ c) $a_n = a_{n-1} + a_{n-2}, \quad a_1 = 5.$

4   a) In each sequence explain how you can find the next term from the terms before it.
    A   2, 4, 8, 16, …
    B   7, 10, 13, 16, 19, …
    C   1, 4, 9, 16, 25, …
    D   1, 1, 2, 3, 5, 8, …

b) Match each sequence with one of these formulas, and write down the value of a_1 in each case.

   (i) $a_n = a_{n-1} + a_{n-2}, \quad a_1 = \dots$ (ii) $a_n = a_{n-1} + 3, \quad a_1 = \dots$
   (iii) $a_n = 2a_{n-1}, \quad a_1 = \dots$ (iv) $a_n = (\sqrt{a_{n-1}} + 1)^2, \quad a_1 = \dots$

B1

━━━━━━━━ TAKE NOTE ━━━━━━━━

There are two main ways of writing the formula for a sequence.

a) By giving a formula for the nth term.

For example, $a_n = 2n+3$ is the formula for the sequence 5, 7, 9, 11, 13,

... Unless otherwise stated we assume $n = 1, 2, 3, 4, 5, \ldots$

b) By giving a formula which connects two or more terms.

For example, $a_n = a_{n-1}+2, \quad a_1 = 5$, also produces the sequence 5, 7, 9, 11, 13, ...

Formulas like that in b) are called *iterative* formulas. With an iterative formula we need also to specify one of the terms (normally, but not always, a_1).

5 a) Find the next term in the sequence

3, 7, 15, 31, ...

b) Complete this iterative formula for the sequence

$a_n = 2a_{n-1}$
$a_1 = \square$

6 a) Write down the first five terms of the sequence

$u_{n+1} = u_n + 6, \quad u_1 = 4$

b) Draw a flow chart to represent the iteration (that is, to show how the terms of the sequence are obtained).

c) What is the 100th term of the sequence?

7 a) Write down the first five terms of each sequence.

(i) $u_{n+1} = \dfrac{1}{u_n}, \quad u_2 = 2$ (ii) $u_{n+1} = (u_n)^2, u_4 = 1$

(iii) $u_{n+1} = (^-u_n)^n, \quad u_1 = 2$ (iv) $u_{n+1} = \sqrt{u_n}, \quad u_1 = 100$.

b) Do any of the sequences have a limit? If so, say what it is.

━━━━━━━━ THINK IT THROUGH ━━━━━━━━

8 Write each of these sequences using an iterative formula. (Start by writing down some terms for them.)

a) $a_n = 4n+3$ b) $a_n = 3-n$ c) $a_n = n^2$.

━━━━━━━━ CHALLENGE ━━━━━━━━

9 a) What is the next term in this sequence?   b) Find an iterative formula for the sequence.

$3, 4, 3\frac{1}{2}, 3\frac{3}{4}, 3\frac{5}{8}, \ldots$

ENRICHMENT

Solving equations using iteration

━━━━━━━━ CHALLENGES ━━━━━━━━

16

1 a) The sequence $u_n = \dfrac{u_{n-1}+6}{2}, \quad u_1 = 8$, has a limit. What is it? (Find successive terms of the sequence until you are sure.)

b) Solve the equation $x = \frac{1}{2}(x+6)$.

c) Compare your results in a) and b). Why is the limit to the sequence also the solution to the equation?

2   a) Investigate the limit of the sequence $u_{n+1} = 5 - \frac{5}{u_n}$, $u_1 = 2$.

What do you think it is?

b) For values of n from 1 to 10, compare the sizes of u_{n+1} and u_n. What do you notice?

c) Imagine that n is very large (say, greater than 10 million). What can you say about u_{n+1} and u_n?

d) Use your calculator to find the two solutions (each correct to 1 DP) of the quadratic equation

$x^2 - 5x + 5 = 0$

each correct to 1 DP. (One solution is between 3 and 4, and the other between 1 and 2.)

e) Explain the connection between your results in a) and d).

3   a) Rearrange $x = \frac{4}{x-3}$ to give an equation of the form $x^2 + bx + c = 0$.

b) Solve the equation you obtain (two solutions).

c) Find the limit of the sequence $u_{n+1} = \frac{4}{u_n - 3}$, $u_1 = 1$

(Calculate $u_1, u_2, u_3, \ldots$ until you think you know the limit.)

d) What is the connection between your results in b) and c)?

e) Rearrange the original equation into the form

$x - 3 = \ldots\ldots$

f) Find the limit of the sequence $u_{n+1} - 3 = \frac{4}{u_n}$, $u_1 = 1$

g) What is the connection between your results in b) and f)?

4   a) Write down an iterative formula to solve the equation

$x = \frac{7}{x+3}$

b) Use your formula in a) to find an approximate solution to the equation

$x^2 + 3x - 7 = 0$ correct to 1 DP.

c) Rearrange the equation in a) into the form

$x + 3 = \ldots\ldots$

and write an iterative formula which will help you to solve it.

d) Use your iterative formula in c) to find the other solution to the equation $x^2 + 3x - 7 = 0$ correct to 1 DP.

CHALLENGE

5   Use iterative formulas to find the two solutions (correct to 1 DP) of the equation $2x^2 + 4x - 3 = 0$

B16

B17 SIMULTANEOUS EQUATIONS

REVIEW

When we search for values which satisfy two equations such as

$$x = 3y$$
and $x + y = 8$

together, we say we are solving the equations *simultaneously*.

The equations are then called *simultaneous equations*.

From the graph we can see that the solution of the equations is $x = 6$, $y = 2$.

(Check: for $x = 3y$: $6 = 3 \times 2$;
           for $x + y = 8$: $6 + 2 = 8$.)

■ Write down examples of a pair of equations which:

a) have the common solution $x = 1$, $y = 2$

b) do not have a common solution

c) have an infinite number of common solutions.

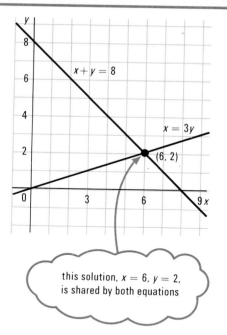

this solution, $x = 6$, $y = 2$, is shared by both equations

CONSOLIDATION

1 a) Which lines on the graph represent the solutions of the following equations:

(i) $y - x = 3$ (ii) $y + 2x = 6$ (iii) $x = y$ (iv) $y + 2x = 0$
(v) $x - y = 3$?

b) Explain how the graphs show that $y + 2x = 6$ and $y + 2x = 0$ do not have a common solution.

c) Use the graph to help you to find the common solutions of these pairs of equations:

(i) $y - x = 3$, $y + 2x = 6$
(iii) $y + 2x = 0$, $y - x = 3$
(v) $x - y = 3$, $y + 2x = 6$
(ii) $y - x = 3$, $x = y$
(iv) $x = y$, $y + 2x = 6$
(vi) $x - y = 3$, $y + 2x = 0$.

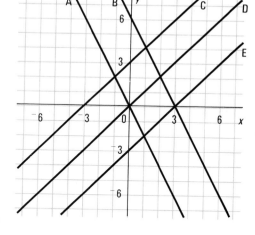

2 You need graph paper.

a) With the same axes, draw the graphs of   (i) $2x + y = 4$ (ii) $3x - 2y = 6$.

b) From your graphs solve the simultaneous equations $2x + y = 4$, $3x - 2y = 6$.

3 You need graph paper.

a) With the same axes, draw the graphs of   (i) $y = 2x^2 - 1$ (ii) $y = 3x + 1$.
Choose values of x from $^-3$ to $^+8$.

b) There are two different solutions of the simultaneous equations $y = 2x^2 - 1$, $y = 3x + 1$.

Find each solution from your graph.

CORE

Method A: Listing solutions of each equation

We can solve simultaneous equations without graphs by various methods. We will look at various methods, beginning with listing solutions of each equation.

1   a) Check that three solutions of the equation $2y-x=8$ are (4, 6) (0, 4) ($^-$2, 3). Write down three more solutions.

   b) Check that three solutions of the equation $y=x+4$ are (0, 4) ($^-$3, 1) (2, 6). Write down three more solutions.

   c) Write down the solution (x, y) which satisfies both $2y-x=8$ and $y=x+4$.

2   By listing some solutions of each equation, solve the simultaneous equations:

  a) $x-y=4$ b) $y=3-2x$ c) $p=3q+1$
     $x+y=10$ $y=x+9$ $q=2p-7$

3   Try to solve the simultaneous equations:

$y=2x-4$
$4x=y-5$

using Method A.
If you do not succeed after five minutes, draw a graph to find the solution.

===== WITH A FRIEND =====

4   Each of you write down a pair of simultaneous equations which are difficult to solve by listing solutions to each equation.
See how long it takes your friend to find the solution (by any method).

Method B: Finding the values of the unknowns by adding

In question 3, you may have found difficulty in identifying the solution. This is often the case when the solutions are not whole numbers, and so we need another method. One possible method is to add the equations in order to eliminate one of the unknowns.

1   a) $x+y=3$
      and $x-y=2$

     are simultaneous equations.

     (i) Explain why this is true:

       $(x+y)+(x-y)=5$

     (ii) Use the equation in (i) to find a value for x.
     (iii) Find y in each equation for the value of x you calculated in (ii).
     (iv) Check that $x=2\frac{1}{2}$, $y=\frac{1}{2}$, satisfies both of the equations.

B17

b) Copy and complete the solution to the simultaneous equations

$$y - 3x = 0$$
$$y + 3x = 2$$

c) Use Method B to solve the simultaneous equations

$$2x - 3y = 0$$
$$4x + 3y = 3$$

Check that your solution fits both equations.

> Adding the lefthand sides and righthand sides of the equations:
> $$(y - 3x) + (y + 3x) = \square$$
> So $\qquad 2y = \square$
> So $\qquad y = \square$
> Put $y = 1$ in $y - 3x = 0$:
> $$1 - 3x = 0$$
> So $\qquad x = \square$
> The solution is $x = \square$, $y = \square$
> Check the original equations:
> $$\square - 3\square = 0 \ \checkmark$$
> $$\square + 3\square = 2 \ \checkmark$$

━━━━━━━ WITH A FRIEND ━━━━━━━

2   In Method B you added the two equations, because by adding you eliminated an unknown.

In these simultaneous equations, adding does not eliminate one of the unknowns:

$$2x + 3y = 8$$
$$x + 3y = 6$$

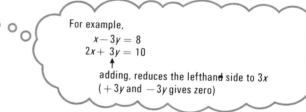

> For example,
> $$x - 3y = 8$$
> $$2x + 3y = 10$$
> adding, reduces the lefthand side to $3x$
> ($+3y$ and $-3y$ gives zero)

Decide between you how to solve the equations (not by drawing graphs, or by listing solutions – use a method similar to Method B).
Each of you use your method to solve the equations. Do not forget to check that your solutions satisfy the two original equations.

3   a) Copy and complete the solution to this pair of simultaneous equations:

$$2y + 3x = 7$$
$$y + 3x = 1$$

b) Solve each pair of equations. Do not forget to check your results.

    (i) $2y + x = 4$
           $y + x = 2$

    (ii) $3x + 2y = 6$
           $x + 2y = 0$

    (iii) $y - x = 9$
            $y - 3x = 11$

> Subtract the lefthand sides and righthand sides of the equations:
> $$(2y + 3x) - (y + 3x) = \square$$
> Simplify: $\qquad y = \square$
> To find x, substitute $y = 6$ in $2y + 3x = 7$
> $$12 + 3x = 7$$
> $$3x = \square$$
> $$x = \dfrac{\square}{\square}$$
> Check in $y + 3x = 1$
> $$6 + (3 \times \dfrac{^-5}{3}) = \square \ \checkmark$$
> Solution: $x = \square$, $y = \square$

CHALLENGE

4   Solve this pair of simultaneous equations by subtracting one equation from the other:

$2x - 4y = 9$
$x - 4y = 6$

5   a) Copy and complete the solution to this pair
       of simultaneous equations:

$5y - x = 10$
$2y - x = 13$

   b) Solve each pair of simultaneous equations.
       Do not forget to check your results.

   (i) $x - y = 9$
         $2x - y = 12$

   (ii) $y - 5x = 8$
         $3y - 5x = 10$

Subtract the lefthand sides and
righthand sides of the equations:
$$(5y - x) - (2y - x) = \square$$
Simplify: $\square y = \square$
                       $y = \square$
To find x, substitute $y = {}^-1$ in $5y - x = 10$
$$(5 \times {}^-1) - x = 10$$
                       ${}^-x = \square$

Check in $2y - x = 13$
$$(2 \times {}^-1) - {}^-15 = 13 \checkmark$$
Solution: $x = \square$, $y = \square$

Method C: Multiplying one equation by a number to obtain equal coefficients of x and y

1   In each pair of simultaneous equations you have solved so far, the x or y coefficients
    have been equal, for example

$3x - y = 12$ $x + 4y = 9$
$3x + 2y = 7$ $3x - 4y = 7$

*i.e. the numbers which
precede x and y*

equal coefficients of x equal coefficients of y

To solve the equations you have therefore been
able to add or subtract to eliminate one of the
unknowns.

a) In these equations the coefficients of x and
    of y are different:

$2x - 3y = 4$
$x + y = 12$

Here is a method for solving a pair of
simultaneous equations of this sort, by
multiplying one equation by a number to
obtain equal coefficients of x and y.
Copy and complete the solution:

---

[1] $2x - 3y = 4$
[2] $x + y = 12$
Multiply the lefthand side and the
righthand side of equation [2] by 3:
[3] $3x + 3y = \square$
Add equations [1] and [3]:
            $5x = \square$
             $x = \square$
Substitute $x = 8$ in equation [1] to find y:
$$(2 \times 8) - 3y = 4$$
             $y = \square$
Check the solution in equation [2]:
        $8 + 4 = 12 \checkmark$

B17

b) Solve this pair of simultaneous equations by first multiplying one equation by
   3:   $3y - x = 6$
        $y - 2x = 3$

c) Solve each pair of simultaneous equations:

   (i) $y - 4x = 5$ (ii) $x + 5y = 0$ (iii) $y - 3x = 8$
         $3y - 2x = 5$ $4x + y = 38$ $3y + x = 4$

CHALLENGE

2 Solve this pair of simultaneous equations by first multiplying equation A by 2 and equation B by 3:

   A $3x + 5y = 7$
   B $2x + 4y = 0$

Method D: Multiplying both equations by a number to obtain equal coefficients of x and y

1 a) In the pair of equations in question 2, that is,

       $3x + 5y = 7$
       $2x + 4y = 0$

       multiplying an equation by a number does not give us equal coefficients, so we multiply each equation by a number, to obtain equal coefficients of x or y.
       Check your solution in question 2 with the one given here:

   b) Solve this pair of simultaneous equations by first multiplying equation A by 5 and equation B by 3.

       A $4x - 3y = 2$
       B $3x + 5y = 16$

   c) Solve each pair of simultaneous equations:

       (i) $2x + 3y = 13$
             $3x + 4y = 16$

       (ii) $4p - 3q = 28$
             $5p - 2q = 21$

---

[1] $3x + 5y = 7$
[2] $2x + 4y = 0$
Multiply equation [1] by 2:
[3] $6x + 10y = 14$
Multiply equation [2] by 3:
[4] $6x + 12y = 0$
Subtract equation [3] from equation [4]:
       $2y = {}^-14$
        $y = {}^-7$
Substitute $y = {}^-7$ in equation [1]:
       $3x + {}^-35 = 7$
          $3x = 42$
           $x = 14$
Check in equation [2]:
       $(2 \times 14) + (4 \times {}^-7) = 0$
Solution: $x = 14$, $y = {}^-7$

THINK IT THROUGH

2 The three lines $2x - 3y = 8$
                      $3x + 4y = 3$
                       $x - 3y = 1$

   meet at the points A, B and C. Find the coordinates of A, B and C.

Method E: Substitution

━━━━━━━━━━ WITH A FRIEND ━━━━━━━━━━

B17

1   Here is a final method of solving two
    simultaneous equations.

    Decide between you how the method works, then
    use it to solve the equations:

    $$p-2q = 14$$
    $$3p+7q = 8$$

[1] $x + 4y = 7$
[2] $2x + 3y = 9$
From equation [1], $x = 7 - 4y$.
Substitute in equation [2]:
        $2(7-4y) + 3y = 9$
Simplify:
        $14 - 8y + 3y = 9$
So $y = 1$
Substitute in equation [1]:
        $x + 4 \times 1 = 7$
So $x = 3$
Check in equation [2]:
        $(2 \times 3) + (3 \times 1) = 9$ ✓
Solution: $x = 3$, $y = 1$

ENRICHMENT

1   a) Guess and test to find the solutions of the simultaneous equations:

    $$y-2 = x^2 + 3x$$
    $$2y = x+2$$

    (There are two pairs of solutions, (x_1, y_1) and (x_2, y_2).)

    b) With the same axes, draw the graphs of

    $$y = x^2 + 3x + 2$$
    and $2y = x + 2$.

    Find where the graphs intersect and explain how the points of intersection relate to your solutions in a).

2   a) Solve the simultaneous equations (by guessing and testing, or otherwise):

    $$y = x^2 + 4$$
    $$y = 12 - x^2$$

    (There are two pairs of solutions, (x_1, y_1) and (x_2, y_2).)

    b) Draw a graph to represent the solutions.

3   This is a set of three simultaneous equations.

    $$x+y+z = 3$$
    $$2x-y+z = 3$$
    $$x-2y-z = 0$$

    Find the values of x, y and z which satisfy the equations (guess and test, or use another method).

B18 TRANSFORMATIONS

REVIEW

- We can use position vectors to represent transformations of the (x, y) plane. For example, we can represent a stretch with invariant line $x = 3$ and scale factor $\times 2$, by the rule

$$\binom{x}{y} \longrightarrow \binom{2x-3}{y}$$

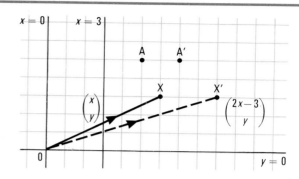

■ Check that the rule takes the position vector of A to A', that is, takes $\binom{5}{5}$ to $\binom{7}{5}$.

- Transformations that leave the origin invariant and transform the plane uniformly are called *linear* transformations.
  A linear transformation can be represented by a rule of the form $\binom{x}{y} \longrightarrow \binom{ax+by}{cx+dy}$.

  In turn, this can be written as $\binom{x}{y} \longrightarrow \begin{pmatrix} a & b \\ c & d \end{pmatrix}\binom{x}{y}$

  and so we can represent linear transformations by a matrix $\begin{pmatrix} a & b \\ c & d \end{pmatrix}$.

■ a) Why is the stretch with invariant line $x = 3$ and rule $\binom{x}{y} \longrightarrow \binom{2x-3}{y}$ *not* a linear transformation?

  b) Why can't the stretch be represented by a matrix $\begin{pmatrix} a & b \\ c & d \end{pmatrix}$?

- We can find the matrix of a linear transformation by first finding the images of the base vectors, that is, of the vectors $\binom{1}{0}$ and $\binom{0}{1}$.

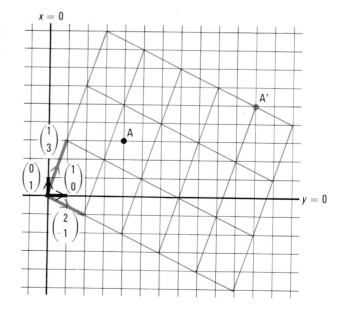

The transformation represented in the diagram

maps $\binom{1}{0}$ onto $\binom{2}{-1}$ and $\binom{0}{1}$ onto $\binom{1}{3}$.

The image of the position vector of point A is $4\binom{2}{-1} + 3\binom{1}{3}$, which can be written as $\begin{pmatrix} 2 & 1 \\ -1 & 3 \end{pmatrix}\binom{4}{3}$.

The matrix of the transformation is thus

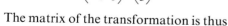

$$\begin{pmatrix} 2 & 1 \\ -1 & 3 \end{pmatrix}$$

where the columns of the matrix are the image of $\binom{1}{0}$ and $\binom{0}{1}$ respectively.

CONSOLIDATION

1   A reflection in the line $x = 0$ maps $\begin{pmatrix} 1 \\ 0 \end{pmatrix} \longrightarrow \begin{pmatrix} -1 \\ 0 \end{pmatrix}$ and $\begin{pmatrix} 0 \\ 1 \end{pmatrix} \longrightarrow \begin{pmatrix} 0 \\ 1 \end{pmatrix}$.

Write down the matrix of the transformation.

2   Write down the matrix for a rotation of 90° anticlockwise about the origin.

3   What transformation does the matrix $\begin{pmatrix} 4 & 0 \\ 0 & 4 \end{pmatrix}$ represent?

4   The (x, y) plane is given a stretch, scale factor × 3, invariant line $x = 0$; it is then reflected in the line $y = x$.

a)   Write down the final images of $\begin{pmatrix} 1 \\ 0 \end{pmatrix}$ and $\begin{pmatrix} 0 \\ 1 \end{pmatrix}$ and hence find the matrix of the combined transformation.

b)   Check that your matrix maps $\begin{pmatrix} 10 \\ 2 \end{pmatrix}$ onto $\begin{pmatrix} 2 \\ 30 \end{pmatrix}$.

B18

CORE

Determinants and area

1   a)   (i)   Check that the transformation with matrix

$\begin{pmatrix} 2 & 3 \\ 1 & 1\frac{1}{2} \end{pmatrix}$ maps A onto A'.

(That is, check that the matrix multiplication

$\begin{pmatrix} 2 & 3 \\ 1 & 1\frac{1}{2} \end{pmatrix} \begin{pmatrix} 3 \\ 4 \end{pmatrix}$ is equal to $\begin{pmatrix} 18 \\ 9 \end{pmatrix}$.)

(ii)   Find the images of B, C and D under the

matrix $\begin{pmatrix} 2 & 3 \\ 1 & 1\frac{1}{2} \end{pmatrix}$.

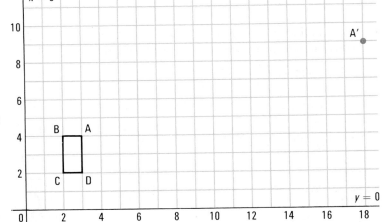

(iii)   Draw the image of the rectangle ABCD. What do you notice?

b)   Draw the image of rectangle ABCD under the transformation $\begin{pmatrix} \frac{1}{2} & -1 \\ -1 & 2 \end{pmatrix}$. What do you notice?

c)   Find another matrix that has the same kind of effect as the matrices in a) and b).

d)   What effect do the matrices in a), b) and c) have

(i)   on the area of rectangle ABCD   (ii)   on the base vectors $\begin{pmatrix} 1 \\ 0 \end{pmatrix}$ and $\begin{pmatrix} 0 \\ 1 \end{pmatrix}$?

CHALLENGE

2 For a matrix $\begin{pmatrix} a & b \\ c & d \end{pmatrix}$, the expression $ad - bc$ is called the *determinant* of the matrix.

For example, in question 1, the determinant of each matrix was zero (for example, $2 \times 1\frac{1}{2} - 3 \times 1 = 0$).

a) Make up some matrices whose determinant is equal to 2, for example, $\begin{pmatrix} 2 & 0 \\ 0 & 1 \end{pmatrix}$.

Draw the image of rectangle ABCD under each matrix. Try at least two different matrices. Find out what happens to the area of the rectangle.

b) Try matrices whose determinant is equal to 3, say, or 1, etc. Describe how the determinant is related to the area of a shape and its image.

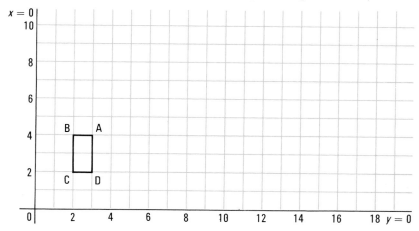

c) The diagram shows the effect of the matrix $\begin{pmatrix} a & b \\ c & d \end{pmatrix}$ on the unit square OABC.

(i) Find the area of OA′B′C′. What is the ratio of the area of OA′B′C′ to the area of the unit square, OABC?

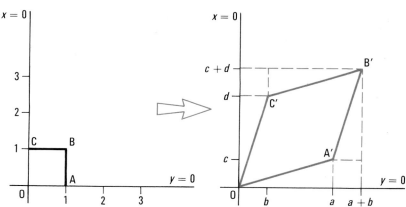

(ii) What do your results tell you about the determinant of a matrix and the areas of shapes in the (x, y) plane?

TAKE NOTE

The expression $ad - bc$ is called the *determinant* (det) of the matrix $\begin{pmatrix} a & b \\ c & d \end{pmatrix}$.

The value of the determinant gives the area factor of the transformation; that is, it gives us the ratio $\dfrac{\text{Area of image shape}}{\text{Area of object shape}}$

For example, the matrix $\begin{pmatrix} 3 & 0 \\ 0 & 3 \end{pmatrix}$ is an enlargement, scale factor $\times 3$. Its determinant is 9 ($3 \times 3 - 0 \times 0$) and it enlarges area by $\times 9$.

3   a) Find the determinant of each of these matrices:

$$\begin{pmatrix} 1 & 0 \\ 0 & {}^-1 \end{pmatrix} \begin{pmatrix} {}^-3 & 0 \\ 0 & 3 \end{pmatrix} \begin{pmatrix} 1 & {}^-1 \\ 0 & {}^-1 \end{pmatrix} \begin{pmatrix} 1 & 2 \\ 0 & 1 \end{pmatrix} \begin{pmatrix} 0 & 2 \\ {}^-2 & 0 \end{pmatrix}$$

b) For each matrix draw a shape in the (x, y) plane, and its image under the transformation.

c) You will have seen in a) that the determinants of some matrices are negative. Investigate what the negative sign tells us.
   Write down what you decide.

4   a) Think of   (i) a rotation   (ii) a reflection   (iii) a stretch   (iv) a shear   (choose transformations that keep the origin invariant).
   Write down the matrix for each of your transformations.

b) Find the value of the determinant of each matrix.

c) Which of your transformations preserve area? Check that their matrices have a determinant of 1 or $^-1$.

5   a) Find the matrix of the transformation which transforms the unit square OABC
   to   (i) OA′B′C′   (ii) OA″B″C″.

b) What is the area
   of   (i) OA′B′C′   (ii) OA″B″C″?

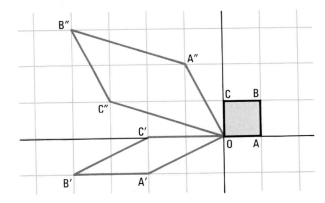

THINK IT THROUGH

6   What is the area factor of the transformation $\begin{pmatrix} x \\ y \end{pmatrix} \longrightarrow \begin{pmatrix} 3x - y \\ y + 3x \end{pmatrix}$?

Combining transformations

1   a) Write down the matrix for each of these transformations:

   (i) a reflection in $y = 0$
   (ii) a reflection in $y = x$
   (iii) a reflection in $x = 0$
   (iv) a reflection in $y = {}^-x$.

b) Predict the resulting matrix for pairs of combined transformations (for example, a reflection in $x = 0$ followed by a reflection in $y = x$), by considering what happens to the base vectors.

c) Multiply together the matrices for the original pairs of transformations in b).

d) Explain the connection between your results in b) and your results in c).

2   a) By thinking about what happens to the base vectors, write down the matrix for

     (i) a reflection in $y = 0$
     (ii) an enlargement, scale factor $\times 2$, centre $(0, 0)$
     (iii) a reflection in $y = 0$, followed by an enlargement, scale factor $\times 2$, centre $(0, 0)$
     (iv) an enlargement, scale factor $\times 2$, centre $(0, 0)$, followed by a reflection $y = 0$.

  b) On a diagram show what happens to the unit square under each transformation (i) to (iv), for example,

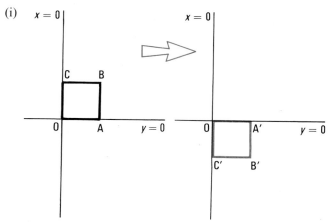

  c) Check that your matrices in (iii) and (iv) have the correct effect upon $\begin{pmatrix} x \\ y \end{pmatrix}$ (that is, write down the image of $\begin{pmatrix} x \\ y \end{pmatrix}$ from your diagrams in b) and also multiply $\begin{pmatrix} x \\ y \end{pmatrix}$ by the matrices).

3   Transformation **A** is a half turn, centre $(0, 0)$.
   Transformation **B** is a reflection in $x = y$.

  a) By thinking about what happens to the base vectors, find the matrix
     for (i) **A** (ii) **B** (iii) **AB** (iv) **BA** (that is, transformation **A** *first* and then transformation **B** applied to the (x, y) plane).

  b) Are **AB** and **BA** identical transformations?

  c) Are the matrices for **AB** and **BA** identical?

  d) Check that the matrices for **AB** and **BA** give the correct images of $\begin{pmatrix} x \\ y \end{pmatrix}$ for each of the combined transformations.

4   Transformation **X** is a quarter turn anticlockwise, centre $(0, 0)$; transformation **Y** is a reflection in $x = y$.

  a) Find the matrix for (i) **X** (ii) **Y** (iii) **XY** (iv) **YX**.

  b) Are **XY** and **YX** identical transformations?

  c) Are the matrices for **XY** and **YX** identical?

  d) Check that the matrices for **XY** and **YX** give the correct images of $\begin{pmatrix} x \\ y \end{pmatrix}$ for each of the combined transformations.

5   Some pairs of transformations produce the same effect on the (x, y) plane no matter in what order they are applied.
For example,

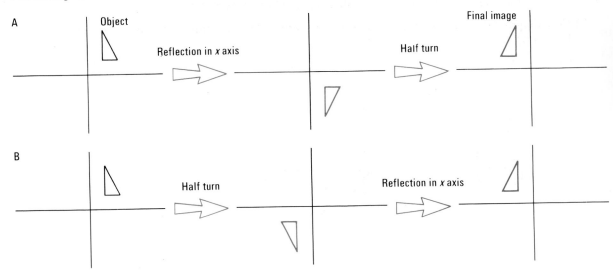

Other pairs of transformations produce different outcomes when combined in different ways. For example,

a) Find the matrices for each of the four combined transformations above. Check that in A and B the matrices are identical, whilst in X and Y they are not.

b) Investigate other pairs of transformations.
Which transformations combine in any order to produce the same result, and which do not?
Draw up as complete a list of each as you can.

If **A** and **B** are transformations then

AB represents the transformation **B** first, then **A**.
BA represents the transformation **A** first, then **B**.

The matrix of **AB** is the matrix of **A** × the matrix of **B**;
the matrix of **BA** is the matrix of **B** × the matrix of **A**.

6   $\mathbf{A} = \begin{pmatrix} ^-1 & 0 \\ 0 & 1 \end{pmatrix}$ (a reflection in $x = 0$)

$\mathbf{B} = \begin{pmatrix} 0 & 1 \\ 1 & 0 \end{pmatrix}$ (a reflection in $y = x$)

a) Check that $\mathbf{AB} \neq \mathbf{BA}$.

b) Check that under the transformation **AB**

$$\begin{pmatrix} x \\ y \end{pmatrix} \longrightarrow \begin{pmatrix} ^-1 & 0 \\ 0 & 1 \end{pmatrix} \begin{pmatrix} 0 & 1 \\ 1 & 0 \end{pmatrix} \begin{pmatrix} x \\ y \end{pmatrix} \longrightarrow \begin{pmatrix} ^-y \\ x \end{pmatrix}$$

c) What happens to $\begin{pmatrix} x \\ y \end{pmatrix}$ under the transformation **BA**?

7   Here are two transformation matrices **X** and **Y**: $\mathbf{X} = \begin{pmatrix} 1 & 0 \\ 2 & 3 \end{pmatrix}$, $\mathbf{Y} = \begin{pmatrix} 2 & 4 \\ 0 & 1 \end{pmatrix}$.

We want to find the effect that **X** followed by **Y** has on the position vector $\begin{pmatrix} 1 \\ 5 \end{pmatrix}$.

Here are two possible methods:

Method 1   Multiply the position vector by **X** (that is, $\begin{pmatrix} 1 & 0 \\ 2 & 3 \end{pmatrix} \begin{pmatrix} 1 \\ 5 \end{pmatrix}$),

then multiply the new position vector by **Y** (that is, $\begin{pmatrix} 2 & 4 \\ 0 & 1 \end{pmatrix} \begin{pmatrix} \square \\ \square \end{pmatrix}$).

Method 2   Multiply **X** and **Y** *in the order* **Y** × **X** (that is, $\begin{pmatrix} 2 & 4 \\ 0 & 1 \end{pmatrix} \begin{pmatrix} 1 & 0 \\ 2 & 3 \end{pmatrix}$).

then multiply the position vector by the resulting matrix (that is, $\begin{pmatrix} \square & \square \\ \square & \square \end{pmatrix} \begin{pmatrix} 1 \\ 5 \end{pmatrix}$).

a) Check that the two methods give the same result.

b) Draw a diagram to show the effect that   (i) **XY**   (ii) **YX** has upon the position vector $\begin{pmatrix} 1 \\ 5 \end{pmatrix}$.

8   a) Multiply   (i) $\begin{pmatrix} 1 & 0 \\ 0 & ^-1 \end{pmatrix} \begin{pmatrix} 1 & 0 \\ 0 & ^-1 \end{pmatrix}$ (ii) $\begin{pmatrix} 2 & 0 \\ 0 & 2 \end{pmatrix} \begin{pmatrix} \frac{1}{2} & 0 \\ 0 & \frac{1}{2} \end{pmatrix}$ (iii) $\begin{pmatrix} 1 & 1 \\ 0 & 1 \end{pmatrix} \begin{pmatrix} 1 & ^-1 \\ 0 & 1 \end{pmatrix}$ (iv) $\begin{pmatrix} 2 & 0 \\ 0 & 3 \end{pmatrix} \begin{pmatrix} \frac{1}{2} & 0 \\ 0 & \frac{1}{3} \end{pmatrix}$

b) Explain what effect each combined transformation in a) has upon the (x, y) plane.

c) Think of the (x, y) plane transformed by the transformation with matrix $\begin{pmatrix} 3 & 0 \\ 0 & 1 \end{pmatrix}$.

What transformation will return the (x, y) plane to its original position and shape?
Write down the matrix for the transformation.

Identity and inverse

1 a) Write down the matrix for the transformations: (i) $\begin{pmatrix} x \\ y \end{pmatrix} \longrightarrow \begin{pmatrix} 4x \\ x+y \end{pmatrix}$ (ii) $\begin{pmatrix} x \\ y \end{pmatrix} \longrightarrow \begin{pmatrix} x \\ y \end{pmatrix}$.

b) Draw a diagram to show the effect that each of these matrices has upon the unit square:

(i) $\begin{pmatrix} 4 & 0 \\ 1 & 1 \end{pmatrix}$ (ii) $\begin{pmatrix} 1 & 0 \\ 0 & 1 \end{pmatrix}$

c) Find the missing matrix (you might find it easier to think geometrically, that is, think about what is happening to the plane).

$$\begin{pmatrix} 2 & 0 \\ 0 & 4 \end{pmatrix} \begin{pmatrix} \square & \square \\ \square & \square \end{pmatrix} = \begin{pmatrix} 1 & 0 \\ 0 & 1 \end{pmatrix}$$

─── TAKE NOTE ───

$\begin{pmatrix} 1 & 0 \\ 0 & 1 \end{pmatrix}$ is called the *identity* matrix.

The transformation which it represents has no effect upon the (x, y) plane:

$$\begin{pmatrix} 1 & 0 \\ 0 & 1 \end{pmatrix} \begin{pmatrix} x \\ y \end{pmatrix} = \begin{pmatrix} x \\ y \end{pmatrix}$$

We use the letter **I** to represent the identity matrix.
A matrix **X** is called the *inverse* of a matrix **Y** if the product of the two matrices gives the identity matrix, that is, if **XY = YX = I**.
We often write the inverse of **Y** as $\mathbf{Y}^{-1}$.
The transformation which **X** represents is also called the inverse of the transformation which **Y** represents.

For example, $\begin{pmatrix} 0 & 1 \\ -1 & 0 \end{pmatrix}$ (a rotation of 90° clockwise about the origin) is the inverse of $\begin{pmatrix} 0 & -1 \\ 1 & 0 \end{pmatrix}$ (a rotation of 90° anticlockwise about the origin).

2 a) Check that the product $\begin{pmatrix} 0 & 1 \\ -1 & 0 \end{pmatrix} \begin{pmatrix} 0 & -1 \\ 1 & 0 \end{pmatrix}$ gives $\begin{pmatrix} 1 & 0 \\ 0 & 1 \end{pmatrix}$.

b) What are the inverse matrices of   (i) $\begin{pmatrix} 0 & 1 \\ -1 & 0 \end{pmatrix}$ (ii) $\begin{pmatrix} 0 & -1 \\ 1 & 0 \end{pmatrix}$?

3 $\mathbf{P} = \begin{pmatrix} 2 & 0 \\ 0 & 2 \end{pmatrix}$. Check that $\mathbf{P}^{-1} = \begin{pmatrix} \frac{1}{2} & 0 \\ 0 & \frac{1}{2} \end{pmatrix}$

4 Transformation **Q** transforms the unit square O (0, 0), A (1, 0), B (1, 1), C (0, 1) into the parallelogram O (0, 0), A′ (4, 0), B′ (6, 2), C′ (2, 2).

a) Find the matrix for the transformation.

b) Check that $\begin{pmatrix} \frac{1}{4} & -\frac{1}{4} \\ 0 & \frac{1}{2} \end{pmatrix}$ is the inverse matrix.

c) On a diagram show the effect that $\begin{pmatrix} \frac{1}{4} & -\frac{1}{4} \\ 0 & \frac{1}{2} \end{pmatrix}$ has upon the unit square.

5 a) Describe the inverse transformations of each of the following (that is, the transformations which 'restore' the (x, y) plane).

   (i)   A 90° clockwise turn, centre $(0, 0)$
   (ii) An enlargement centre $(0, 0)$, scale factor $\times 2$
   (iii) A reflection in $x = y$
   (iv) A one-way stretch, scale factor $\times 2$, with $x = 0$ invariant
   (v)   A shear with $y = 0$ invariant, which maps $(1, 1) \rightarrow (2, 1)$.

   b) By thinking about the base vectors, write down the matrix of each transformation in a).

   c) By thinking about the base vectors, write down the matrix of each inverse transformation in a).

   d) Multiply each pair of matrices found in b) and c). Check that each product gives the identity matrix. If it does not, check the inverse transformations and inverse matrices.

6 A transformation increases the areas of shapes in the (x, y) plane by scale factor $\times 4$.

   a) What is the determinant of the transformation?

   b) How does the inverse transformation affect the areas of shapes?

   c) What is the determinant of the inverse transformation?

EXPLORATION

7 a) Write down the matrices of some familiar transformations (include rotations, reflections, enlargements, stretches and shears).
   For each matrix, write down its inverse (think about the geometrical transformation that 'restores' the (x, y) plane).

   Check each time that the product of the matrix pair is equal to $\begin{pmatrix} 1 & 0 \\ 0 & 1 \end{pmatrix}$.

   Try to find a rule for obtaining the inverse matrix directly from the original matrix (without thinking about the transformations).

   b) Apply your rule to some more complex matrices like $\begin{pmatrix} 2 & ^-1 \\ 3 & 5 \end{pmatrix}$.

   If necessary modify your rule.
   (Hint: a matrix and its inverse have determinants whose product is 1 ... Why?)

8 This is the matrix from question 1, page 201: $\begin{pmatrix} 2 & 3 \\ 1 & 1\frac{1}{2} \end{pmatrix}$ Why does it not have an inverse?

TAKE NOTE

The inverse of the matrix $\begin{pmatrix} a & b \\ c & d \end{pmatrix}$ is $\begin{pmatrix} \dfrac{d}{ad-bc} & \dfrac{^-b}{ad-bc} \\ \dfrac{^-c}{ad-bc} & \dfrac{a}{ad-bc} \end{pmatrix}$ For example, the inverse of $\begin{pmatrix} 2 & 1 \\ ^-2 & 3 \end{pmatrix}$ is $\begin{pmatrix} \frac{3}{8} & ^-\frac{1}{8} \\ \frac{1}{4} & \frac{1}{4} \end{pmatrix}$.

9 Find the inverse of each matrix: a) $\begin{pmatrix} 1 & 0 \\ 0 & 1 \end{pmatrix}$ b) $\begin{pmatrix} 3 & 1 \\ ^-1 & 2 \end{pmatrix}$ c) $\begin{pmatrix} 0 & 4 \\ ^-4 & 0 \end{pmatrix}$

10 a) Find the matrix of the transformation $\begin{pmatrix} x \\ y \end{pmatrix} \longrightarrow \begin{pmatrix} 3x+2y \\ y-x \end{pmatrix}$.

   b) Find the inverse matrix.

   c) Draw diagrams to show the effect of the original transformation, and of the inverse transformation, on the square O (0, 0), A (1, 0), B (1, 1), C (0, 1).

ENRICHMENT

1 Choose any two matrices **A** and **B**.
Check that:

  det **A** × det **B** = det **B** × det **A** = det (**AB**) = det (**BA**).

  What does this result tell you about transformations in the (x, y) plane?

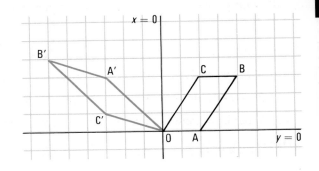

2 Find the matrix of the transformation which maps ABCO to A′B′C′O.

3 Under a transformation, the triangle (0, 0) (1, 0) (0, 1) is transformed to (0, 0) (4, ⁻1) (⁻3, ⁻5).

  a) Find the image of (1, 1) under the transformation.

  b) Find the area of the transformed triangle. (Use matrices!)

4 a) Show that $\begin{pmatrix} e & f \\ g & h \end{pmatrix} \left[\begin{pmatrix} a & b \\ c & d \end{pmatrix} \begin{pmatrix} x \\ y \end{pmatrix} \right] = \left[\begin{pmatrix} e & f \\ g & h \end{pmatrix} \begin{pmatrix} a & b \\ c & d \end{pmatrix} \right] \begin{pmatrix} x \\ y \end{pmatrix}$ b) Explain what the result means.

5 Find the matrix for a $\frac{1}{8}$th clockwise turn, centre (0, 0).
Find the inverse matrix.

6 Find the matrix for a clockwise turn through $\theta°$, centre (0, 0).
Find the inverse matrix.

7 a) Solve the simultaneous equations $3x+2y = 16$
                                 $2x+4y = 12$

   Use any method you wish.

  b) The equations can be written as a *single* matrix equation: $\begin{pmatrix} 3 & 2 \\ 2 & 4 \end{pmatrix} \begin{pmatrix} x \\ y \end{pmatrix} = \begin{pmatrix} 12 \\ 16 \end{pmatrix}$.

   Solve this equation by multiplying both sides of the equation by the inverse of $\begin{pmatrix} 3 & 2 \\ 2 & 4 \end{pmatrix}$,

   that is, $\begin{pmatrix} \square & \square \\ \square & \square \end{pmatrix} \begin{pmatrix} 3 & 2 \\ 2 & 4 \end{pmatrix} \begin{pmatrix} x \\ y \end{pmatrix} = \begin{pmatrix} \square & \square \\ \square & \square \end{pmatrix} \begin{pmatrix} 12 \\ 16 \end{pmatrix}$.

8 Use matrices to solve these simultaneous equations: a) $4x+y = 30$ b) $2x-y = 2$ c) $2x+3y = 10$
                                                     $x+2y = 11$ $x+3y = 29$ $6x+9y = 20.$

CORE

1   The scatter graph shows the
    lengths and masses of a
    sample of a new variety of
    broad bean.

    Masses are measured to the
    nearest $\frac{1}{2}$ g and lengths to the
    nearest $\frac{1}{2}$ cm.

    a) What can you say about
       the lengths of all the beans
       recorded in the shaded
       region?

    b) Graph B shows the lengths
       and masses of a different
       variety of broad bean to
       those recorded in Graph A.

       What can you say about
       the masses of all the beans
       recorded in the shaded
       region?

    c) Imagine that Graph A is
       placed over Graph B.
       There will be a region of
       double shading.
       What can you say about
       any bean recorded in this
       region?

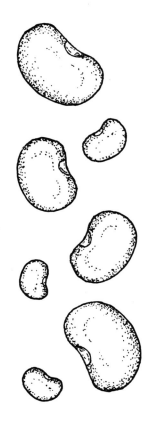

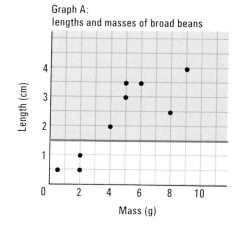

Graph A:
lengths and masses of broad beans

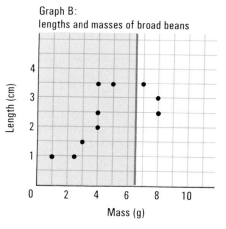

Graph B:
lengths and masses of broad beans

d) Which of these beans would be recorded in the double shaded region?

A
1 g   B
2 g   C
3 g   D
6 g   E
7 g

FULL SIZE

e) In Graph A we can represent the shaded region by the inequality $l \geqslant 1.5$

   (That is, the length of bean in this region is greater than or equal to 1.5 cm.)
   Write a similar inequality for the shaded region in Graph B. Use m to represent mass of beans.

2   Morrisey's frozen baby carrots must be at most
6 cm long and weigh at least 5 g.

a) Which of the five carrots satisfy the conditions?

b) Draw a graph to illustrate the information in
the first sentence. Record each of the five
carrots on the graph.
Leave unshaded the region on the graph where
carrots which satisfy Morrisey's conditions
would be recorded.

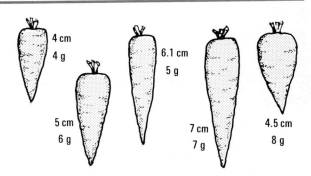

THINK IT THROUGH

3   a) Describe the masses and lengths of the objects which could be recorded in the shaded section in each of
these graphs:

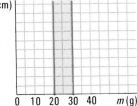

b) Copy and complete the
relations representing the
shaded regions:

(i) ...$\leqslant l \leqslant$...   (ii) ...$\leqslant m \leqslant$...

c) Imagine that the two graphs are superimposed one upon the other. List the mass and length of
(i) the smallest object   (ii) the largest object, which would be recorded in the double shaded region.

4   a) In the diagram, A is the point
(1, 4) and B is the point (4, ⁻2).
Check that the
coordinates of A and B satisfy
the relation $2x+y=6$.

b) C is the point (6, 2). Do the
coordinates of C satisfy the relation
$2x+y>6$ or the relation
$2x+y<6$?

c) Check that the coordinates of
G satisfy the relation
$2x+y<6$.

d) Decide which relation,
$2x+y=6$ or $2x+y>6$ or
$2x+y<6$, each of the points
D, E, F and H satisfy.

e) Sketch the graph of
$2x+y=6$. Shade the region
in which points satisfy the
relation $2x+y\geqslant6$.

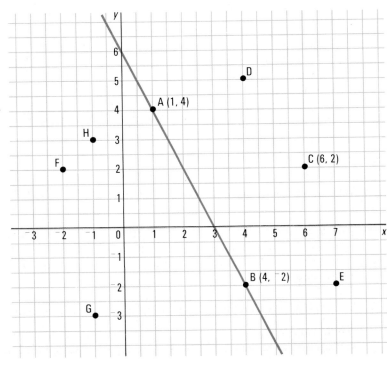

B19

5   The red line shows the
solutions of the equation
$2x - y = 8$.

a) Check that each point
along it satisfies the
relation $2x - y = 8$.

b) What do the red numbers
represent?

c) Find a point (x, y) in the
plane for which

   (i) $2x - y > 8$
   (ii) $2x - y < 8$.

d) Which of these two regions
represents the solutions to
the inequality

   $2x - y \leqslant 8$?

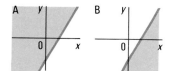

B19

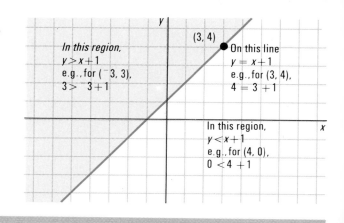

TAKE NOTE

Any line divides the points in a plane into three
regions – the points on the line, and points in the two
regions either side of the line.

The points which satisfy the relation $y = x + 1$ lie on
the line.
The points which satisfy the relation $y > x + 1$ lie in
the red region.
The points which satisfy the relation $y < x + 1$ lie in
the unshaded region.

We can decide which region goes with which relation
by testing individual points in the regions (as shown
in the illustration).

6 a) Match each red region with an inequality:

Inequalities: $y<3$, $x<y$, $x\leqslant 3$, $x+y\geqslant 0$, $2x+y\geqslant 3$, $2x+y\leqslant 3$, $y>x^2+3$, $y\leqslant x^2+3$.

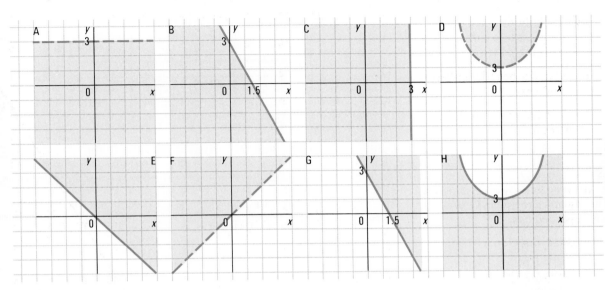

b) Why do you think some lines are shown as broken lines and some as continuous lines, in a)?

7 Copy the diagram.

a) Mark in red (or another colour) all the points which satisfy the relation $y-x=2$.

b) Check that the point (3, 2) satisfies the relation $y-x<2$.
Shade in black the region of the diagram which contains points satisfying this relation (you will need to draw the line as a broken line).

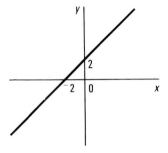

8 a) Draw a graph of the relation $2x-y=3$ for $^-4\leqslant x\leqslant 6$.

b) With the same axes, draw the lines $y=1$ and $x=4$.

c) Check that the point (2, 3) satisfies each of the three relations:

$y>1$, $x<4$, $2x-y<3$.

d) On your graph *leave unshaded* the region of points which satisfy each of the relations in c).

9 The points inside and on the boundary of the rectangle ABCD satisfy these relations simultaneously:

$3\leqslant x\leqslant\square$ $\square\leqslant y\leqslant\square$ Copy and complete each one.

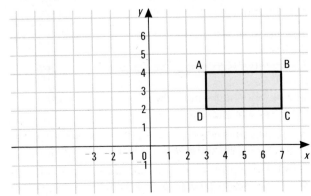

B19

================ THINK IT THROUGH ================

10 Write down three relations which the points in
    the unshaded region and on its boundary satisfy
    simultaneously.

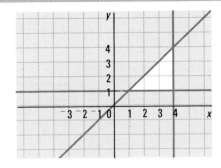

================ TAKE NOTE ================

The *unshaded* region in Graph A
is represented by $x < 3$.

The unshaded region in Graph B
is represented by $x \geqslant 3$.

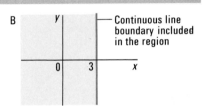

Processes of elimination

1   a) Here are three relations: $x+y \leqslant 10$, $2x-y \geqslant 4$, $y > 2$.
       By thinking and testing, find a point (x, y) in the plane which satisfies all three relations simultaneously.

    b) Here is a way of systematically finding points (x, y) in the plane which satisfy all three inequalities
       simultaneously:

Step 1	*Step 2*	*Step 3*
Draw the graph of $x+y = 10$. Shade out (eliminate) points for which $x+y > 10$.	Draw the graph of $2x-y = 4$. Eliminate points for which $2x-y < 4$.	Draw the graph of $y = 2$. Eliminate points for which $y \leqslant 2$.

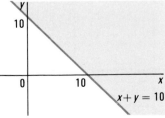 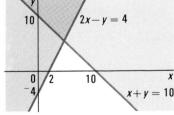 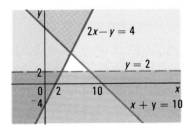

       Notice that the unshaded triangle has two continuous lines and one broken line for its sides.
       The points which satisfy all three relations lie inside the triangle and on the continuous lines.
       Give the coordinates of three such points.

    c) Use a process of elimination to identify the values of (x, y) which simultaneously satisfy the relations:
       $x+y \geqslant 5$, $y > 3+x$, $x > 3$.

2   Write down four relations which are
simultaneously satisfied by the points (x, y) in the
shaded region (all the boundary lines are a part of
the region).

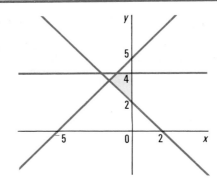

3   Represent the region in the (x, y) plane which is simultaneously satisfied by each set of relations:

a) $y \geqslant 2x$, $2y \leqslant x$, $x > 2$.

b) $x + 8 \leqslant y$, $x + y + 8 \geqslant 0$, $y < 3$, $x < 0$.

ENRICHMENT

Maximizing and minimizing

 CHALLENGE

1   a) Think of all the points (x, y) which simultaneously satisfy the relations:

   $x + y \leqslant 8$, $x > 4$, $y \geqslant 2$.

   Name *three* such points.

   b) Think about the expression $2y + x$.
   Its value changes for different choices of x and y.
   What is the largest possible value of $2y + x$ if x and y also satisfy the relations in a)?

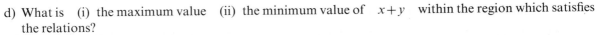

2   a) The unshaded region simultaneously satisfies
these relations:

   $\square \leqslant x \leqslant 5$
   $\square \leqslant y \leqslant \square$

   Copy and complete each relation.

   b) Check that at the point A, the value of the
   expression $x + y$ is 5.

   c) What is the value of the expression $x + y$
   at   (i) B   (ii) C?

   d) What is   (i) the maximum value   (ii) the minimum value of $x + y$ within the region which satisfies
   the relations?

   e) What is the maximum value of   (i) $2y - x$ (ii) $2x + y$ within the region which satisfies the relations?

B19

3   a) The unshaded region (which includes its boundaries)
       simultaneously satisfies the three relations:

   $x ? 5, y ? 1, y ? x.$

   Copy and complete each relation.

   b) Predict the point in the unshaded region where
      you will find

      (i) the maximum value of $x+y$
      (ii) the minimum value of $2y-x.$

   c) Check your predictions in b) by finding values
      of $x+y$ and $2y-x$ in the region.

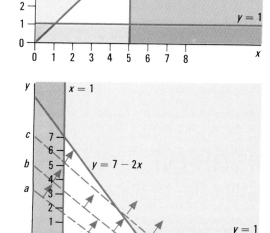

4   (In parts a) to d), ignore the dotted lines.)

   a) In the unshaded region, predict the point
      which gives a maximum value for the
      expression $x+4y.$

   b) Test your prediction in a) by calculating values
      of $x+4y.$

   c) Predict the point in the unshaded region which
      gives a maximum value for the expression $xy.$

   d) Test your prediction in c) by calculating values of $xy.$

   e) What is the value of $x+y$ for each point along
      the lines   (i) a   (ii) b   (iii) c?

   f   Explain how the dotted lines can help you to find the maximum value of $x+y$ within the unshaded region.

5   a) Illustrate on a graph the region of points which satisfy simultaneously the relations:

   $x \geqslant 2, \quad y \geqslant 1$ and $x+2y \leqslant 12.$

   b) Draw the lines (in broken line form) $y-2x = 10, \quad y-2x = 2, \quad y-2x = {}^{-}6, \quad y-2x = {}^{-}10.$
      Find the minimum value of $y-2x$ in the unshaded region.

▓▓▓▓▓▓▓▓▓▓ TAKE NOTE ▓▓▓▓▓▓▓▓▓▓

To find the maximum or minimum value of an
expression (for example, $x+y$) in a region, imagine
lines which represent equal values of the expression.
For example, for $x+y$, imagine $x+y = 1, x+y = 2,$
$x+y = 3, \ldots$
These are the broken lines in the diagram.
As the lines move to the right the value of $x+y$
increases.
Its maximum value within the shaded region is 6 (that
is, at the point A).
Its minimum value is 2 (that is, at the point C).

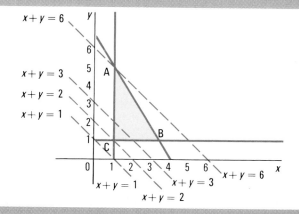

Solving problems

1   Chrissie can lift any load less than 24 kg. She has
to load some tins of paint into a van.
Tins of emulsion have a mass of 3 kg. Tins of
gloss have a mass of 2 kg.

a) Each trip, Chrissie carries x tins of gloss and
y tins of emulsion.
Write down an expression for
(i) the total number of cans she is carrying
(ii) the total mass of paint she is carrying.

b) Explain the significance, in relation to
Chrissie's task, of (i) the crosses (ii) the
circles (iii) the broken line on the graph.

c) Can Chrissie carry 11 cans and still remain inside
her weight-carrying limit? Explain your answer.

d) Which of the relations is the correct condition
for the number of cans which Chrissie can carry:
(i) $x + y < 24$ (ii) $2x + 3y < 24$ (iii) $x + y < 11$?

e) Which of the relations in d) represents the
correct condition for the mass of paint which
Chrissie can carry?

f   Each trip, Chrissie wants to carry the maximum
possible number of cans. How many tins of emulsion
and how many tins of gloss should she
carry on each trip? (Give each of the possibilities.)

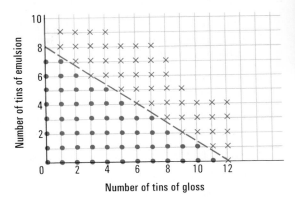

Number of tins of emulsion

Number of tins of gloss

TAKE NOTE

The conditions which govern a problem can often be represented in graphical form, and the problem solved
using graphical methods. The process of eliminating non-viable solutions to arrive at a range of potential
solutions is called *linear programming*.

2   A small engineering firm manufactures a small number of brake drums for 1.3L and 2.0S cars.
The cost of making these parts is
(i) £20 for the 1.3L   (ii) £30 for the 2.0S.
The factory can produce a maximum of 25 parts per day, and the manufacturing costs have to be
restricted to £600 per day at most.

a) Write an expression for the cost restriction on manufacturing x 1.3L brake drums and y 2.0S
brake drums per day.

b) Write an expression for the maximum output of the factory.

c) Draw a graph to illustrate the information. Highlight the region showing possible
manufacturing output.

d) What is the maximum number of 2.0S parts which can be produced when the total
numbers of cars is a maximum?

3 A hotel caters for groups of adults and teenagers of not more than 30 people. Because of room and cost restrictions it has the following conditions:

(i) there must be more than 20 people in the group
(ii) the group must include at least 3 adults
(iii) the group must include not more than 6 adults.

a) Write the four statements above as relations (use *n* for the number of adults, and *m* for the number of teenagers).

b) A youth-club group includes 15 teenagers. How many adults must there be?

c) What is the maximum number of teenagers in a party which includes only 4 adults?

4 A television manufacturer produces two types of set, a 34 cm model and a 58 cm model.
The 34 cm model takes 5 hours to manufacture, and the 58 cm model 10 hours. The company employs 15 people who each work a maximum of 40 hours per week. The maximum output of the factory is 80 sets per week.

a) Write down:

(i) a relation regarding the time taken to produce x 34 cm sets and y 58 cm sets;
(ii) a relation regarding the number of sets produced.

b) Illustrate the information above on a graph.

c) The profit on a 34 cm set is £30 and on a 58 cm set is £45. What is the maximum profit the company can make in one week?